Checklist

nendo office
2007
office
linden plywood
138(m²)

P.3-13

1

vase-vase
2006
vase
one percent products
steel, ceramic
W136×D180×H240(mm)

P.14-17

2

ribbon
2007
stool
Cappellini
steel
W375×D375×H440(mm)

P.19-21

3

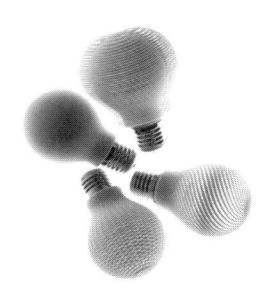

bulb-lamp
2006
lighting
one percent products
nylon
W80×D60×H80(mm)

P.23-29

4

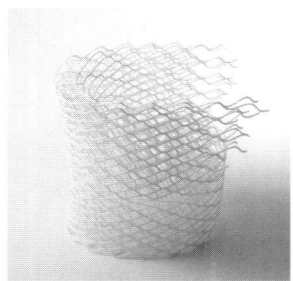

diamond chair
2008
chair
Museo della Permanente, Milan
nylon
W520×D670×H580(mm)

P.31-39

5

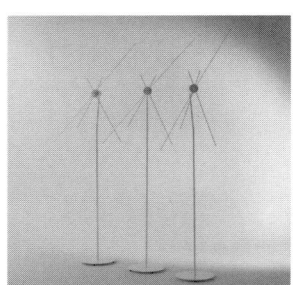

kazadokei
2008
clock
Museum of Contemporary Art Tokyo, Tokyo
steel, aluminium
W400×D400×H2650(mm)

P.41-45

6

cabbage chair
2008
chair
21_21 Design Sight, Tokyo
pleated paper
W750×D750×H650(mm)

P.51-57

7

kuuki
2008
private exhibition
Gallery Le Bain, Tokyo
paper, nylon, porous resin, steel
61(m²)

P.58-83

8

blown-fabric
2009
lighting
La Triennale di Milano, Milan
Smash™ (thermoplastic nonwoven fabric)
W250 × D250 × H250 (mm)

P. 95-109

9

ghost stories
2009
private exhibition
Friedman Benda Gallery, New York
string, felt-tip marker
290 (m²)

P. 110-119

10

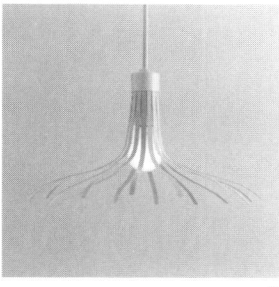

hanabi
2006
lighting
Milan Design Week, Milan
shape memory alloy, steel
W180 × D180 × H1440 (mm)

P. 121-125

11

period, comma, "quote"
2009
paper weight
S6"
aluminium
period: W58 × D58 × H40 (mm)
comma: W53 × D53 × H53 (mm)
quote: W70 × D50 × H50 (mm)

P. 128-131

12

fadeout-chair
2009
chair
Museum of Arts and Design, New York
walnut, acrylic
W410 × D495 × H750 (mm)

P. 132-145

13

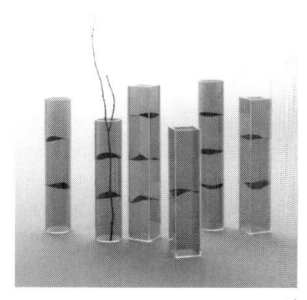

phantom-waves
2009
vase
Museum of Arts and Design, New York
polarizing film, acrylic
W80 × D80 × H350, 400, 450 (mm)
W70 × D70 × H350, 400, 450 (mm)

P. 149-162

14

Kanazawa World Craft Triennial 2010 pre-event
2009
exhibition space
21st Century Museum of
Contemporary Art, Kanazawa
glass, aluminium, acrylic
695 (m²)

P. 164-179

15

cord-chair
2009
chair
Museum of Arts and Design, New York
maple, stainless steel
W420 × D450 × H800 (mm)

P. 185-195

16

cream-chair
2009
chair
prototype
foamed silicone

P. 197-209

17

ghost stories
2009
private exhibition
Museum of Arts and Design, New York
stickers
198(m²)

P. 211-229

18

chair garden
2010
private exhibition
Galleria Antonia Jannone, Milan
ceramic, plastic
63(m²)

P. 230-237

19

clear perfume bottle
2010
perfume bottle
one percent products
acrylic, glass, aluminium
W134 × D60 × H35(mm)

P. 239-243

20

photograph:　Daici Ano　1,15　/　Masayuki Hayashi　2-9,11-14,16,19,20　/　Jimmy Cohrssen　10,18

nendo ghost stories

photograph Kenichi Higuchi

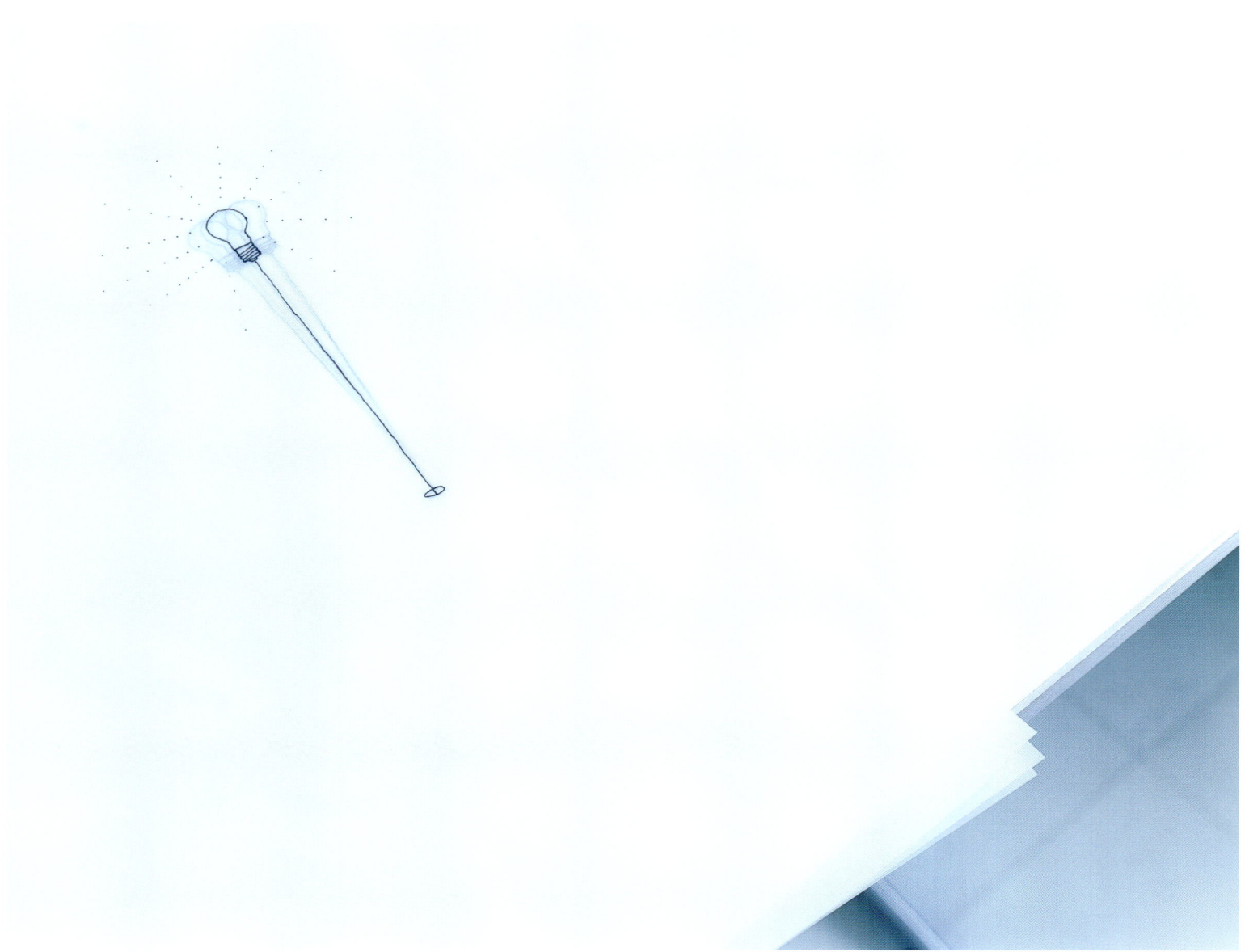

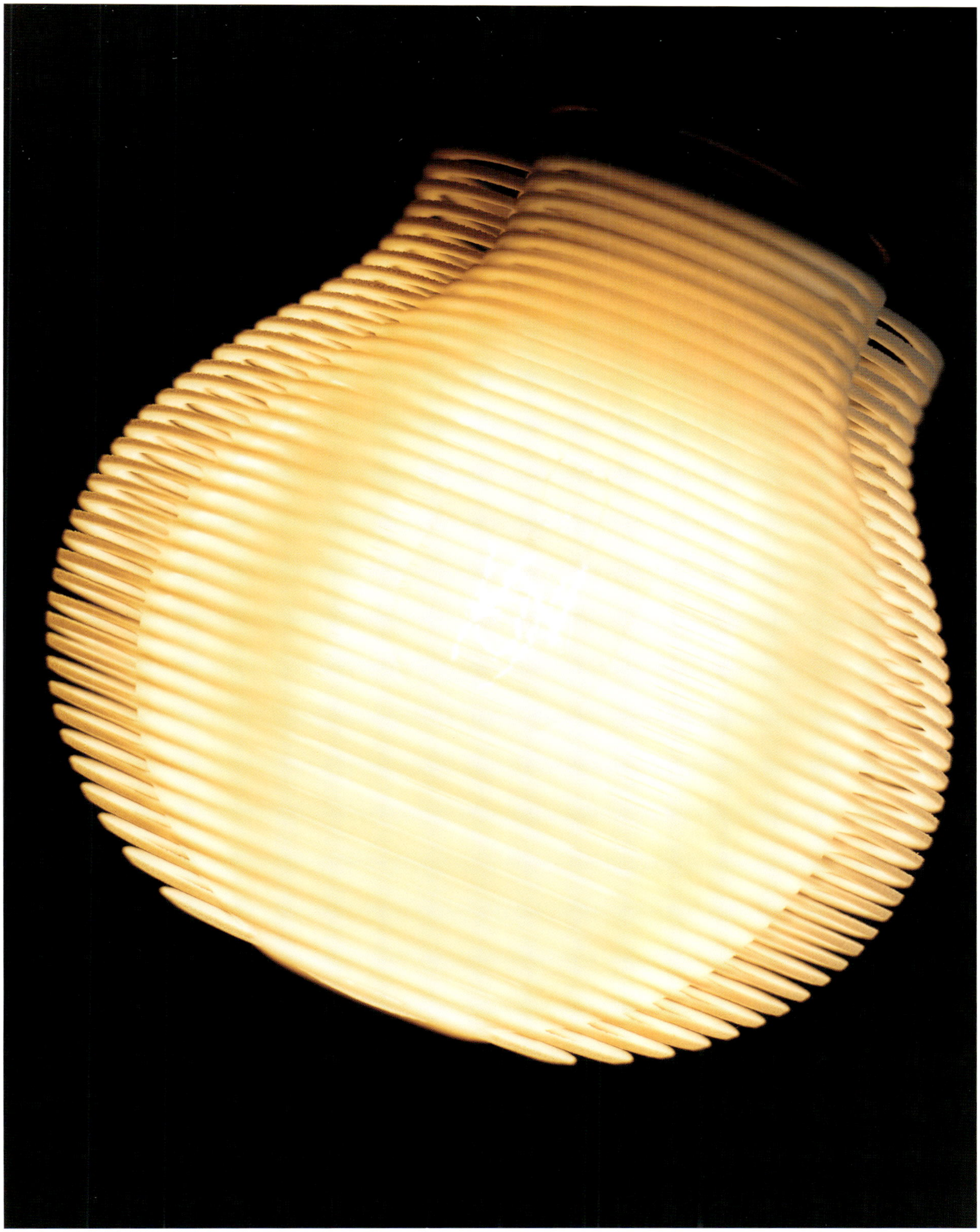

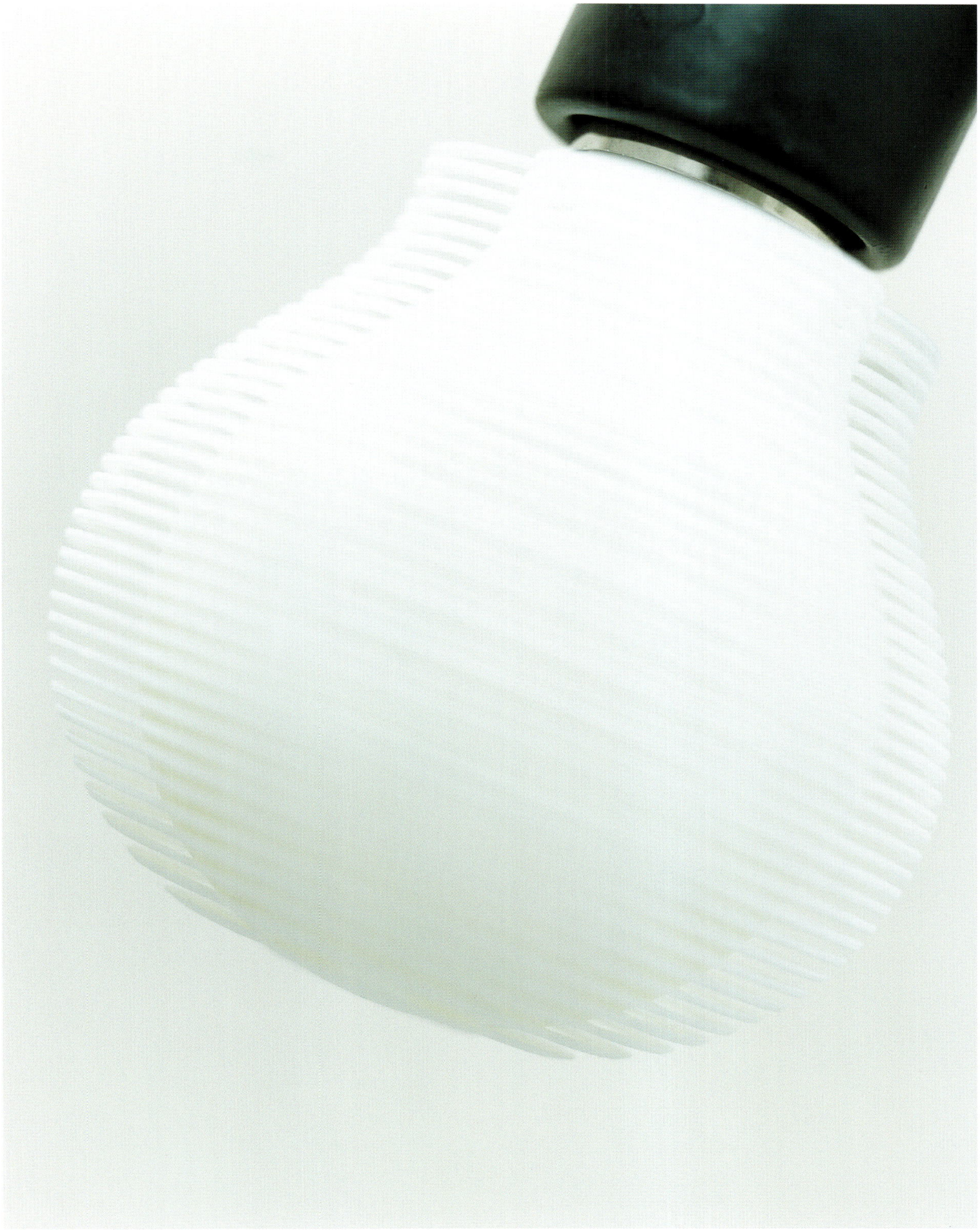

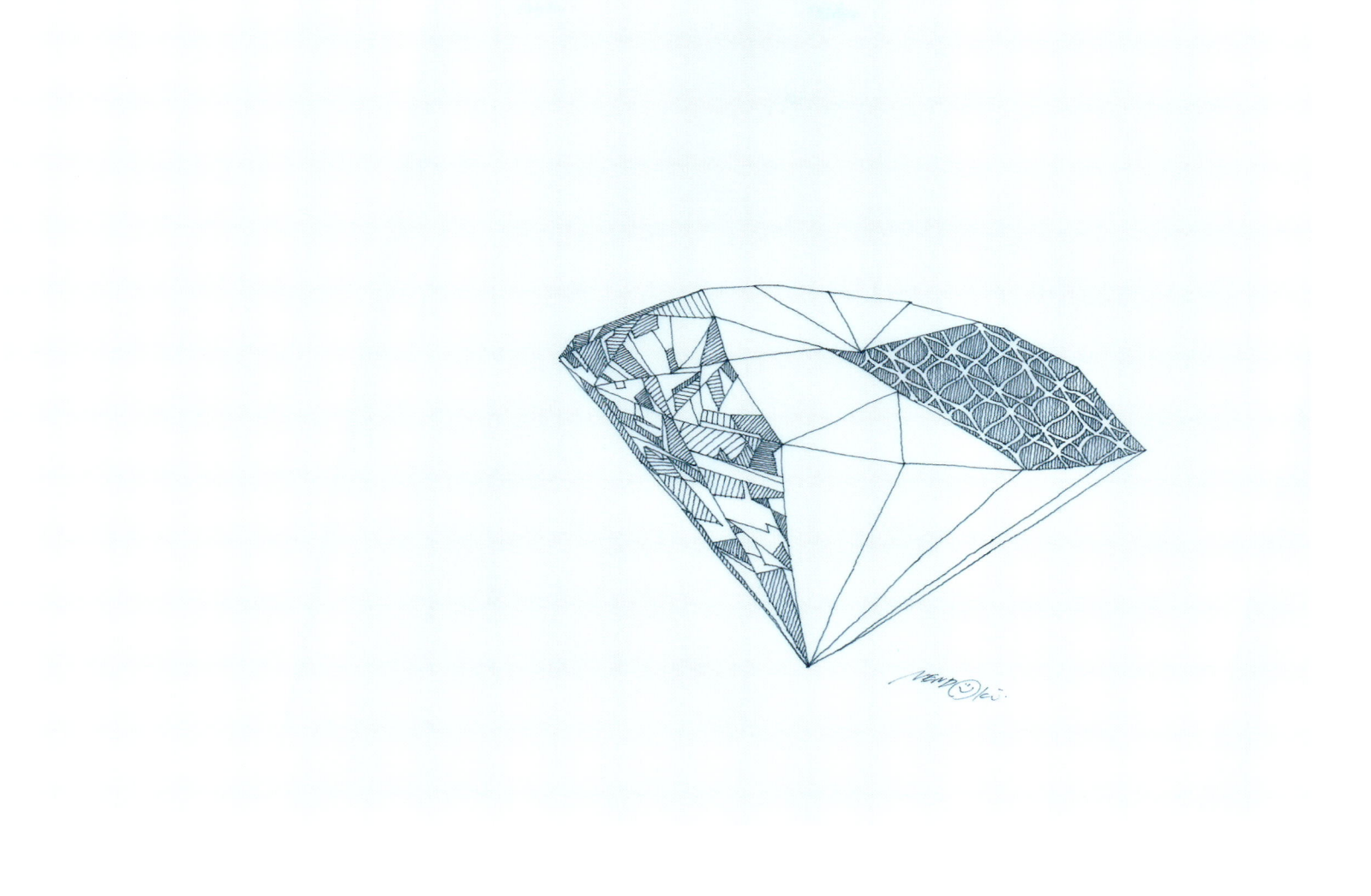

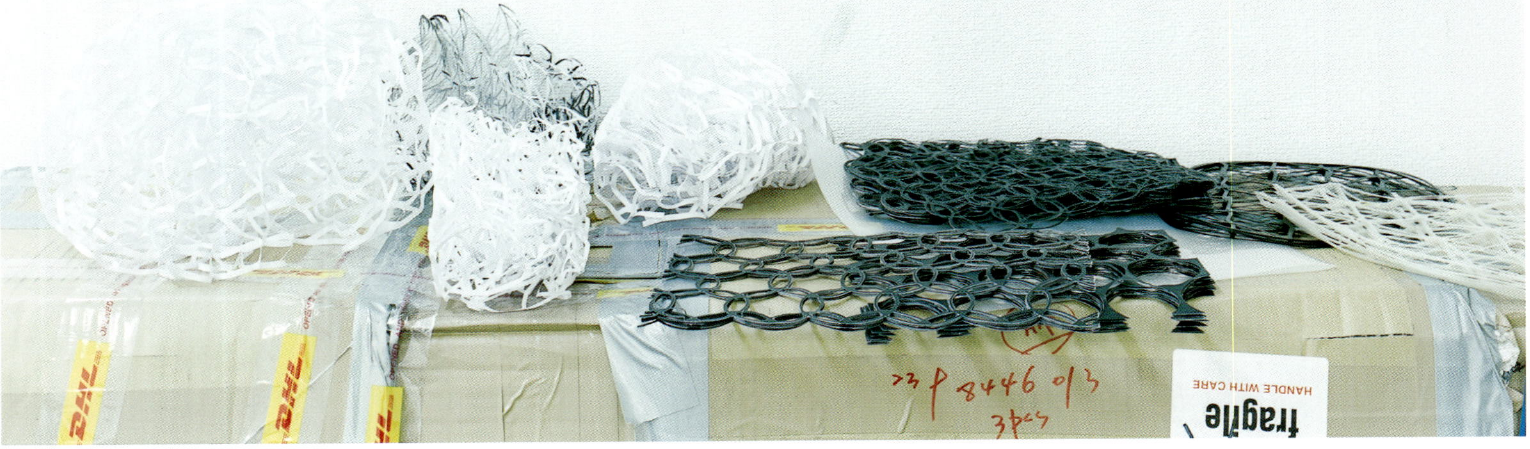
DHL
fragile
HANDLE WITH CARE

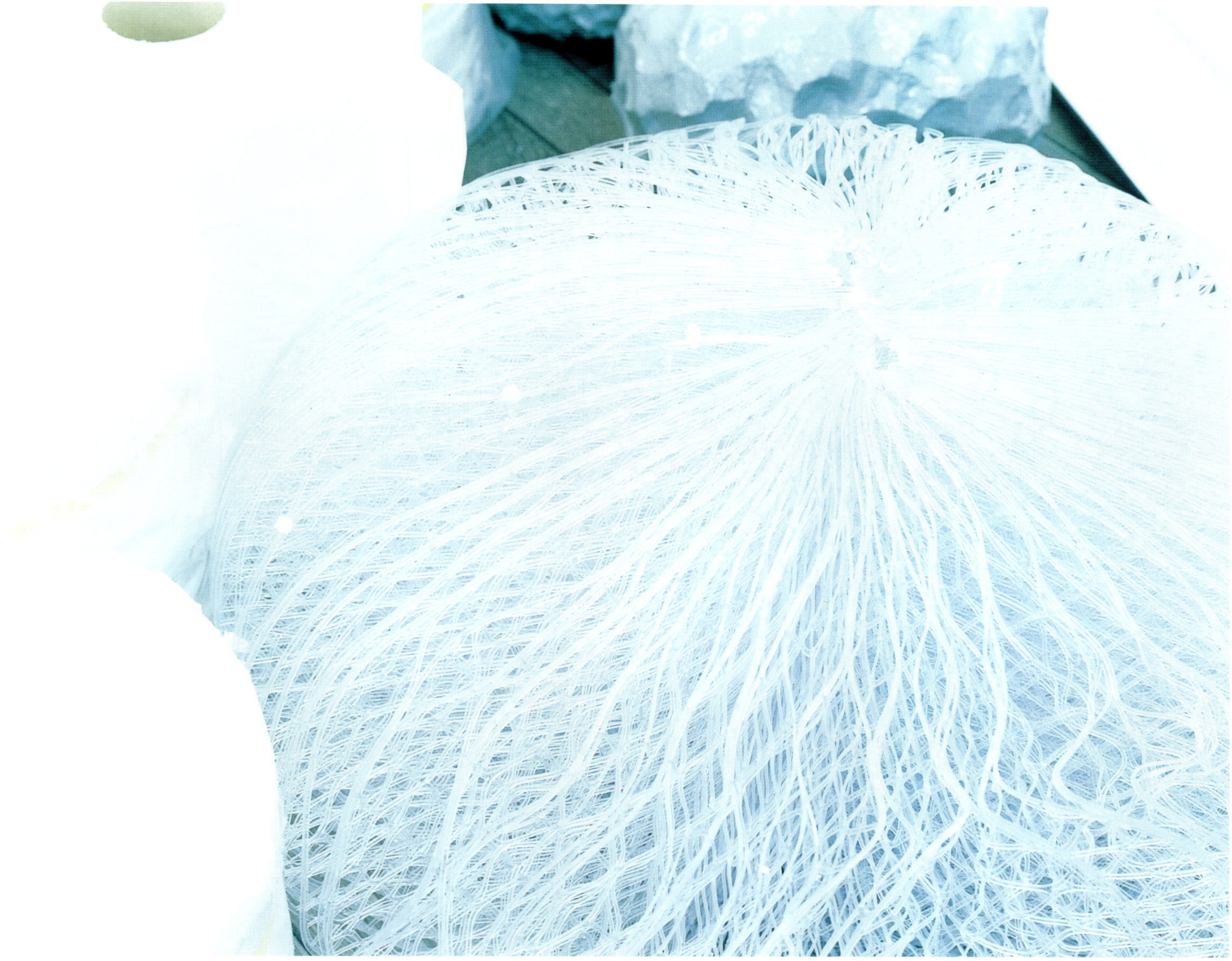

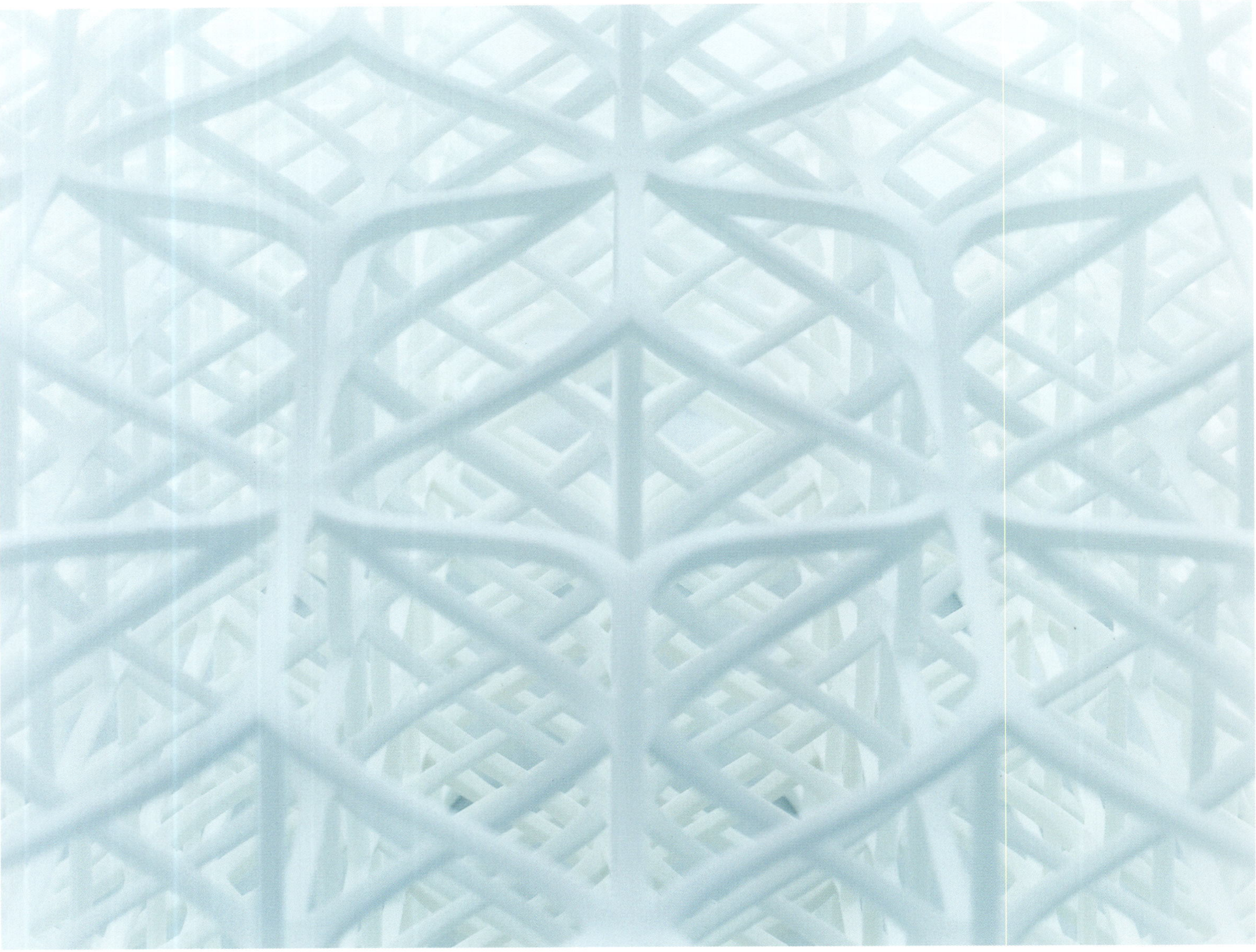

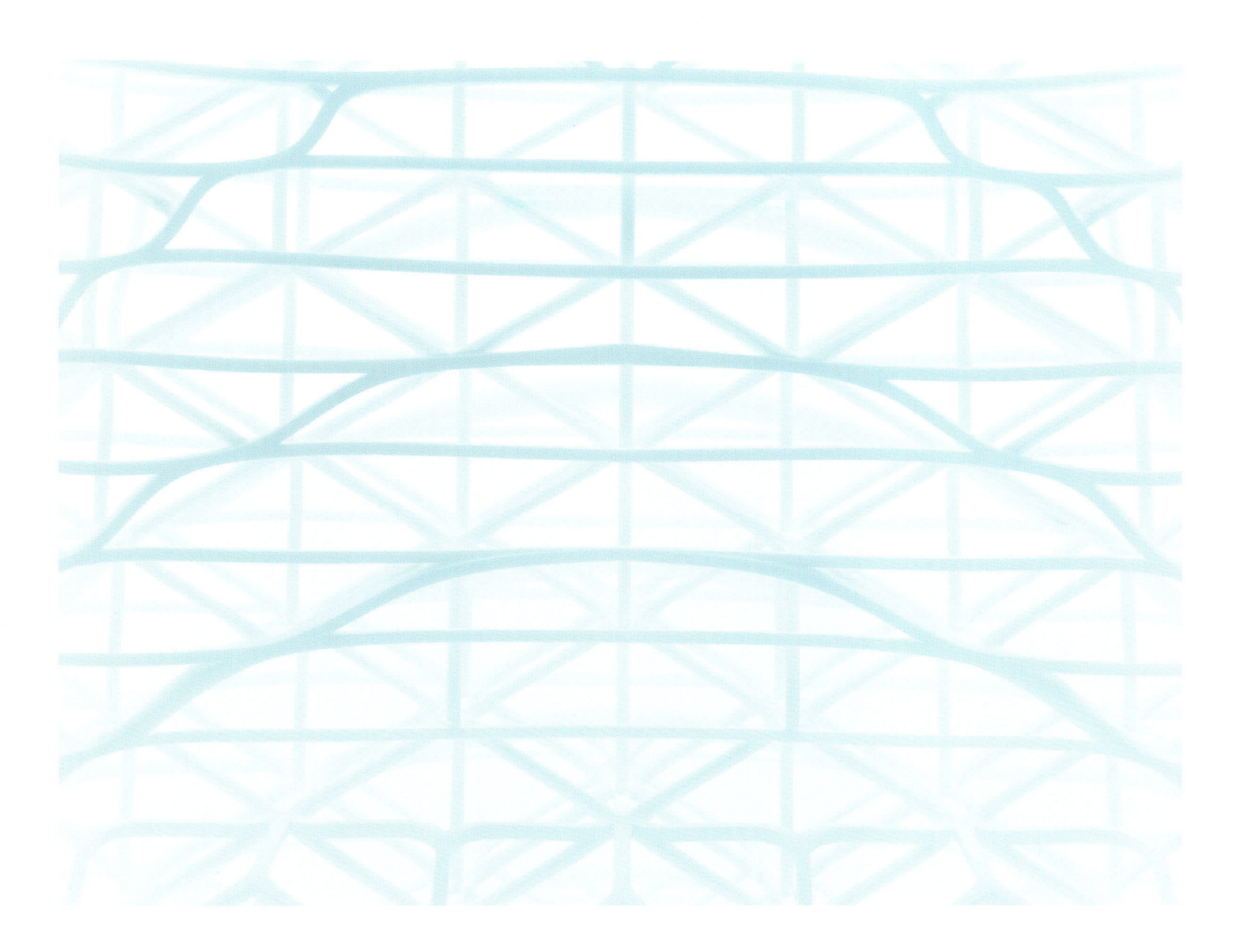

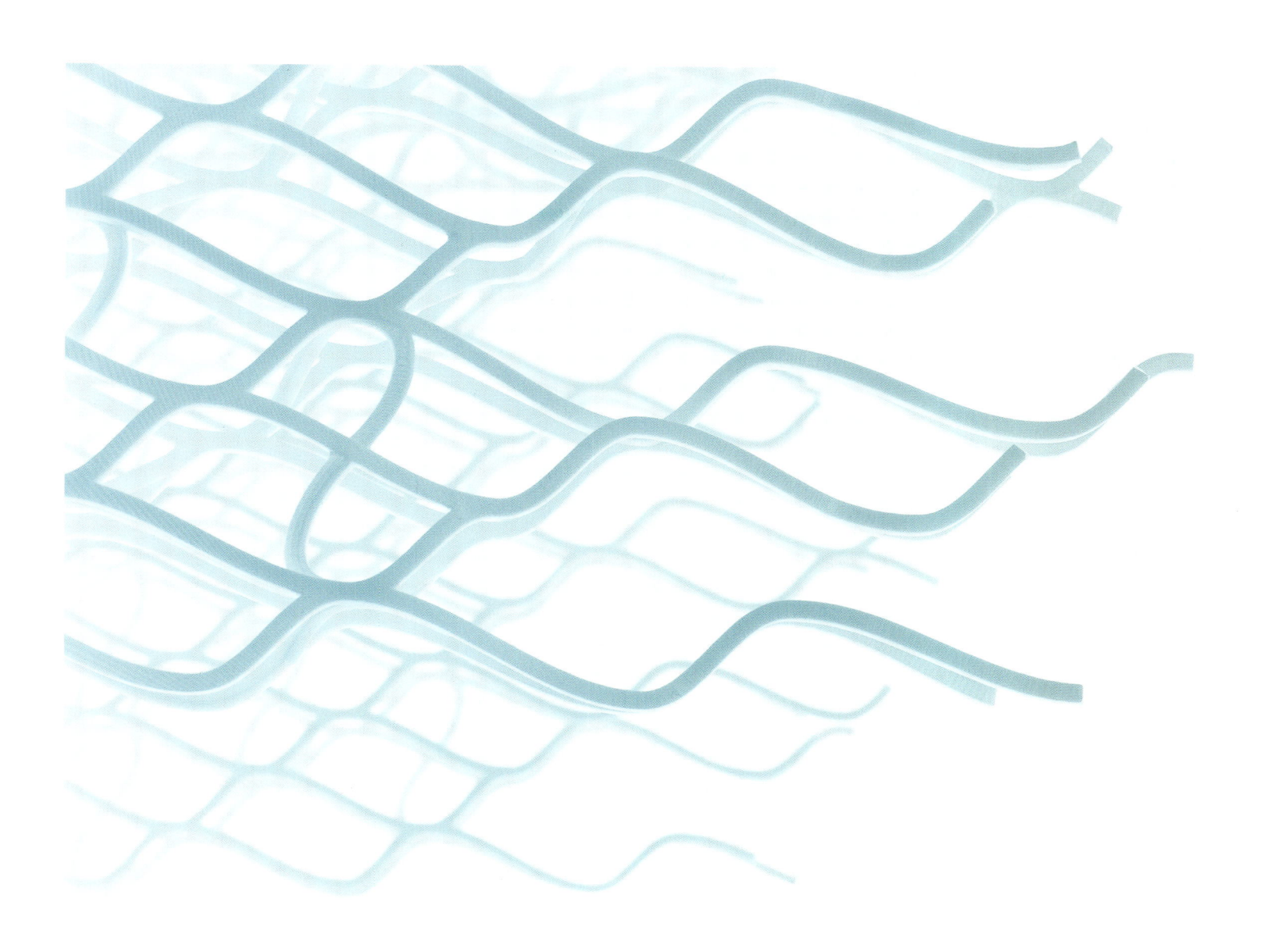

min. sec.
hr.

TIME
=
WIND

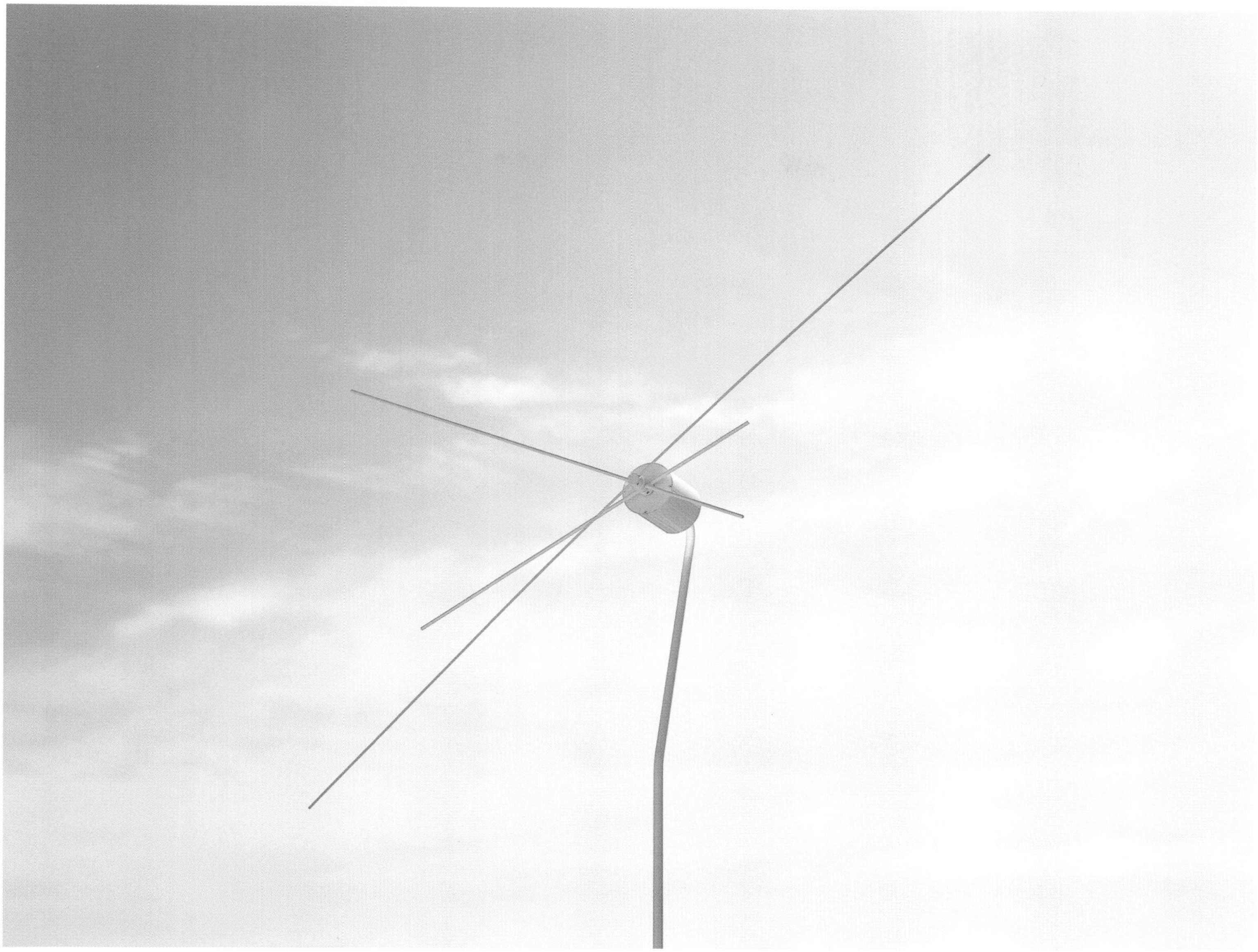

3M
スプレーのり77
タレにくく塗りやすい
多用途タイプ
Creative Life Spray
Spray
SURFACE PRIMER
すばやい仕上り
ガラスクル
ふきムラなし
ピッカピカ
汚れを防ぐ

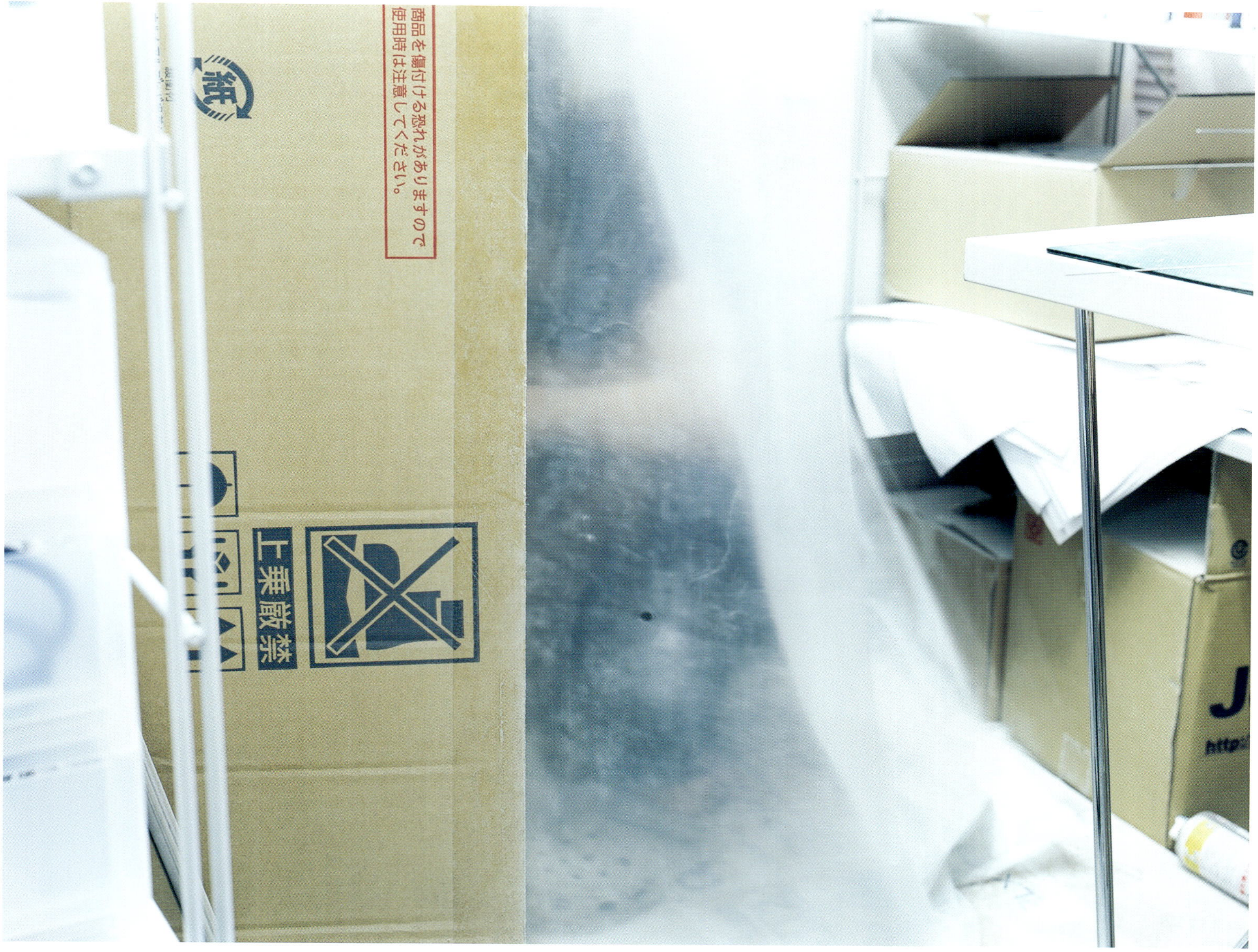
紙
商品を傷付ける恐れがありますので
使用時は注意してください。
上乗厳禁

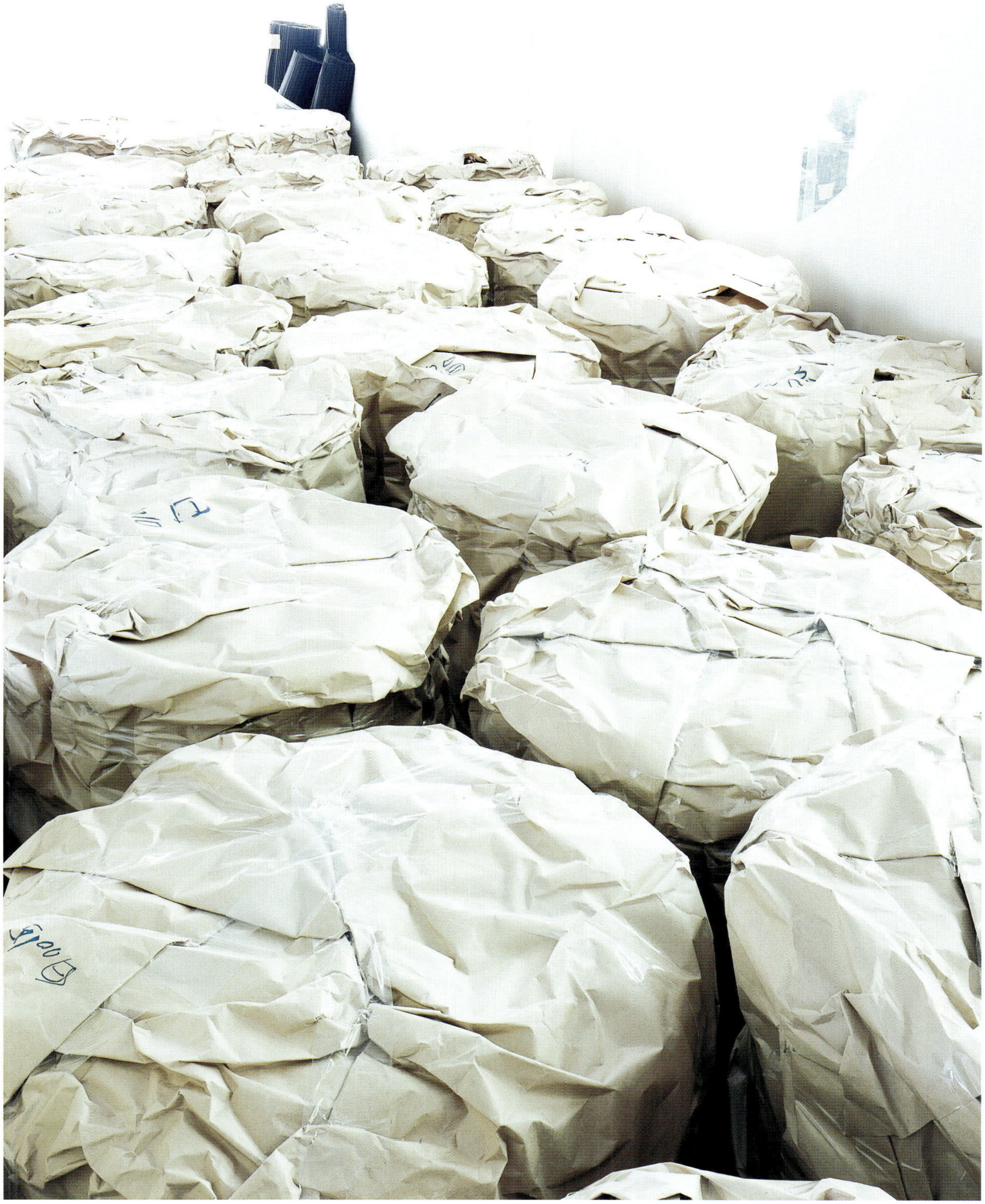

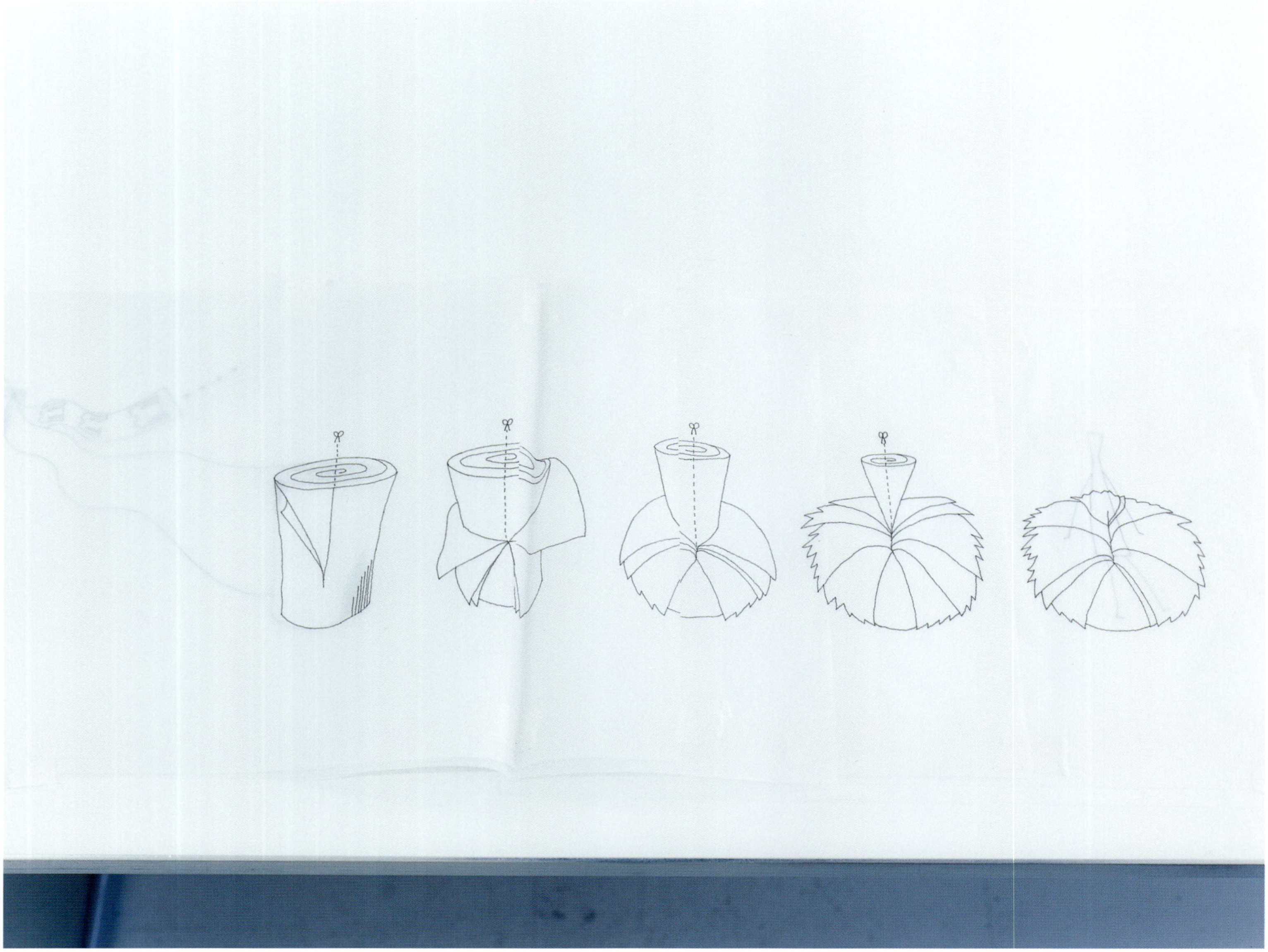

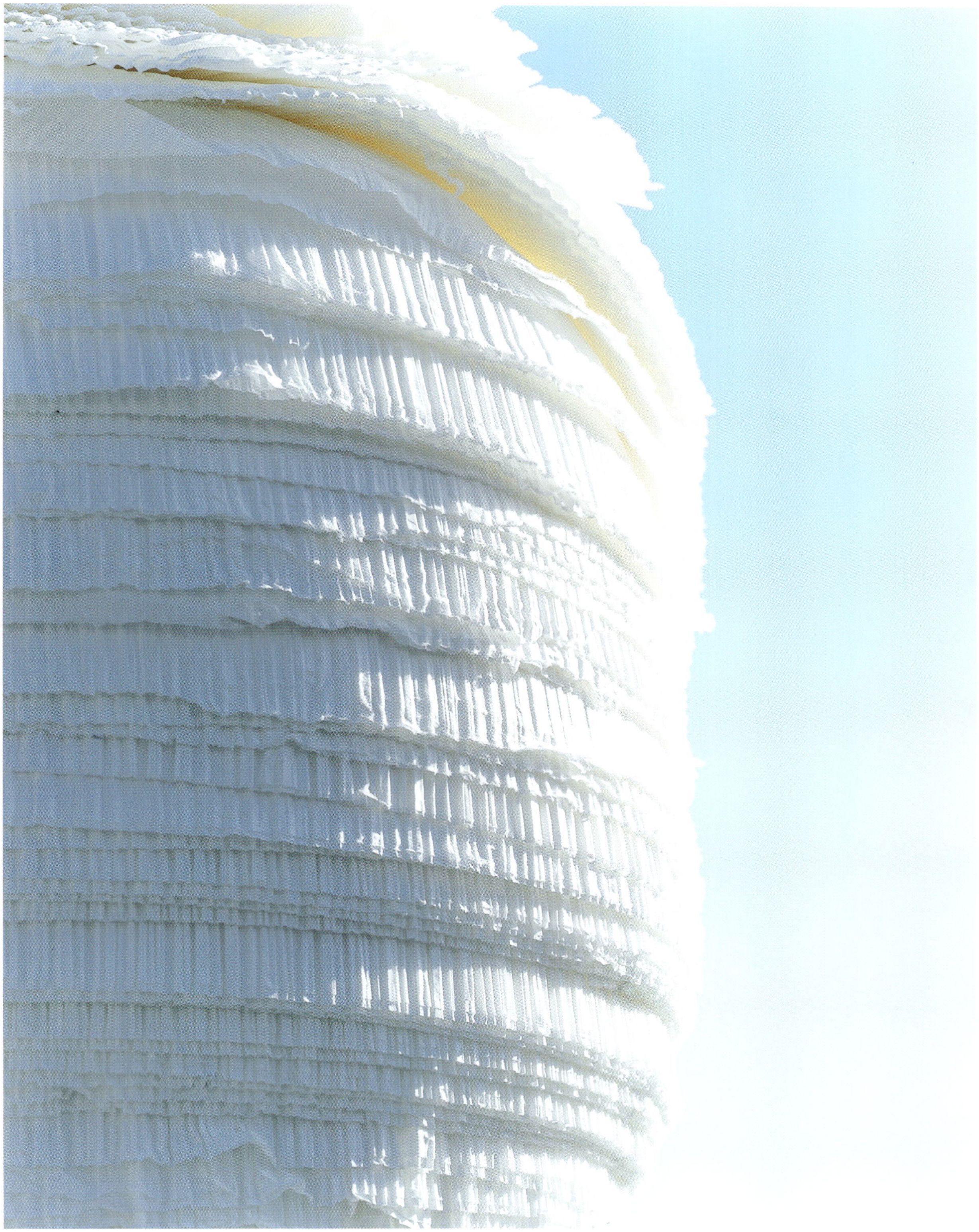

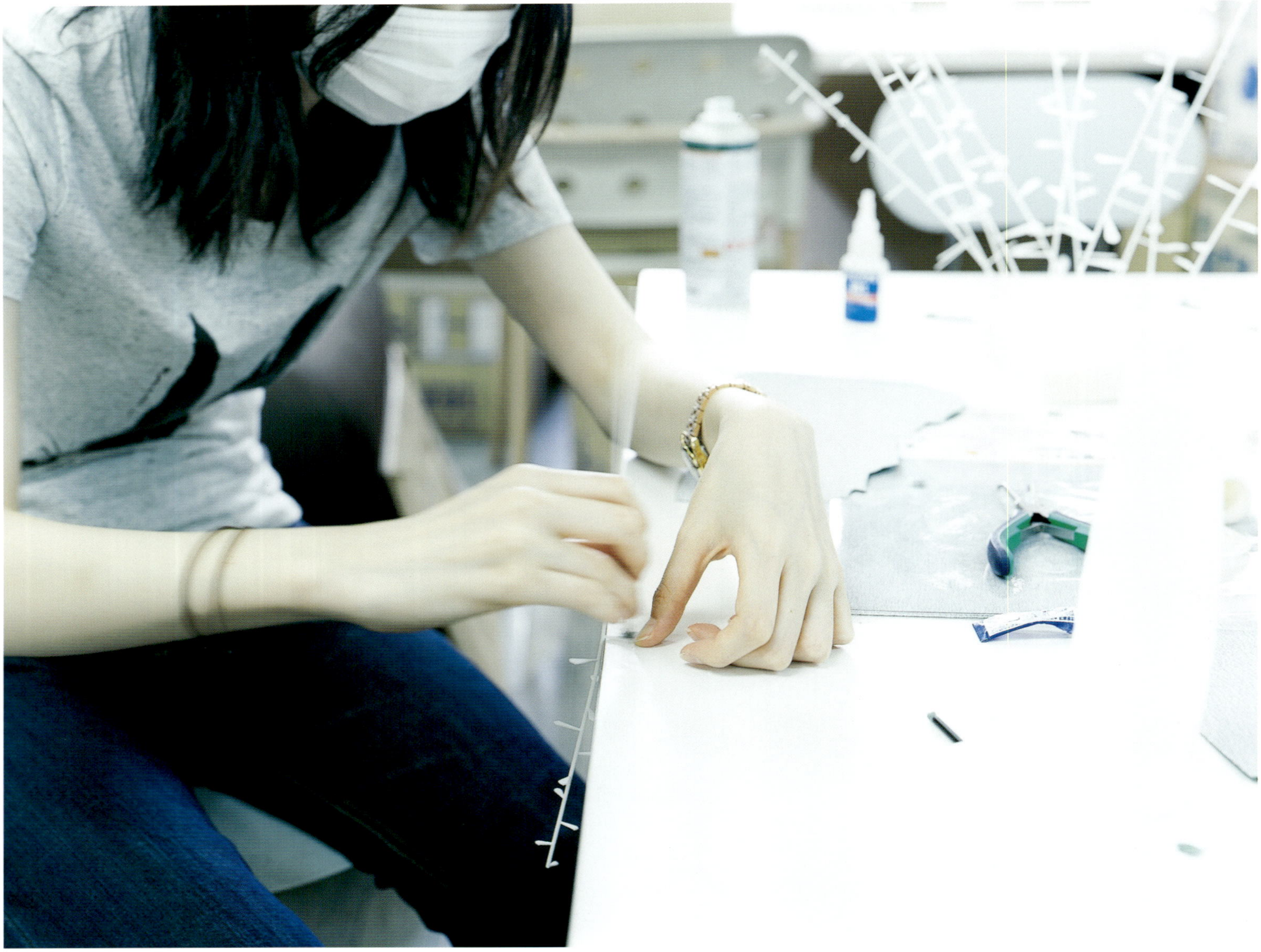

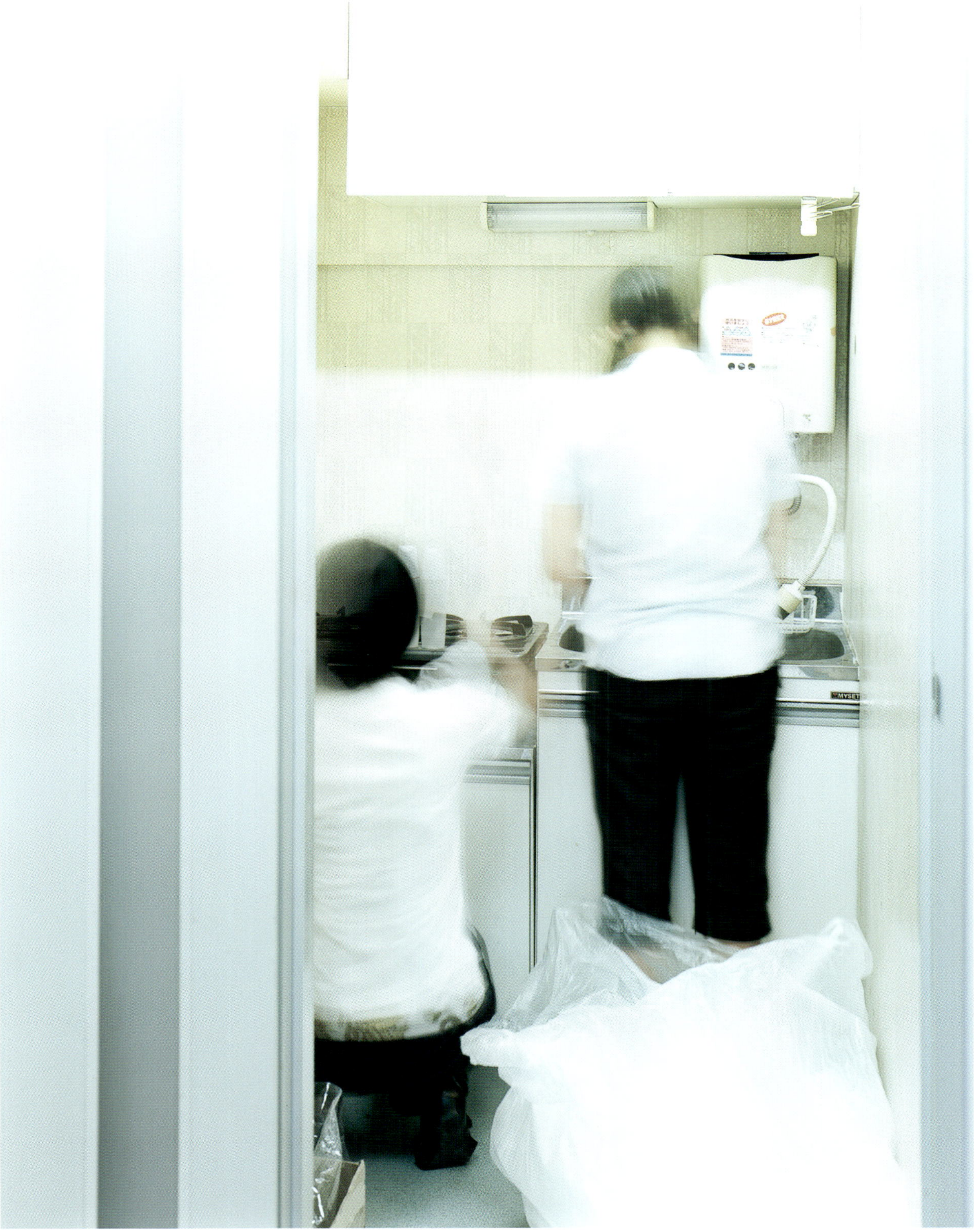
MYSET

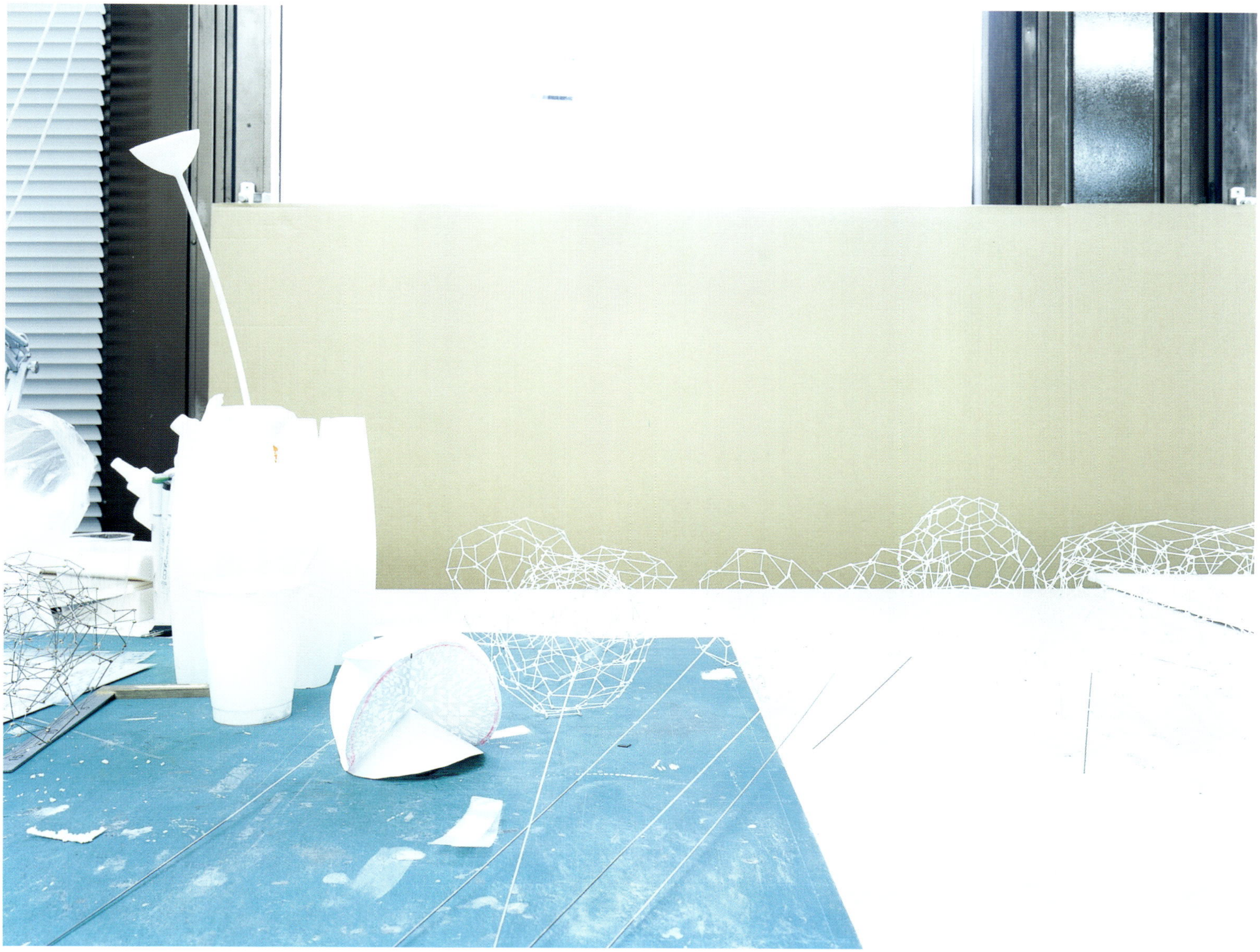

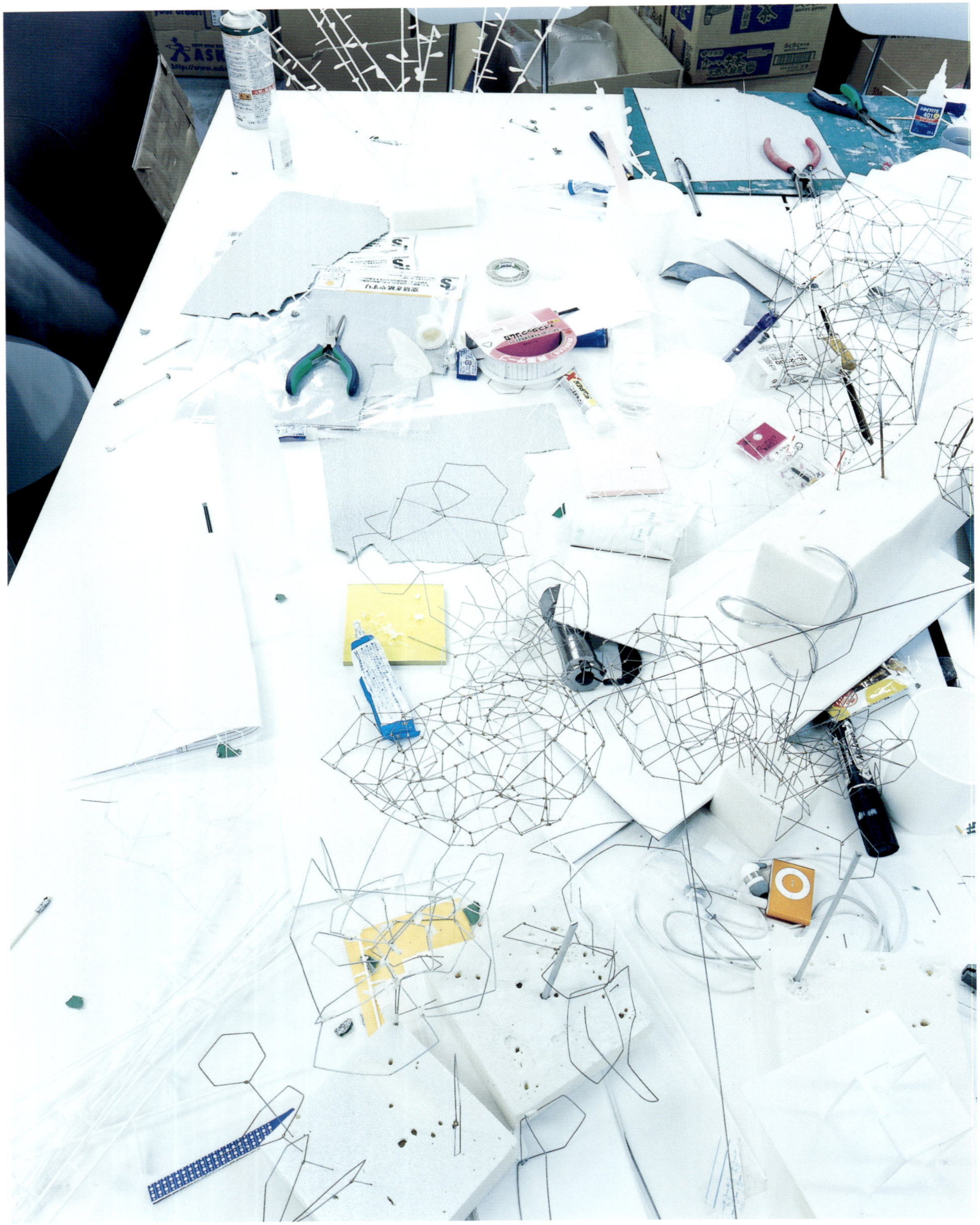

65

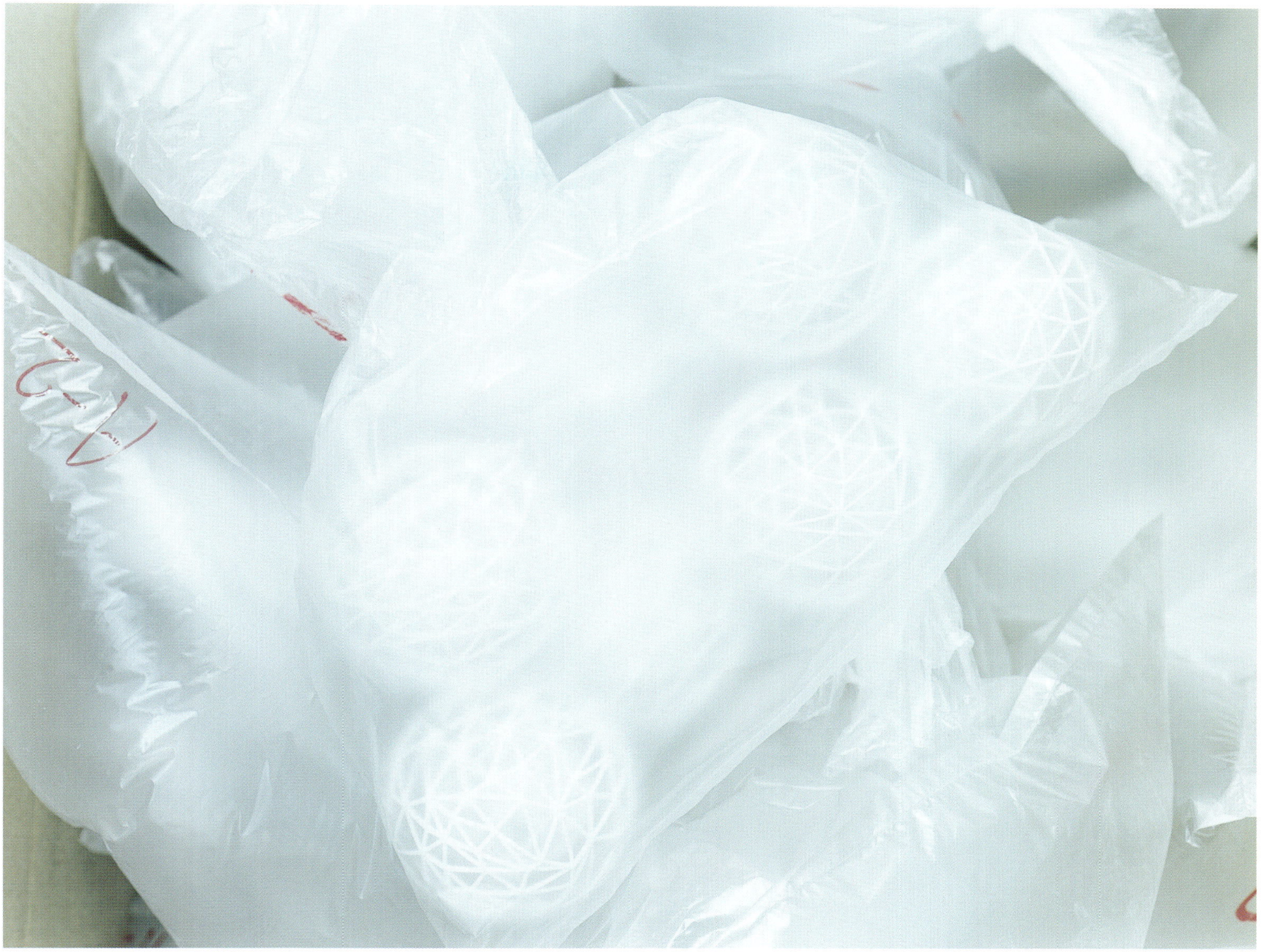

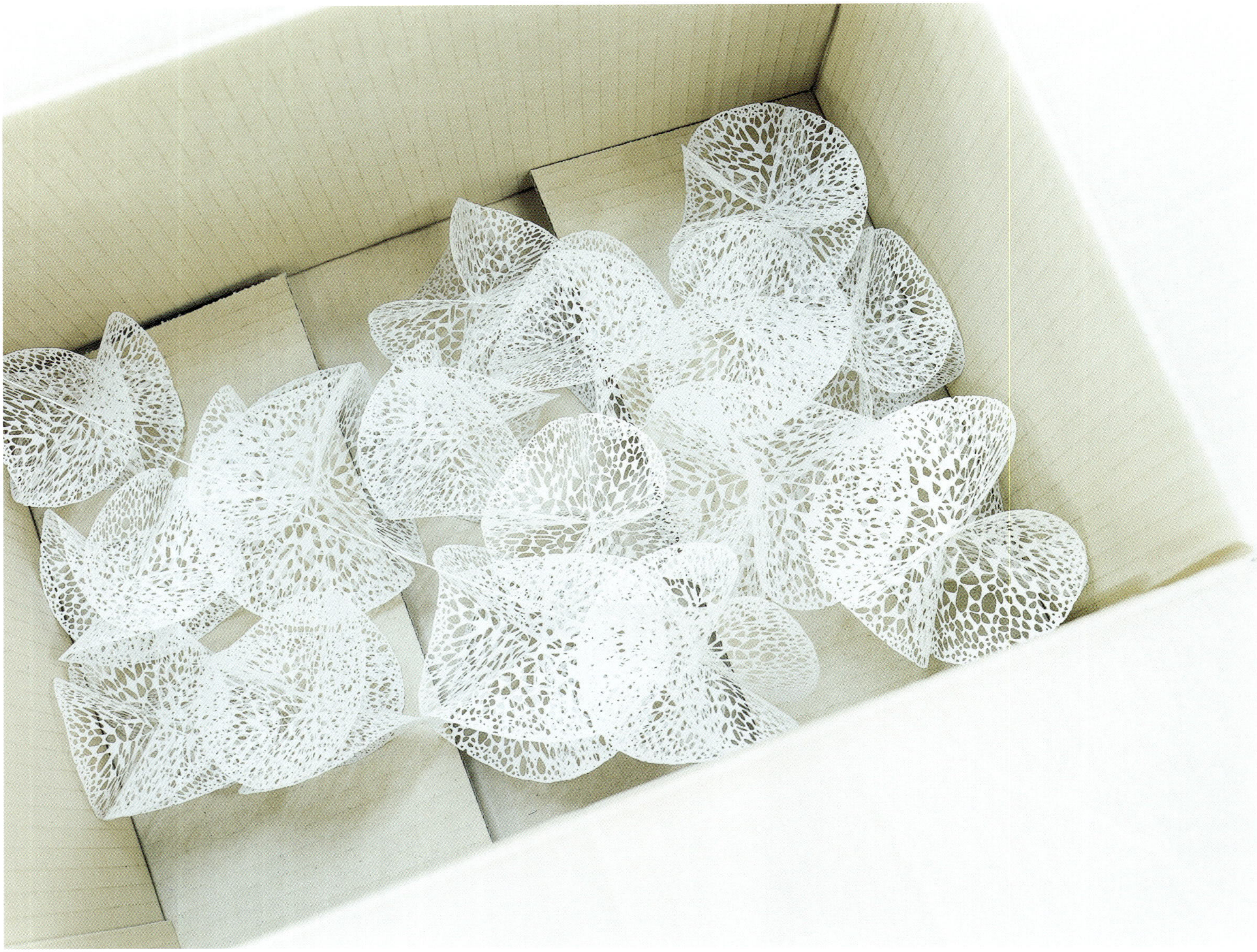

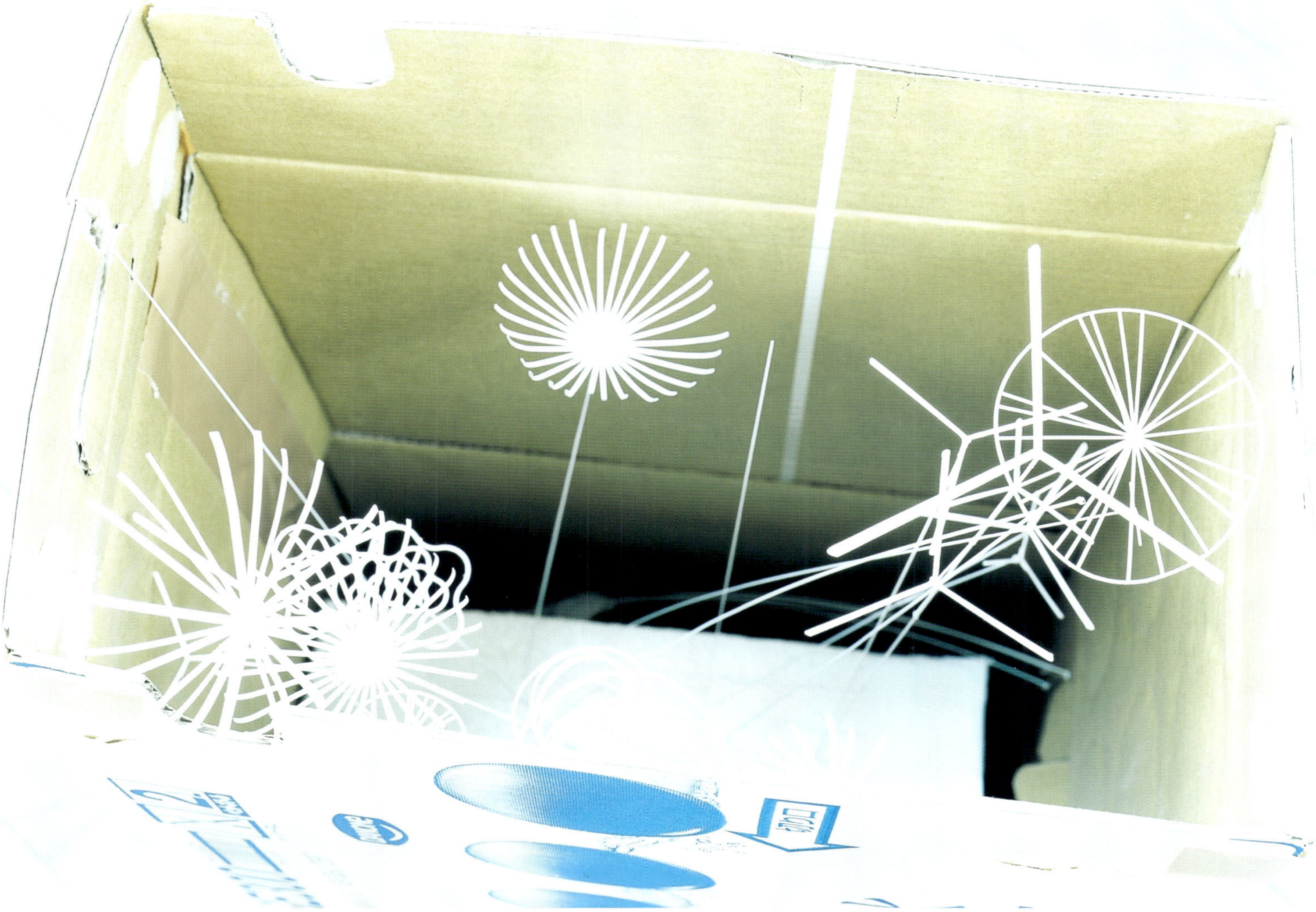

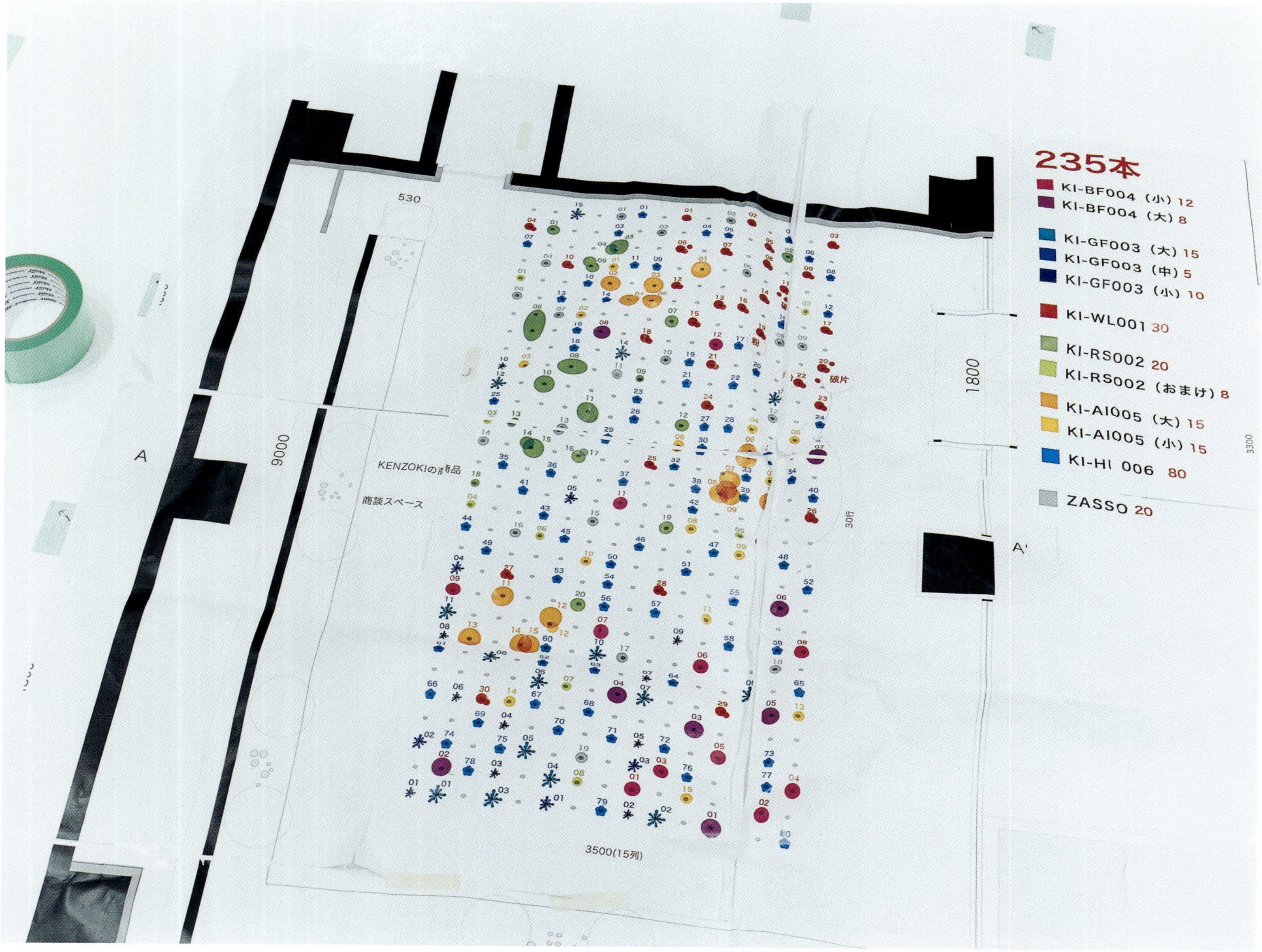
235本
KI-BF004（小）12
KI-BF004（大）8
KI-GF003（大）15
KI-GF003（中）5
KI-GF003（小）10
KI-WL001 30
KI-RS002 20
KI-RS002（おまけ）8
KI-AI005（大）15
KI-AI005（小）15
KI-HI 006 80
ZASSO 20
530
1800
9000
3300
A
A'
KENZOKIの商品
商談スペース
破片
粉
30行
3500(15列)

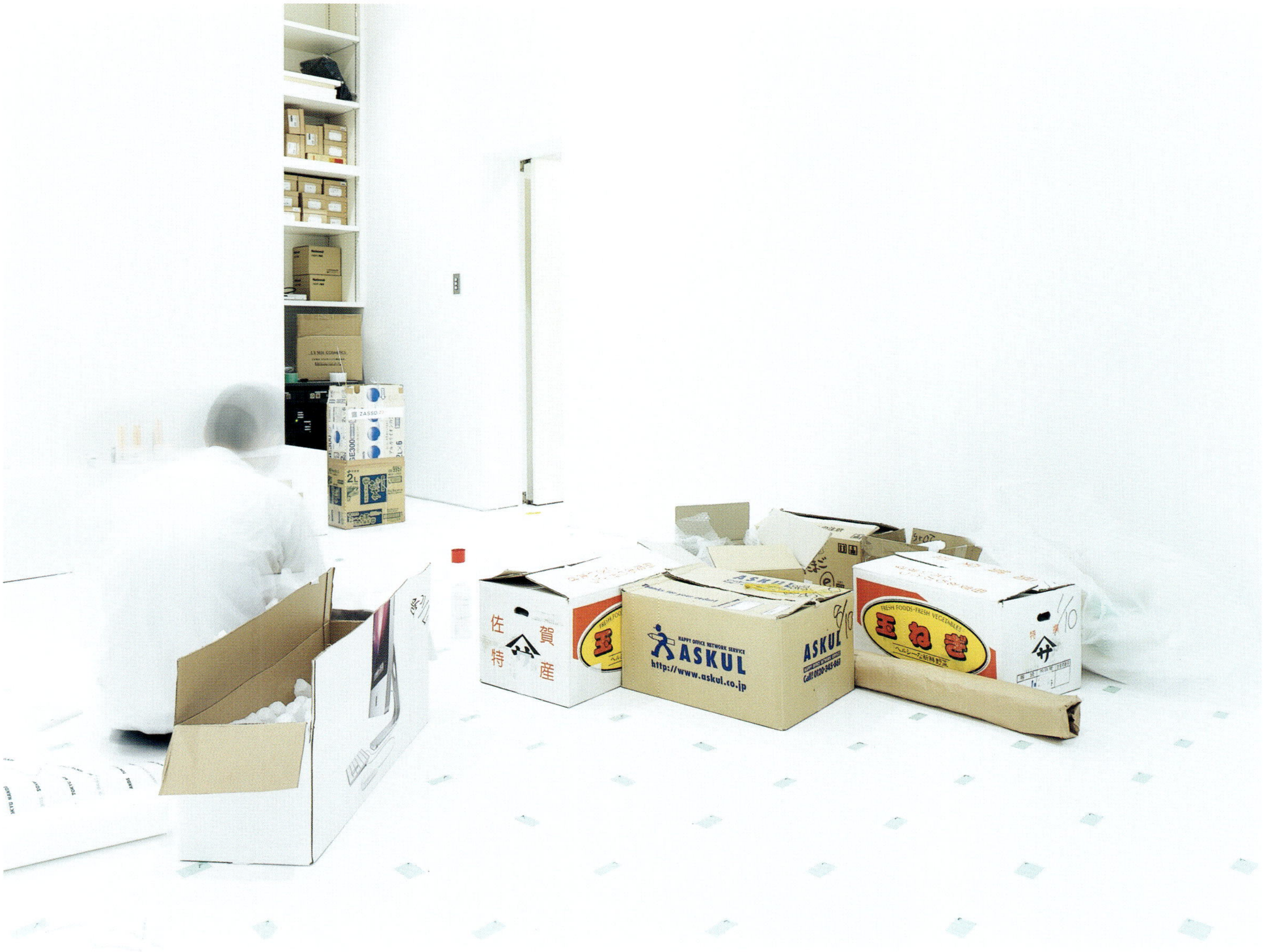

HAPPY OFFICE NETWORK SERVICE
ASKUL
http://www.askul.co.jp
ASKUL
佐賀特産
玉ねぎ

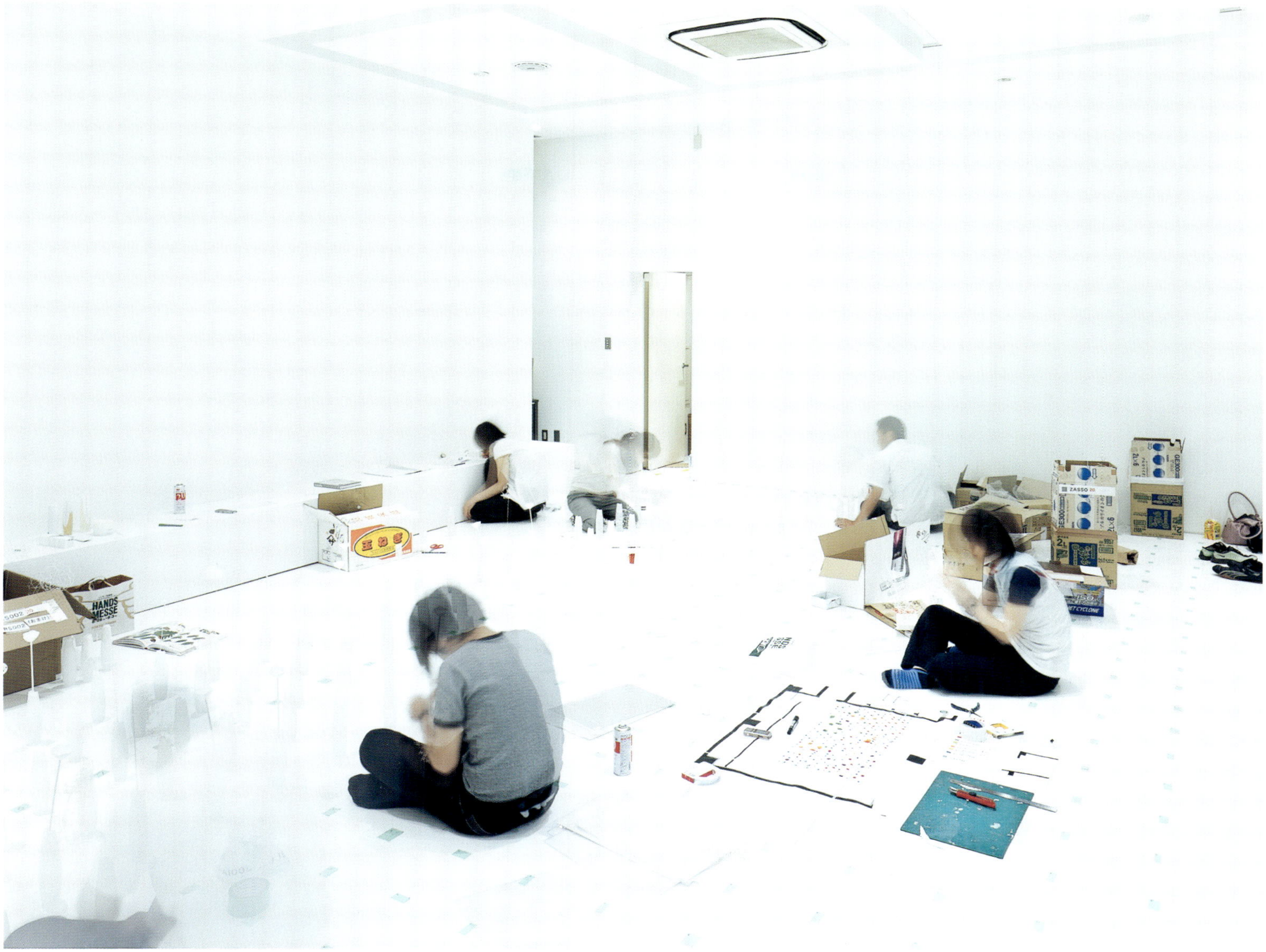
HANDS
MESSE
ZASSO

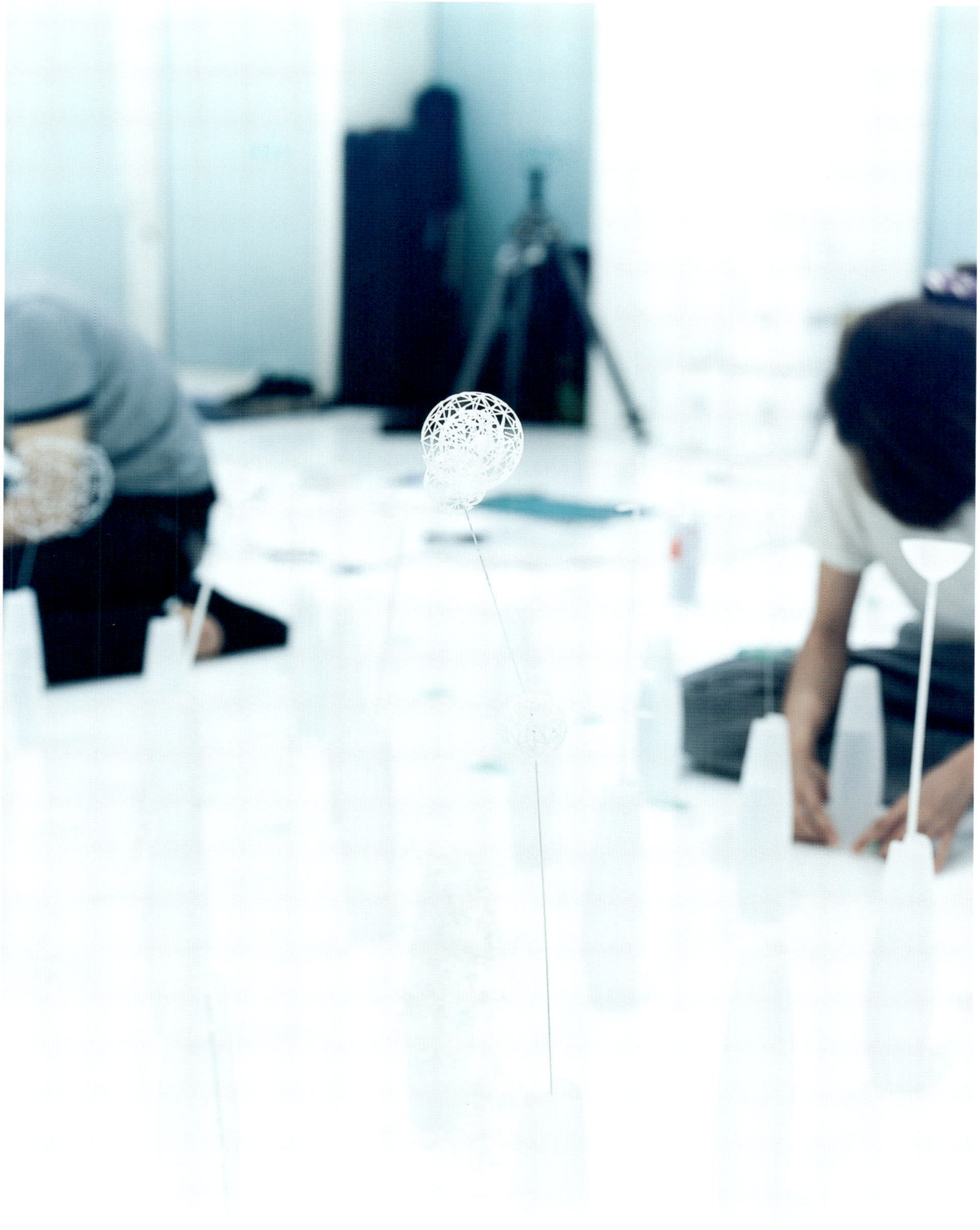

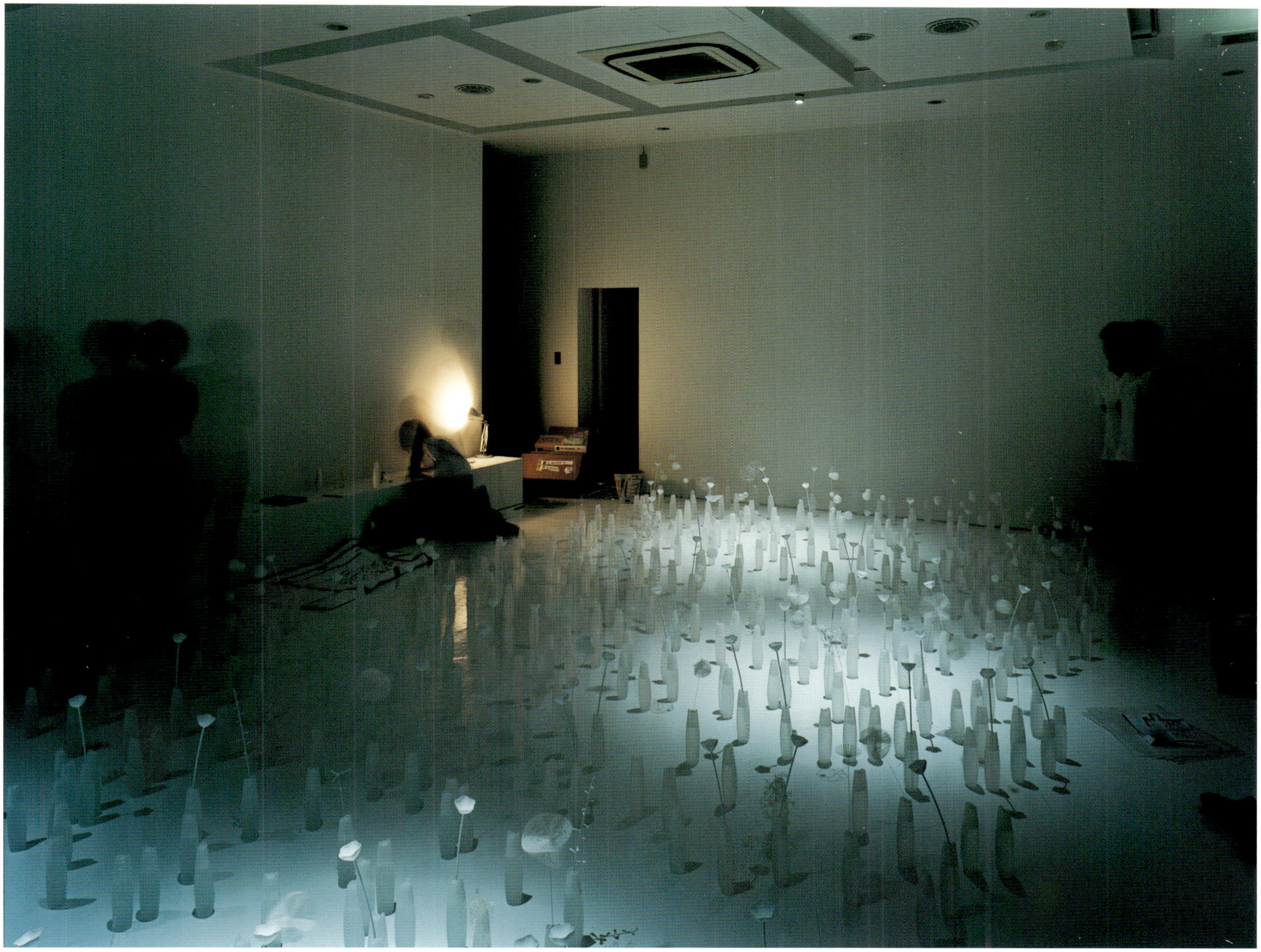

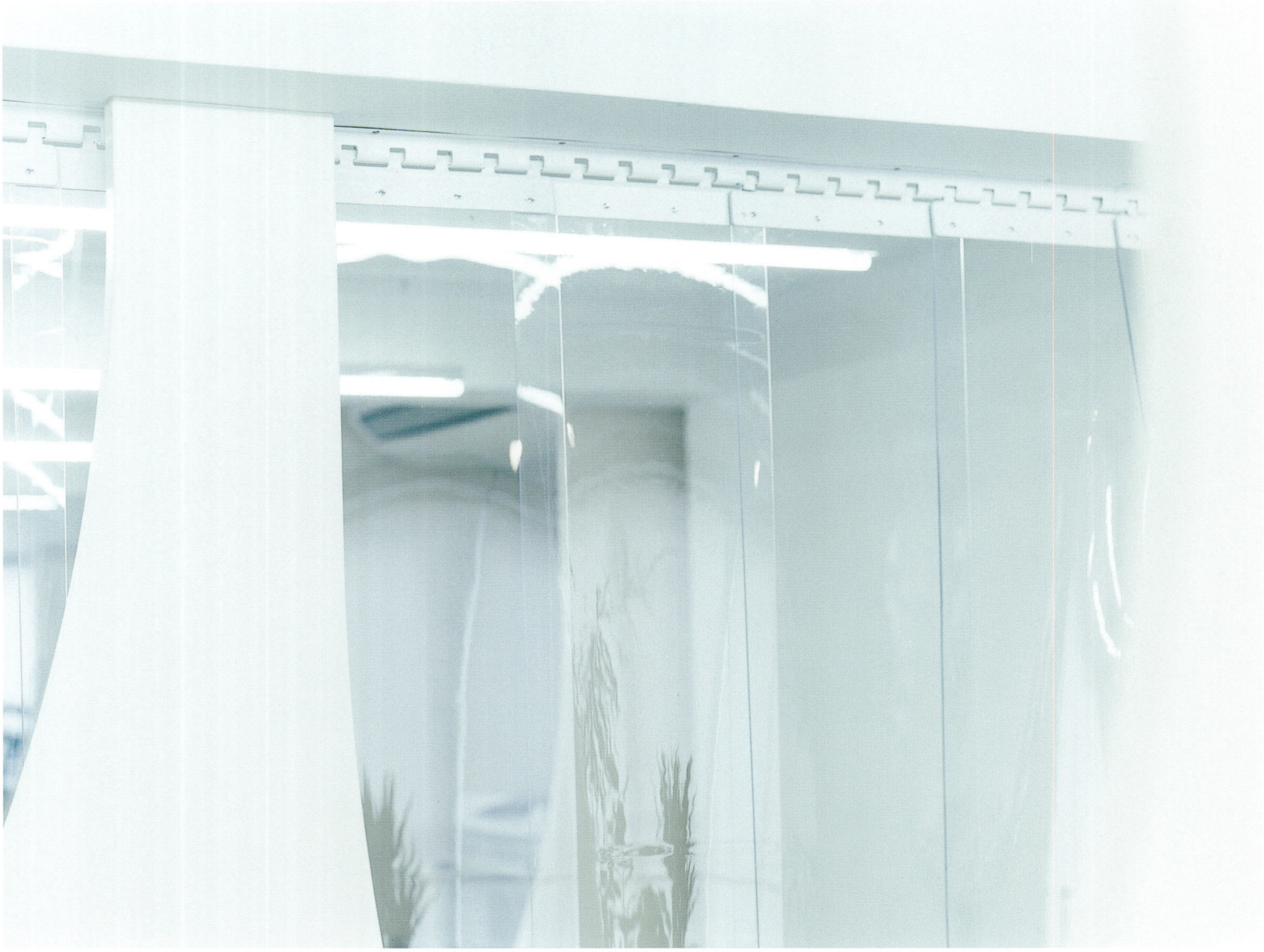

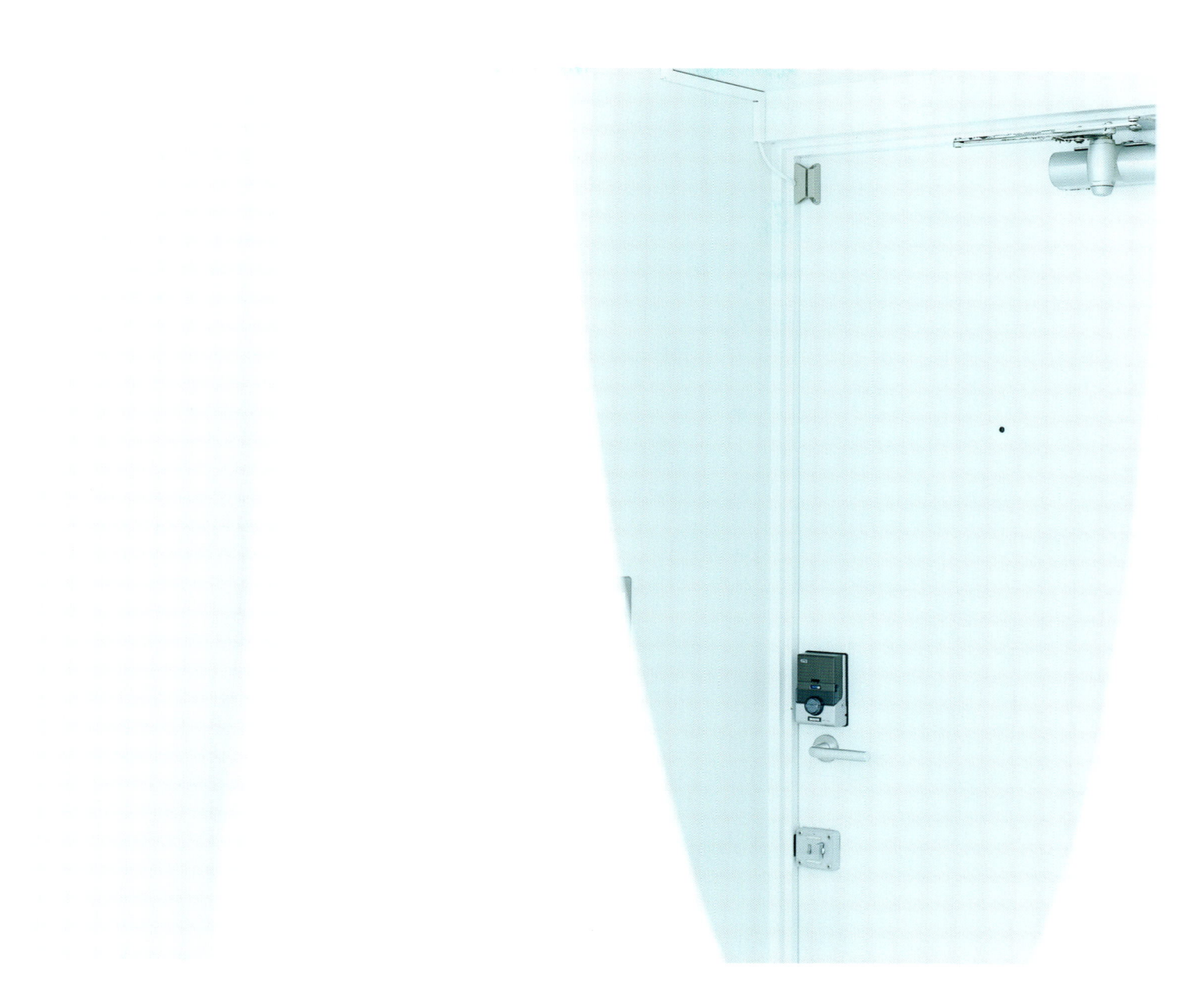

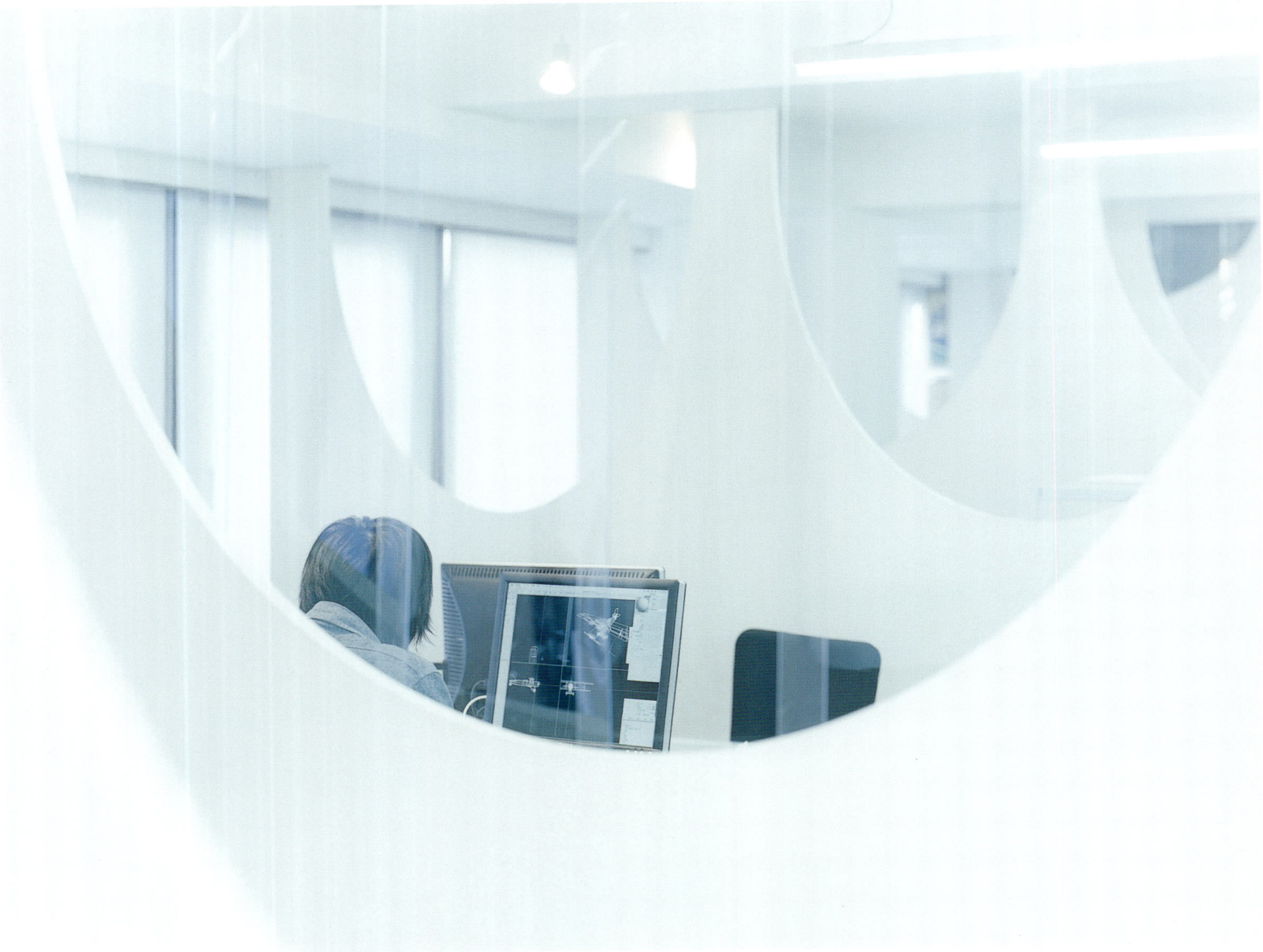

92

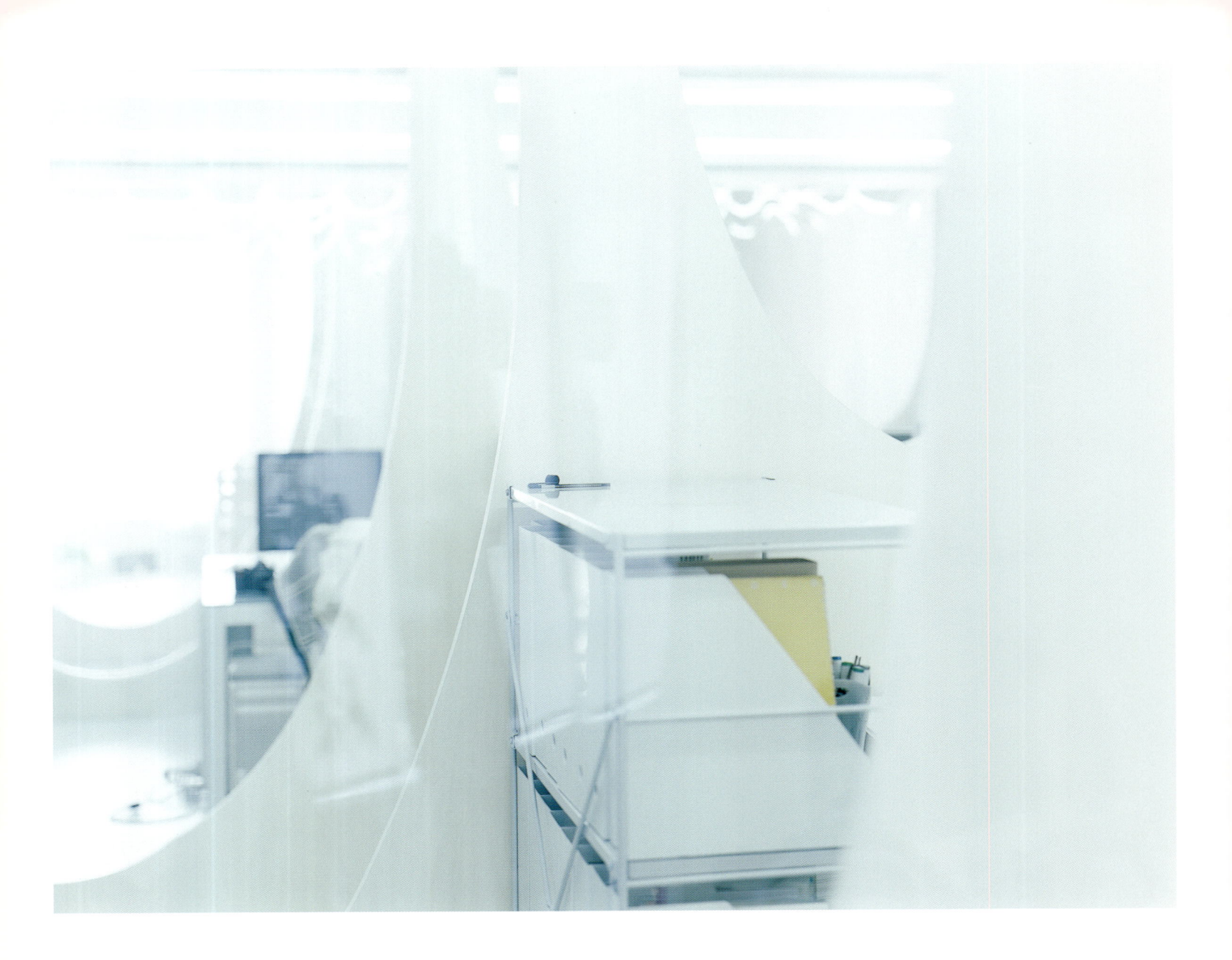

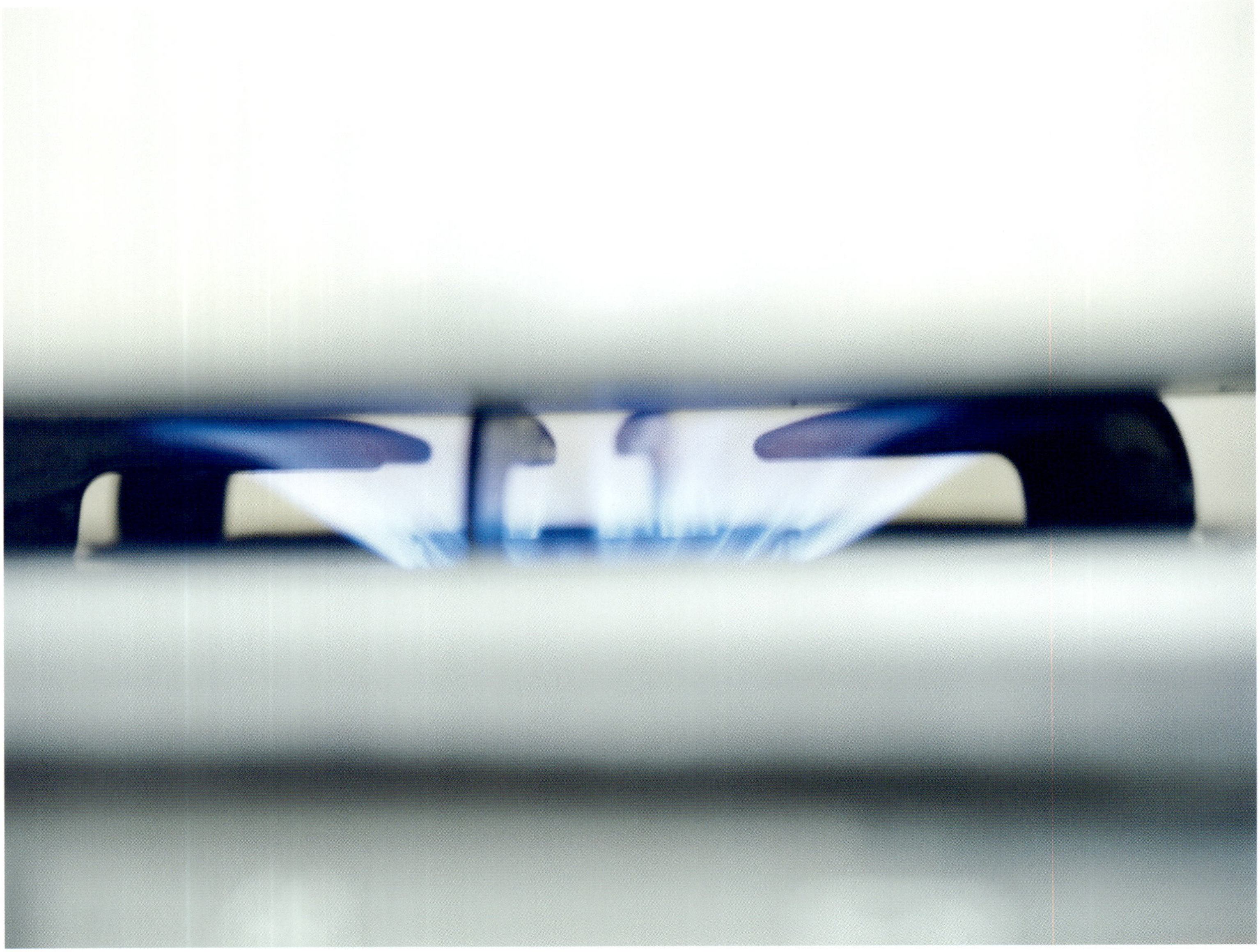

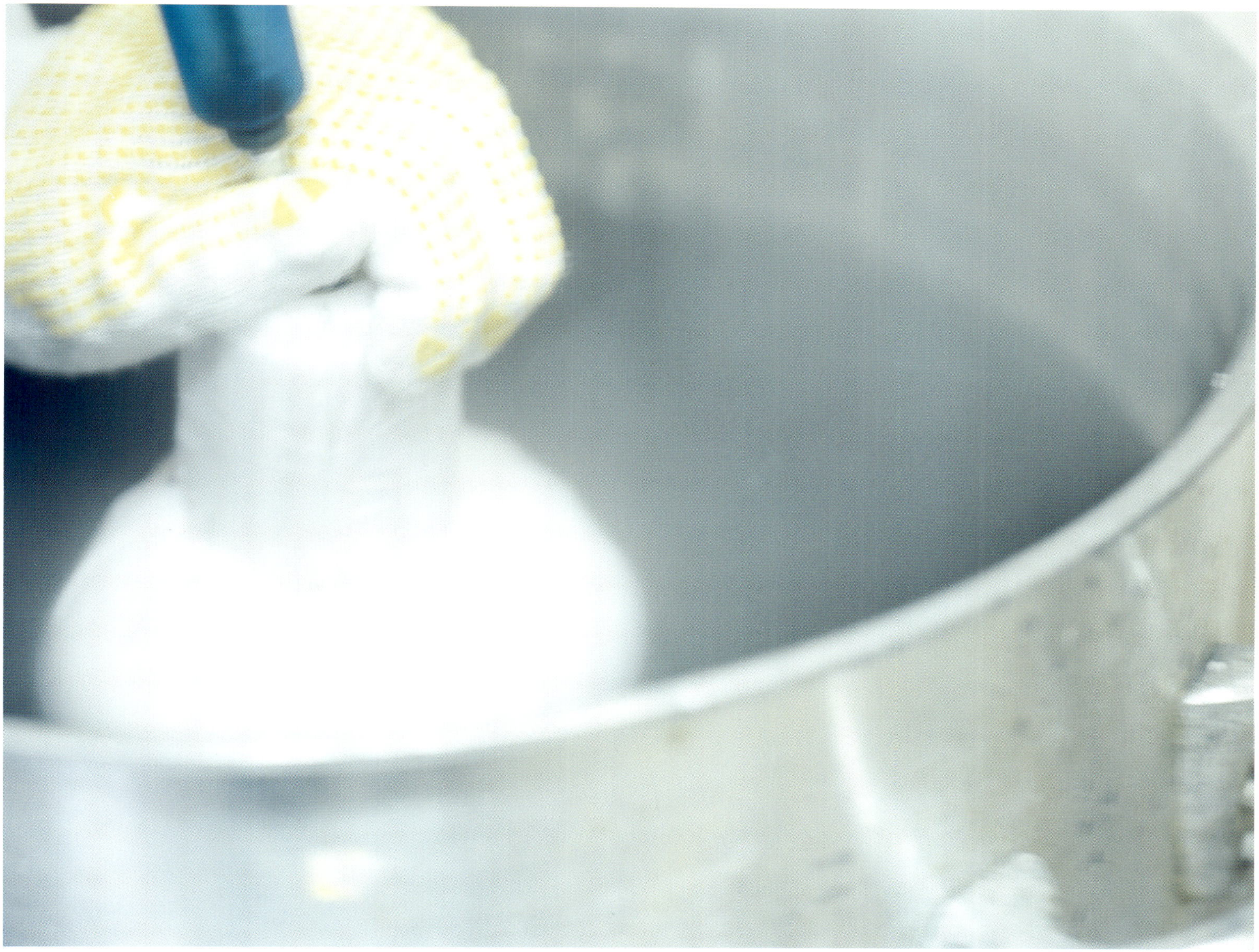

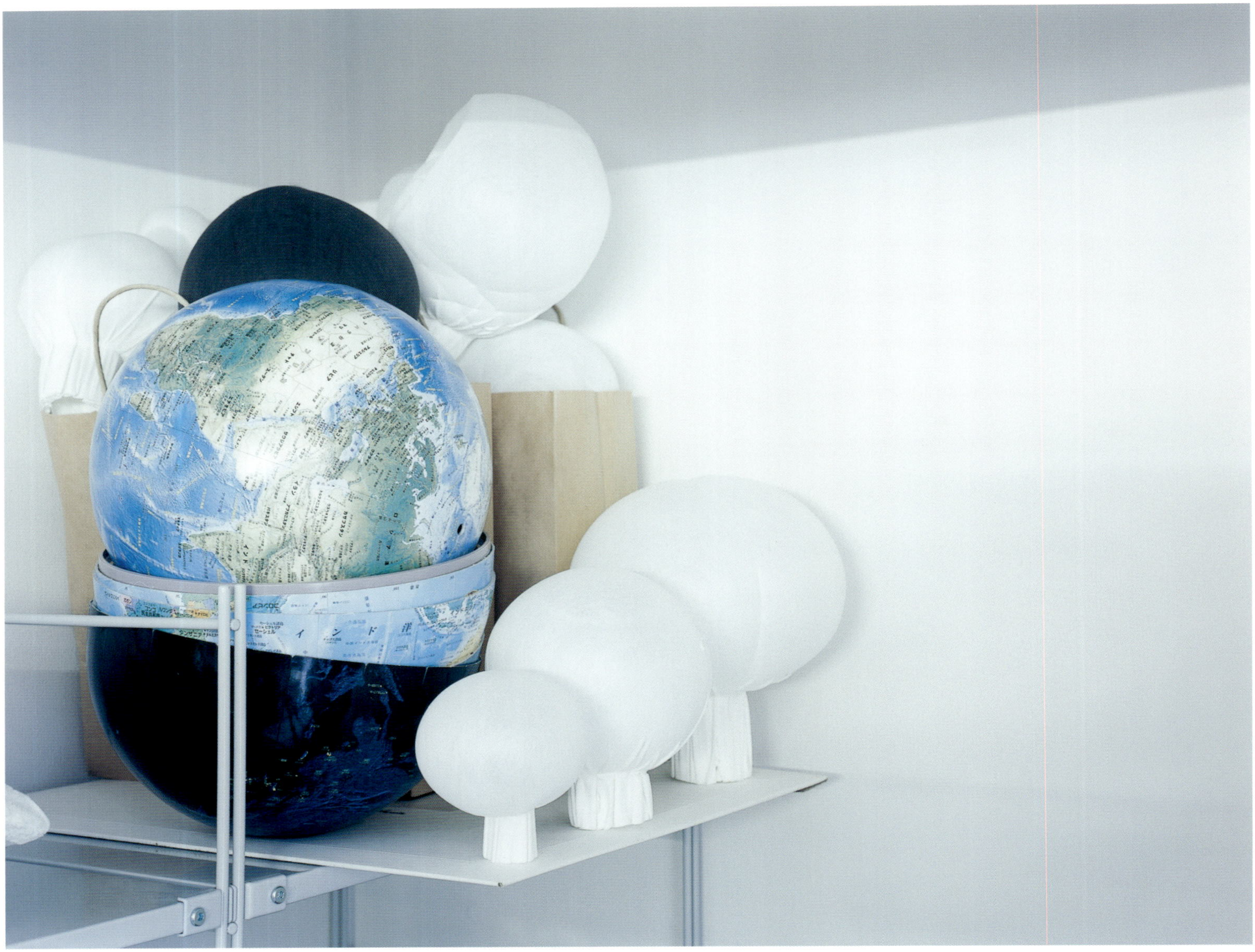
インド洋

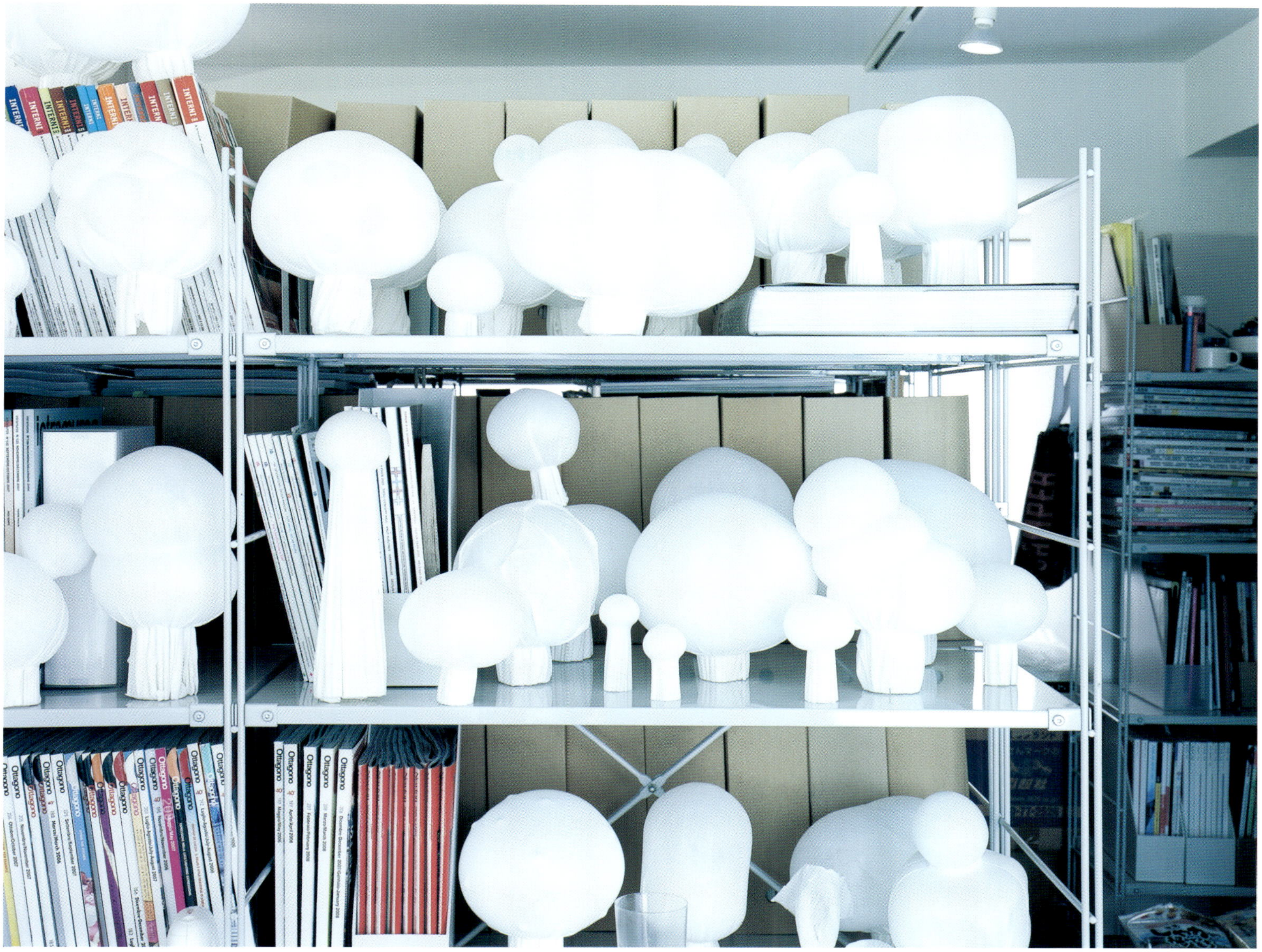

101

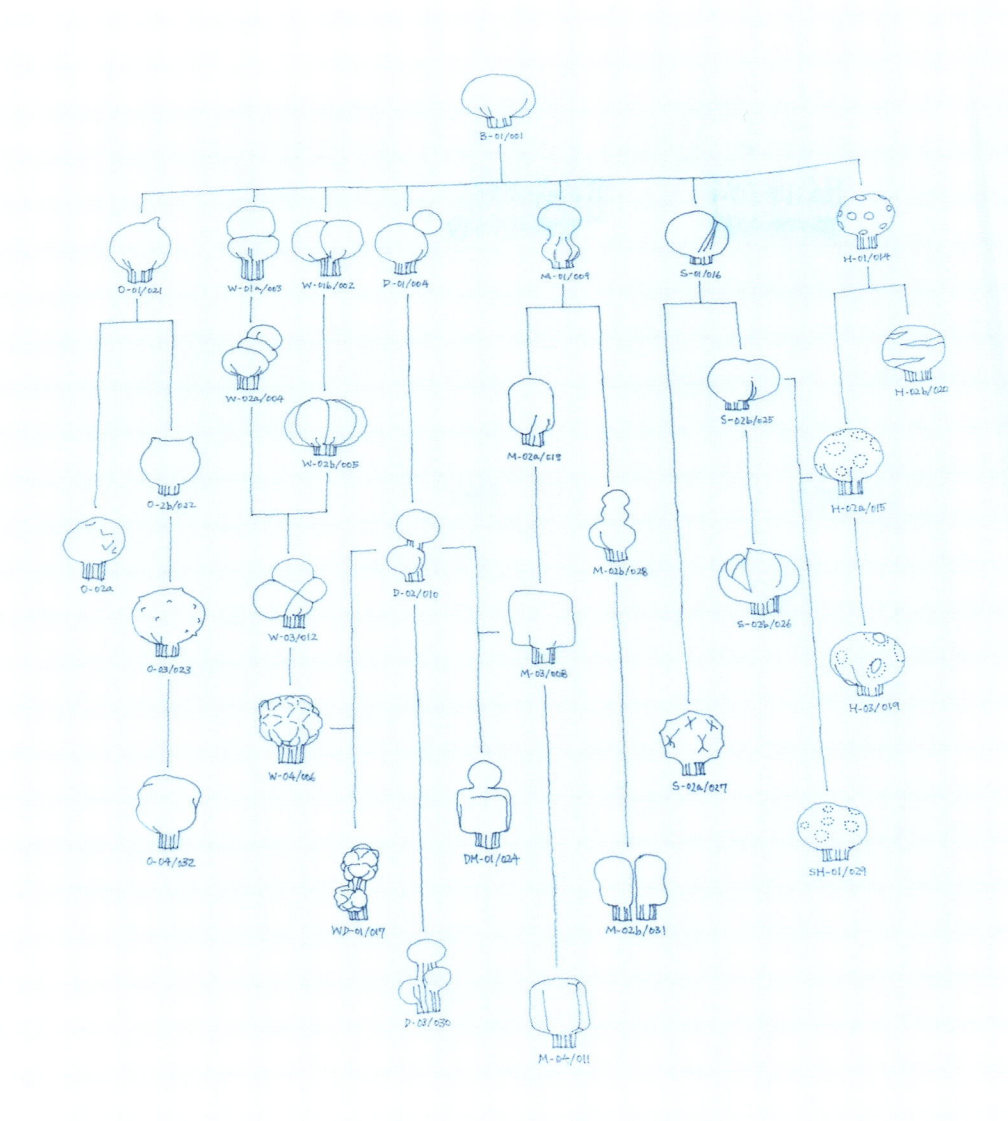

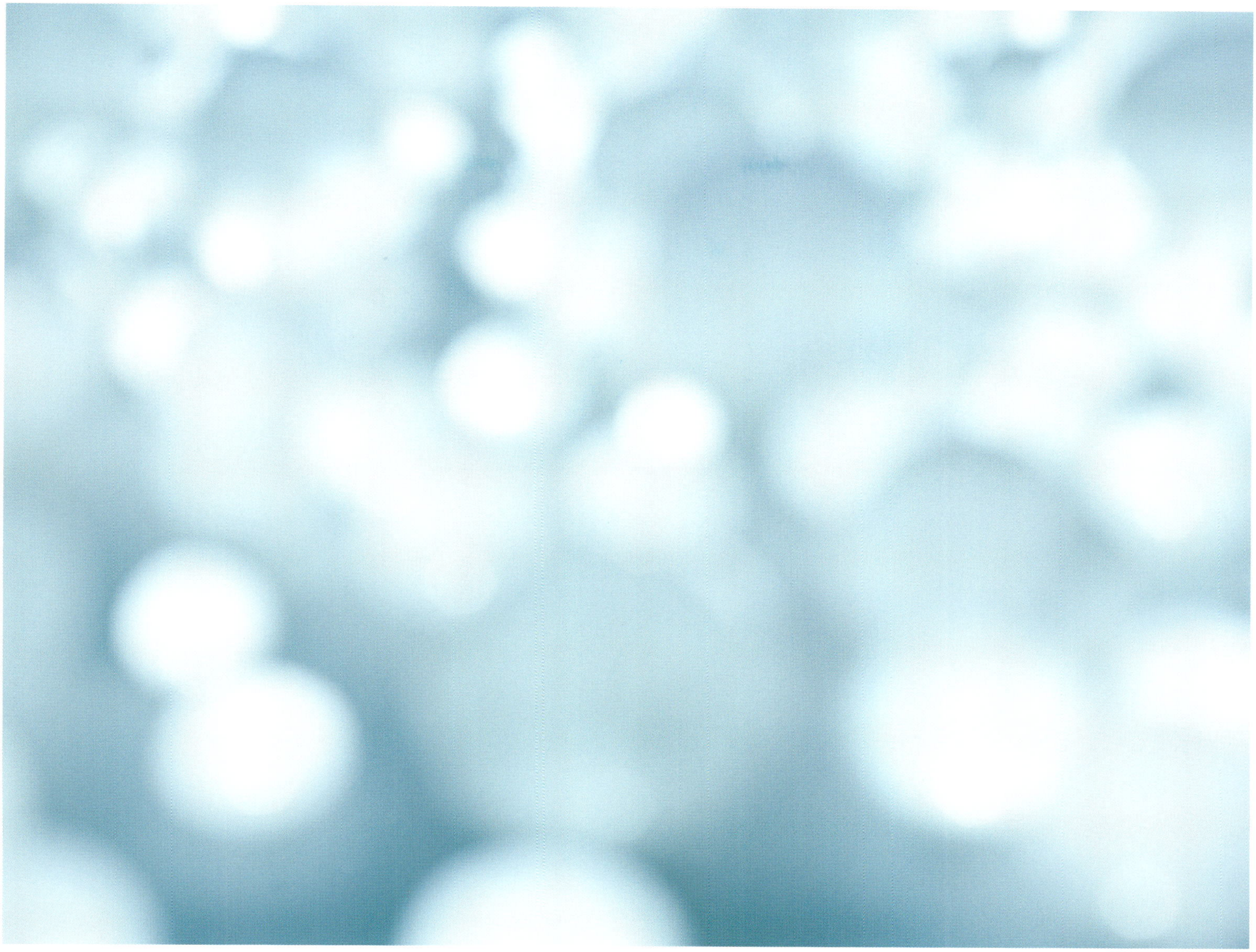

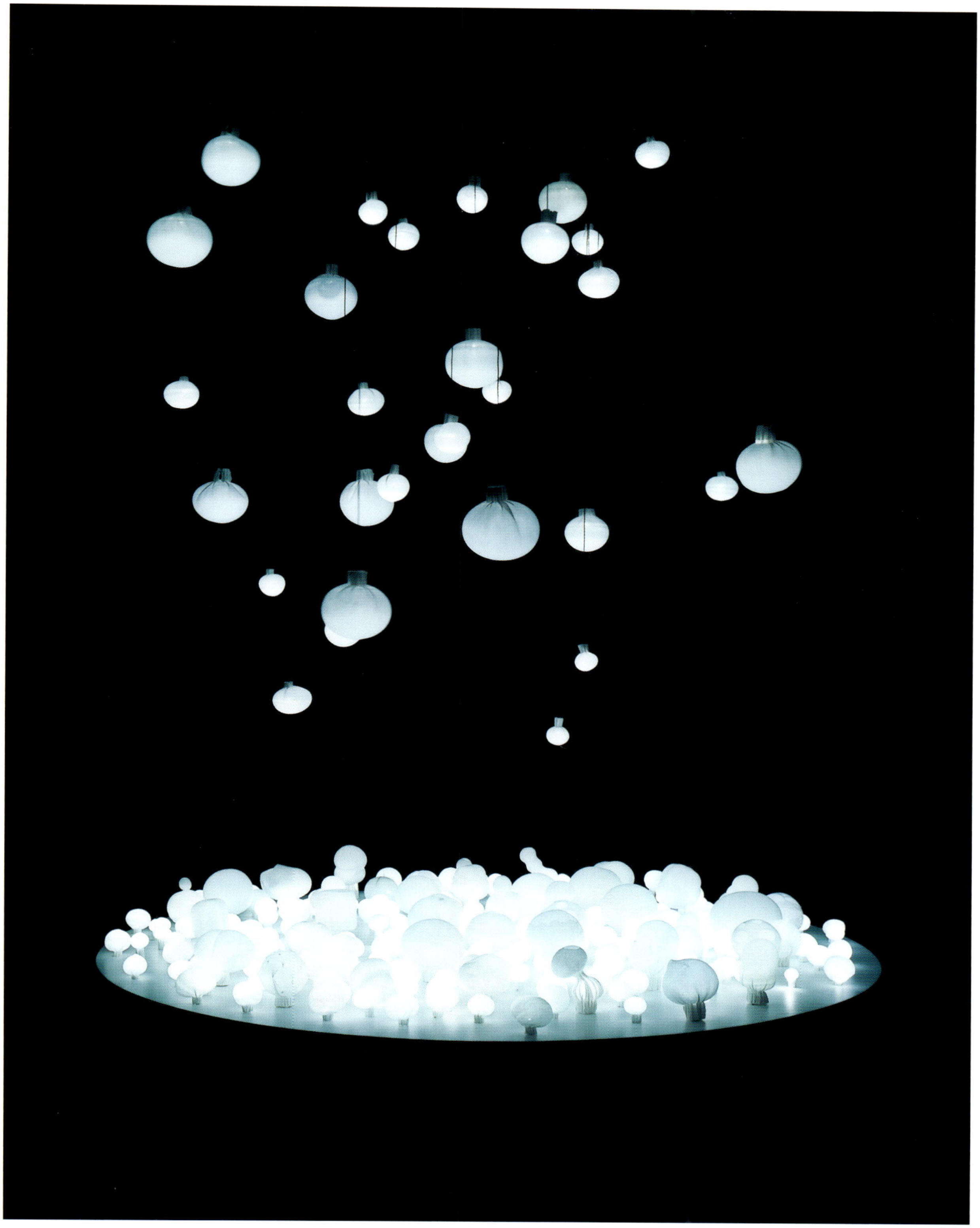

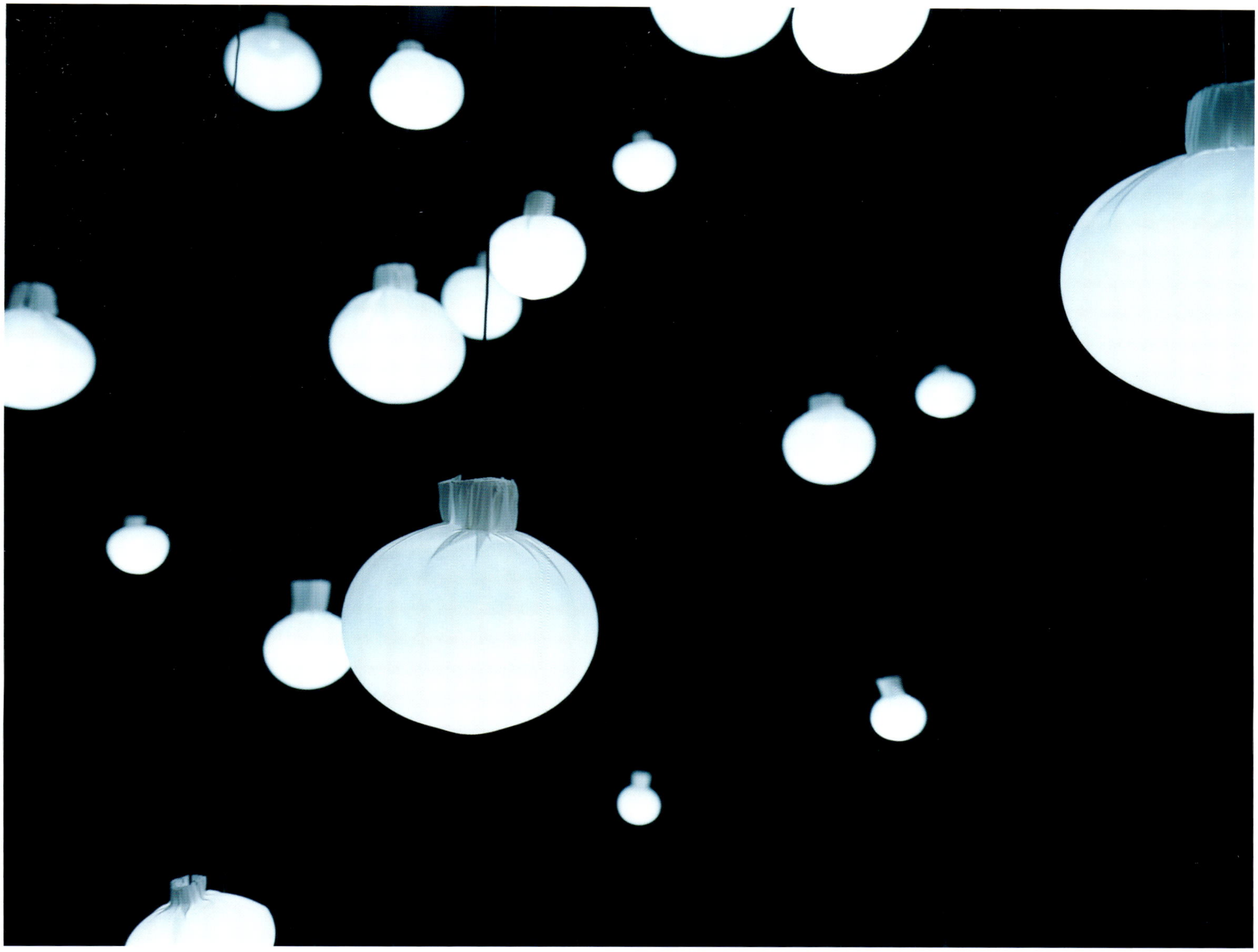

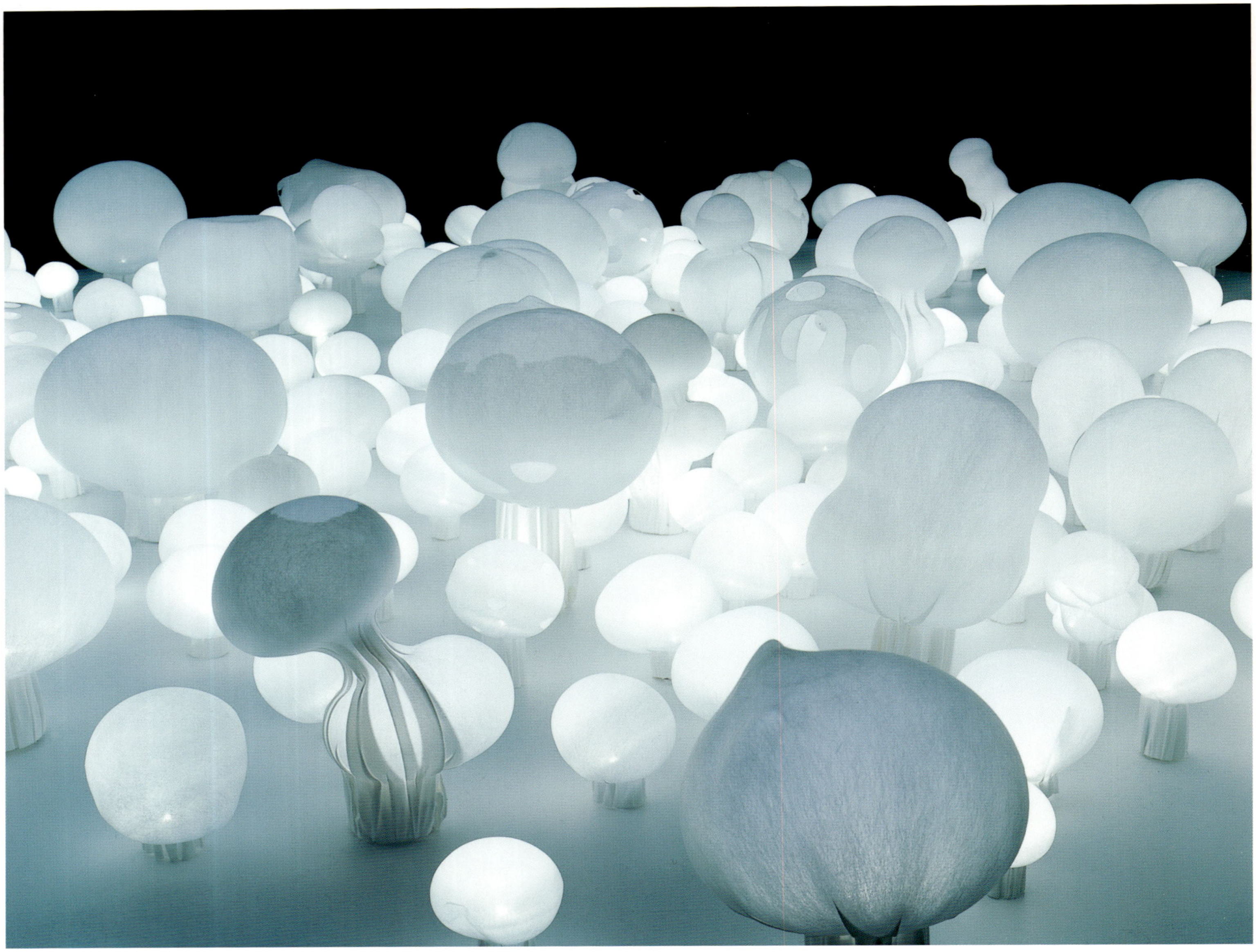

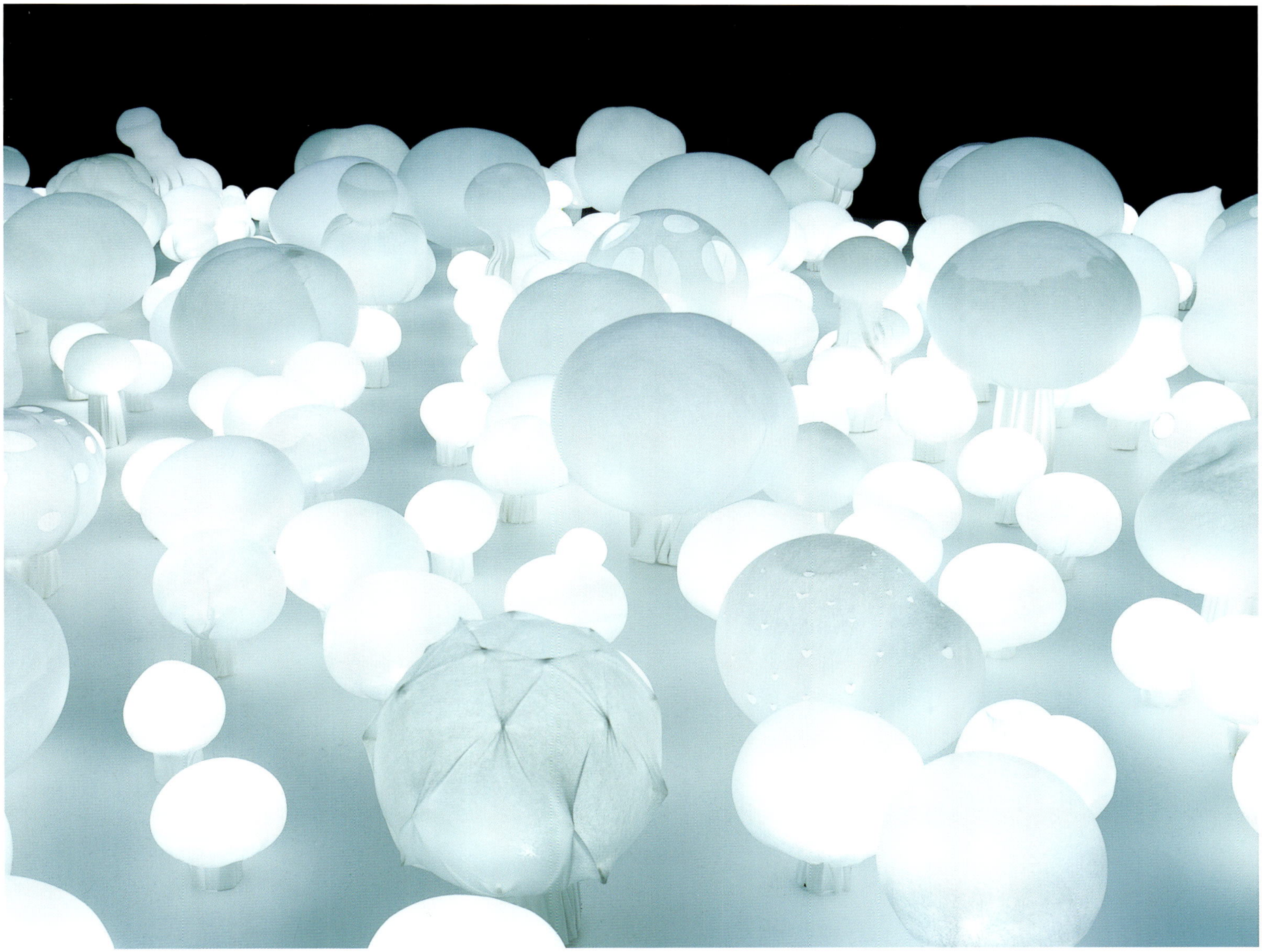

LIGHT — SHADOW

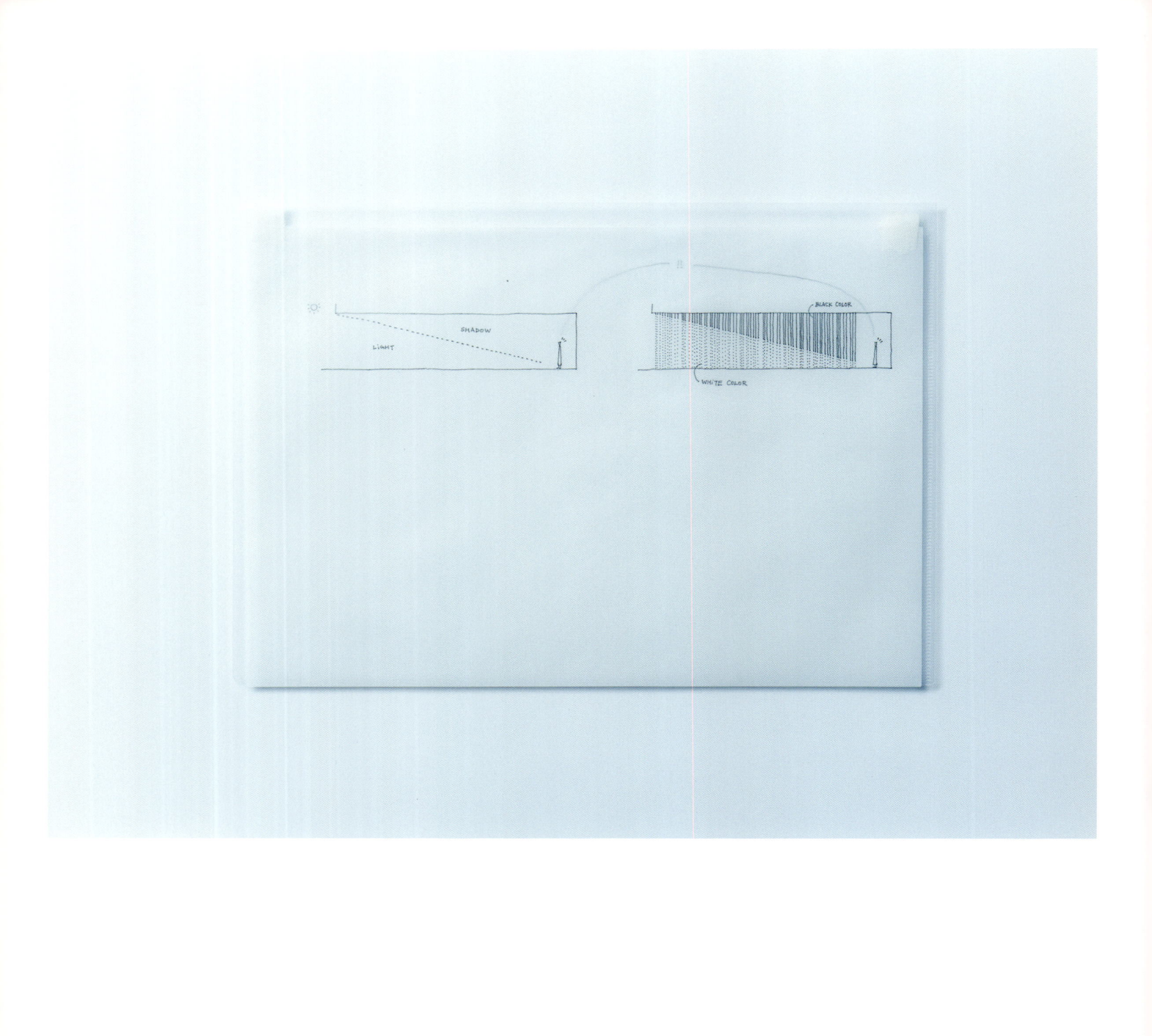

BLACK COLOR
WHITE COLOR

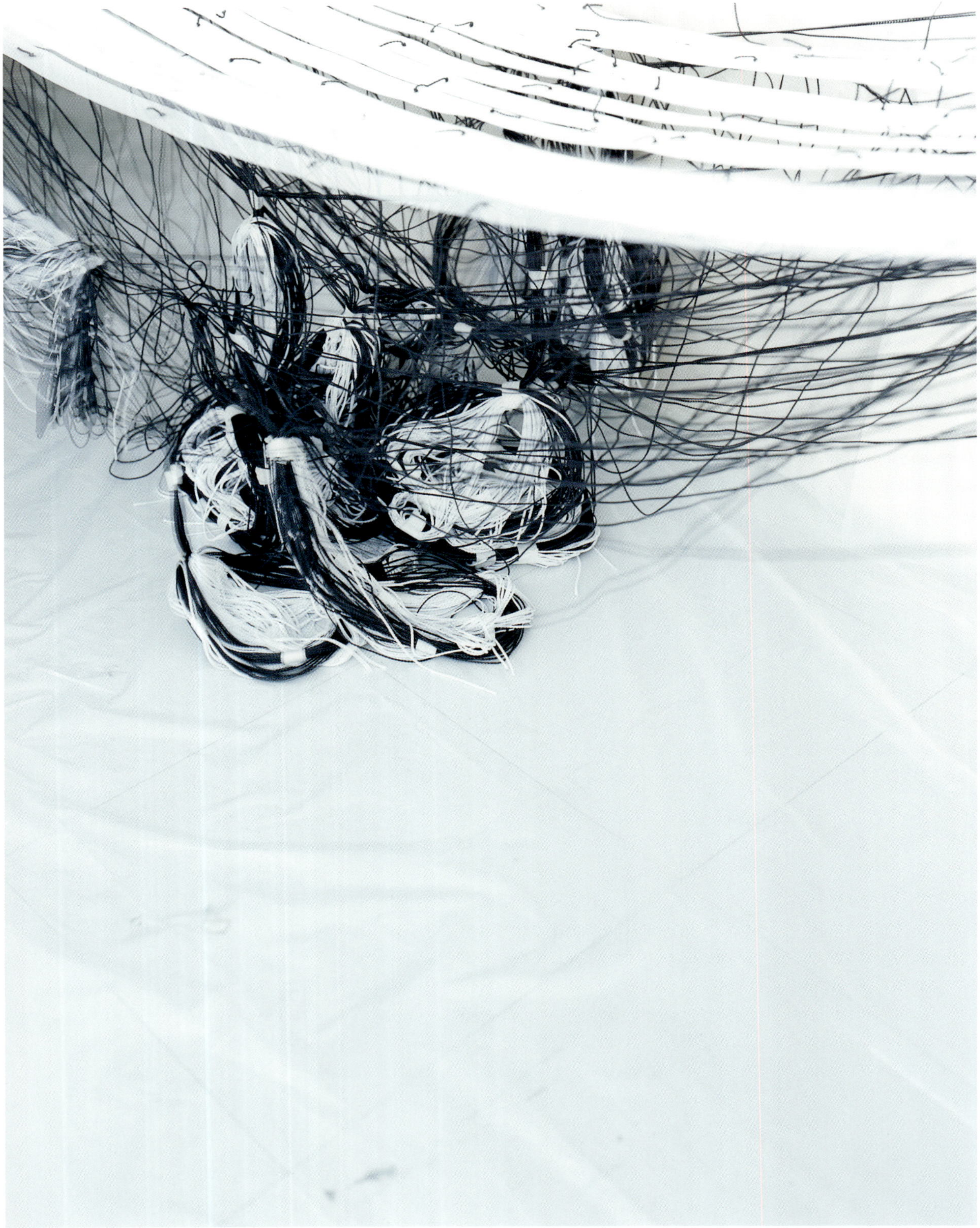

115

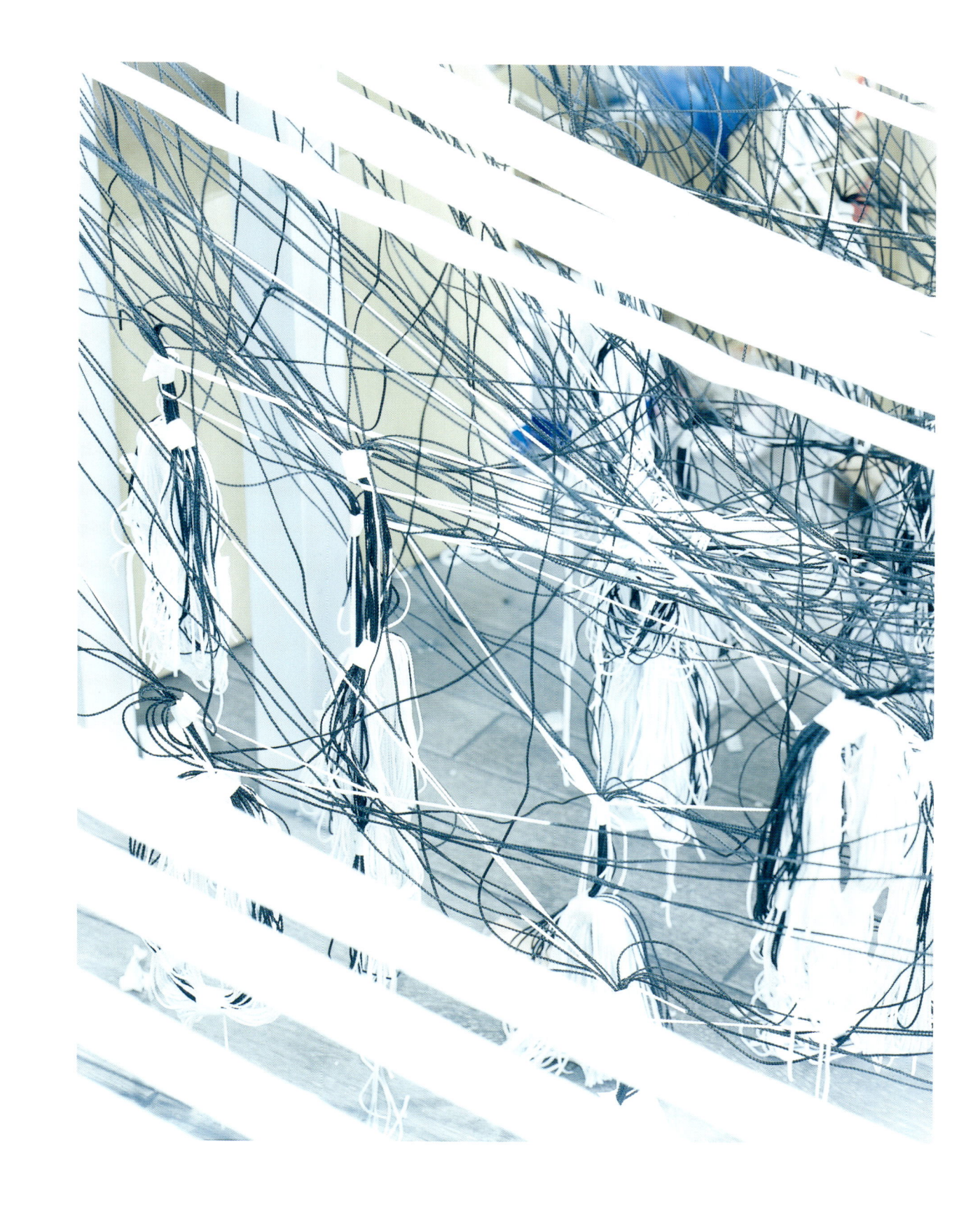

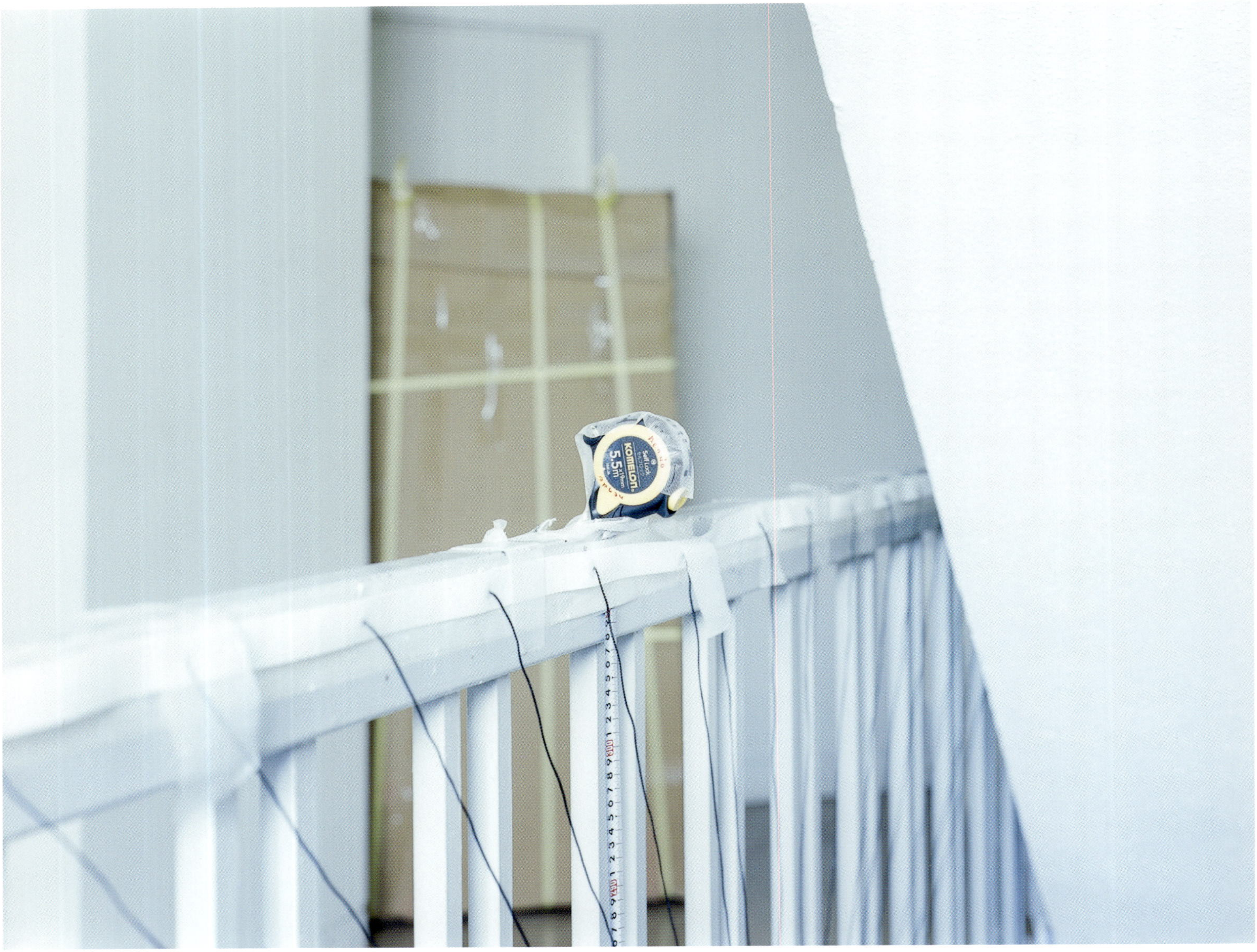

KOMELON
Self Lock
5.5m

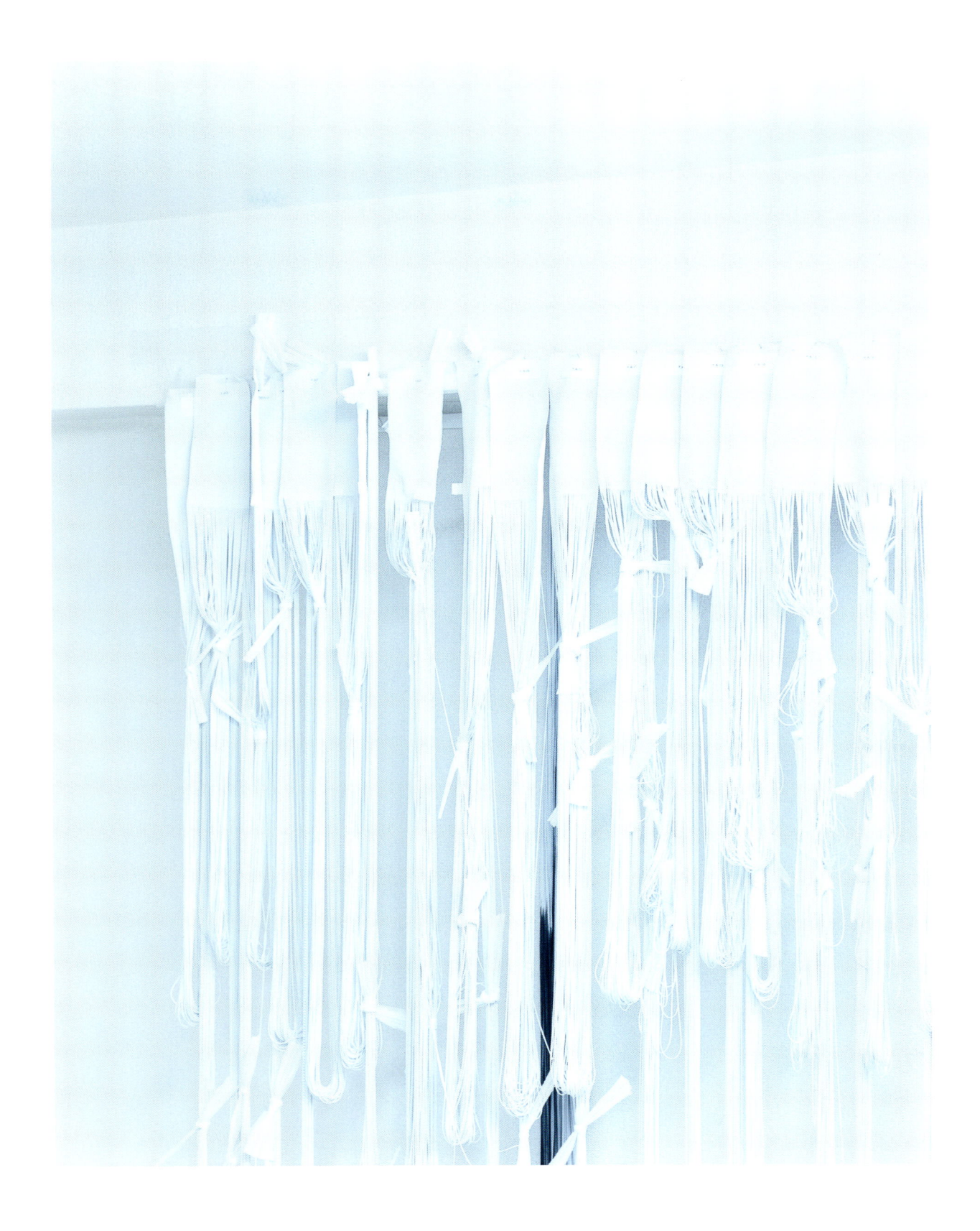

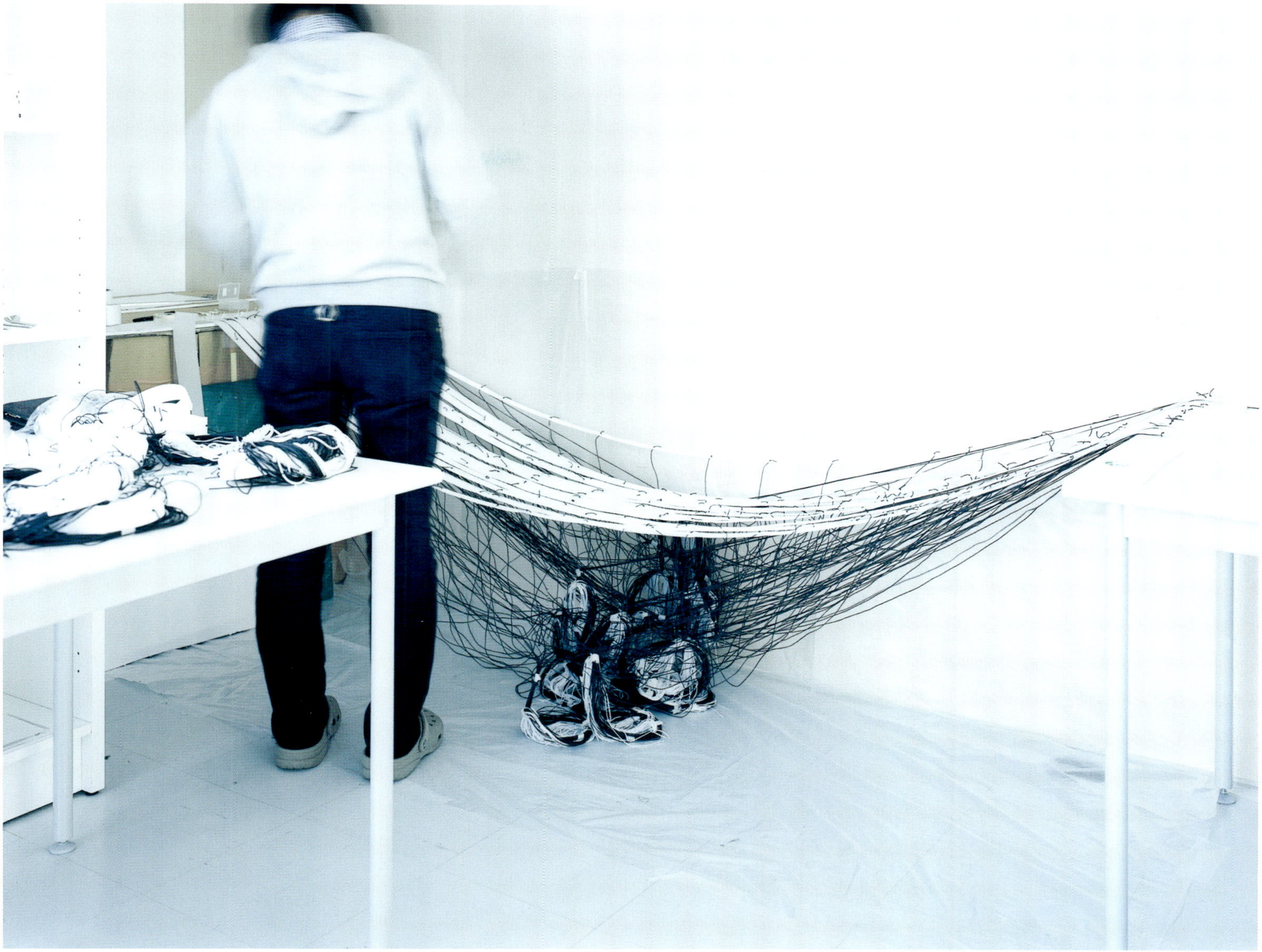

40°C
30°C
20°C
LIGHT BULB
E17. 36W

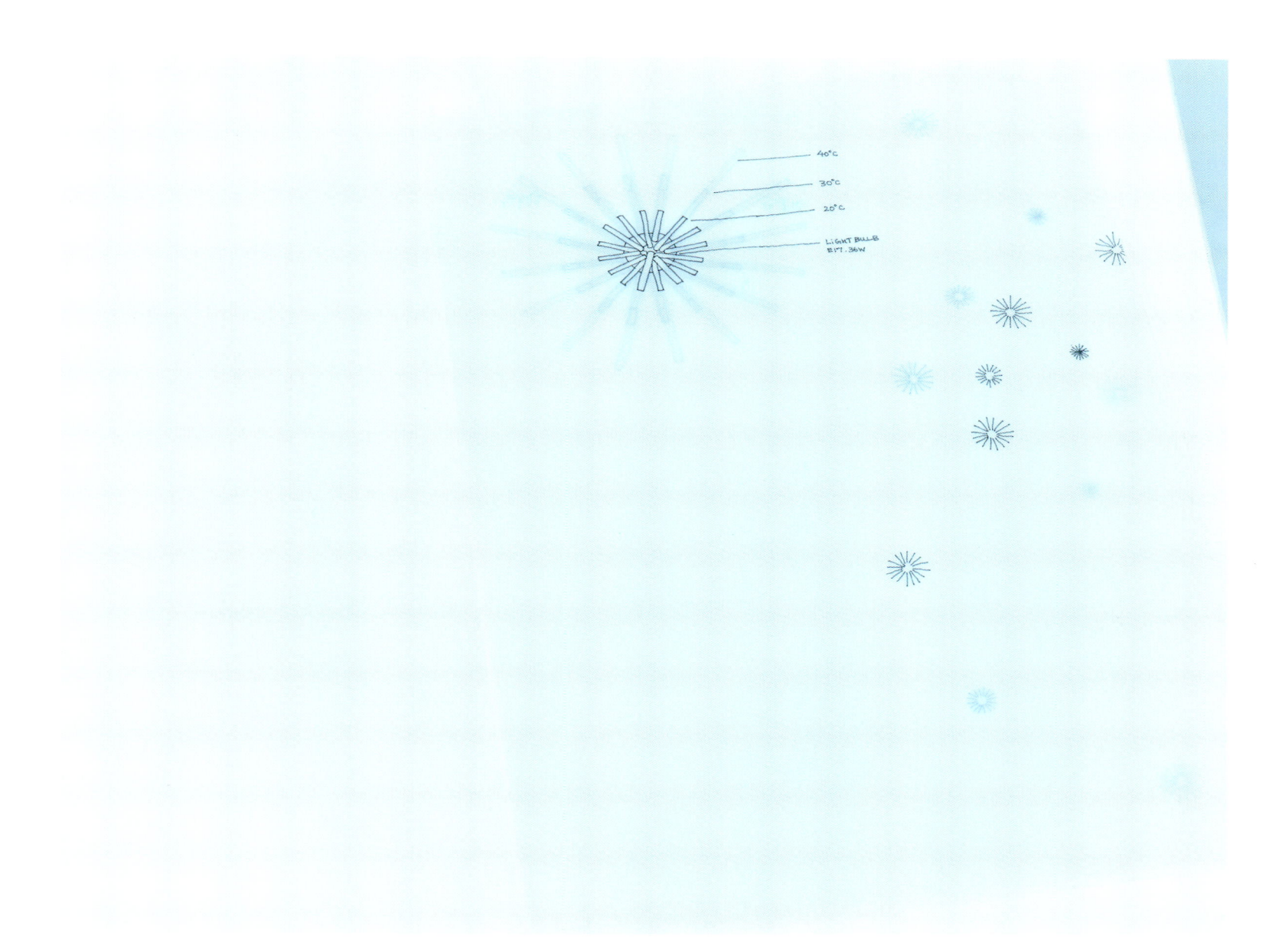

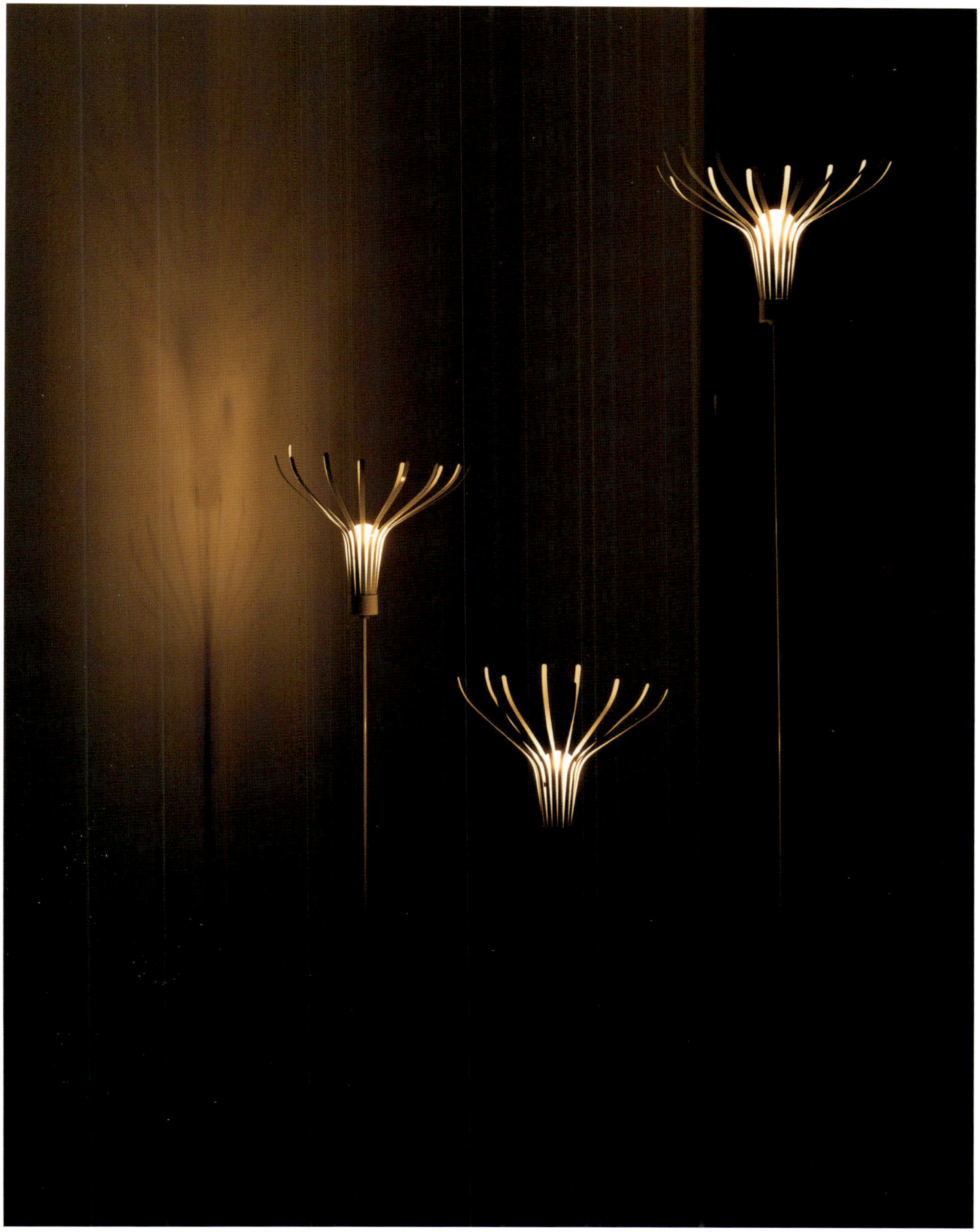

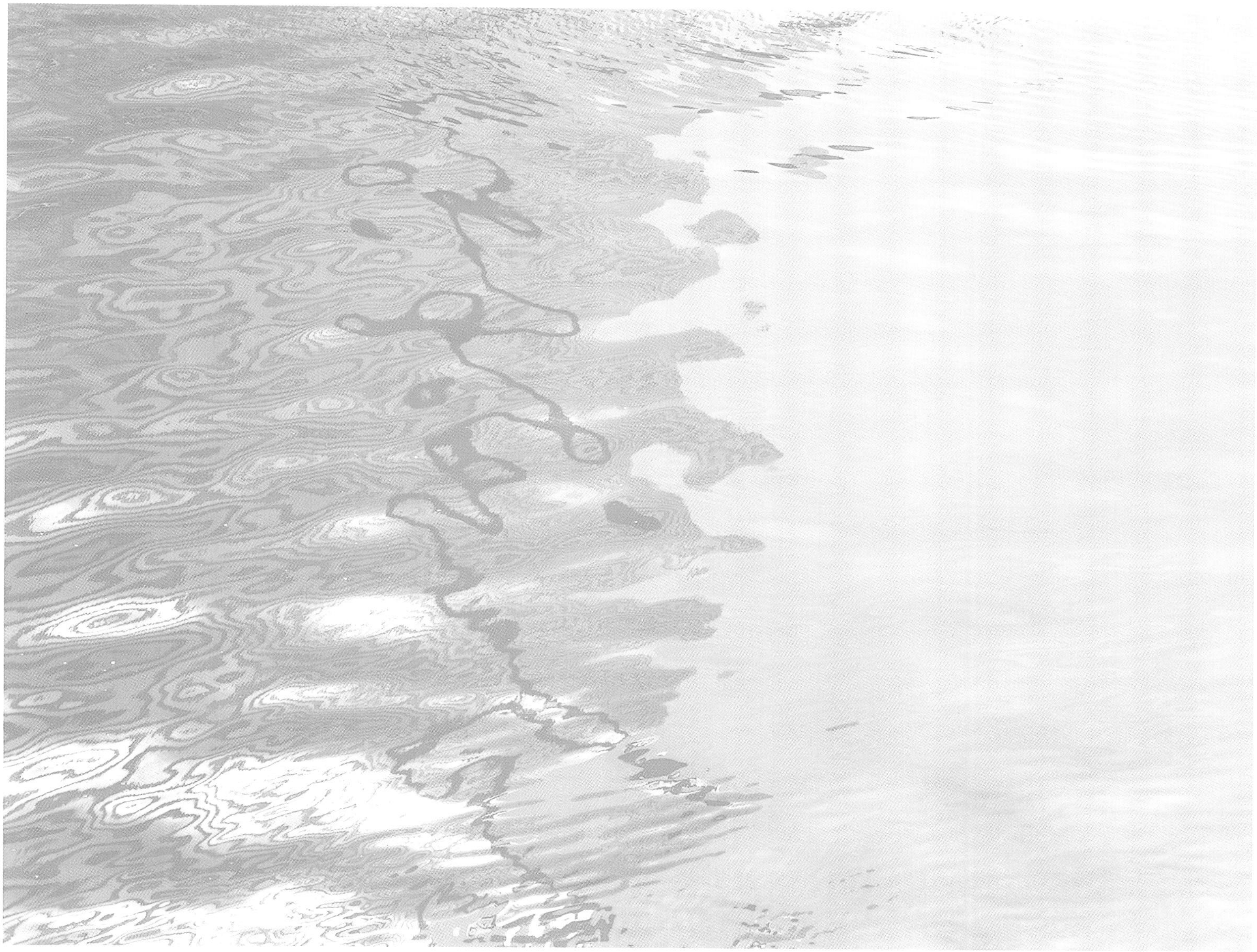

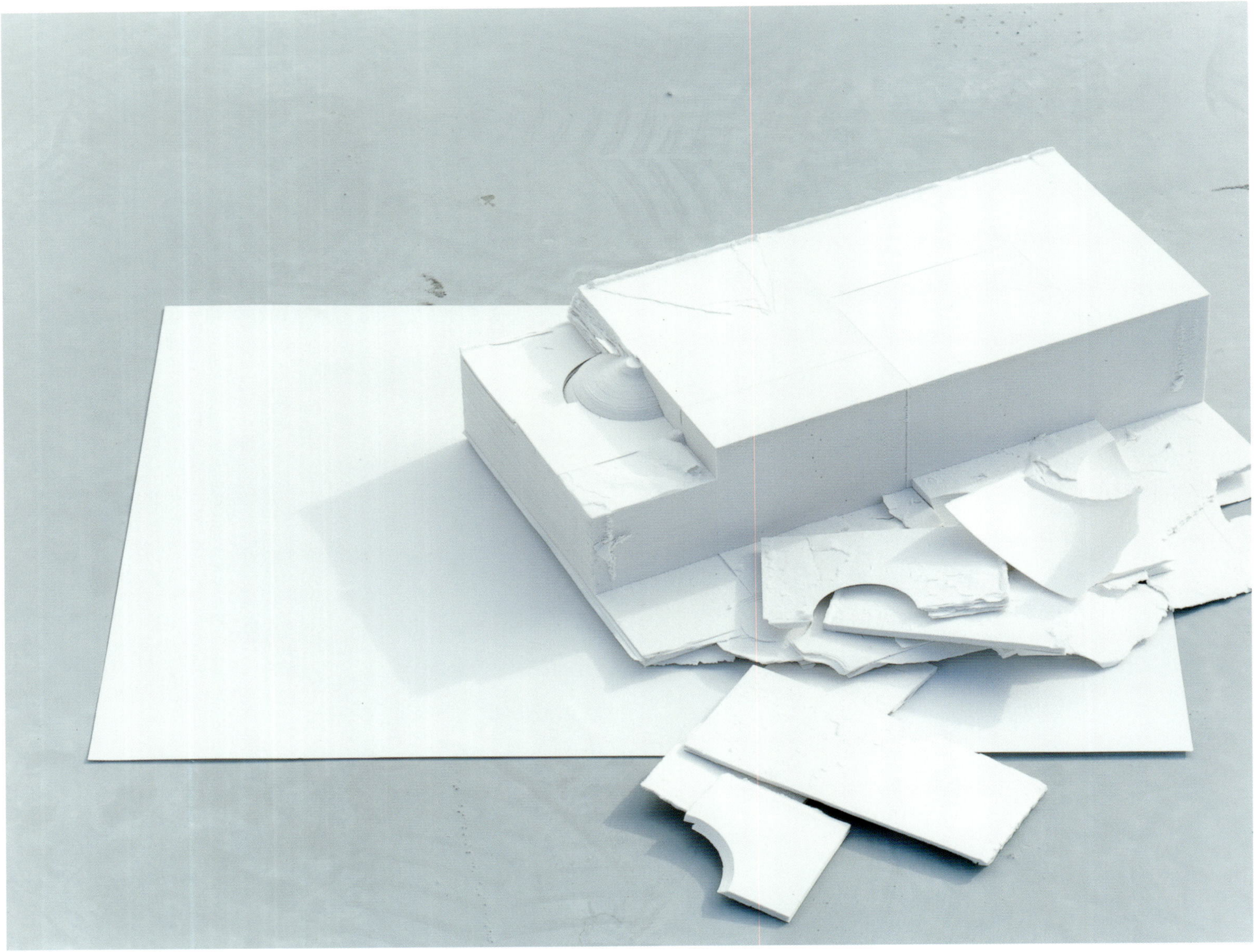

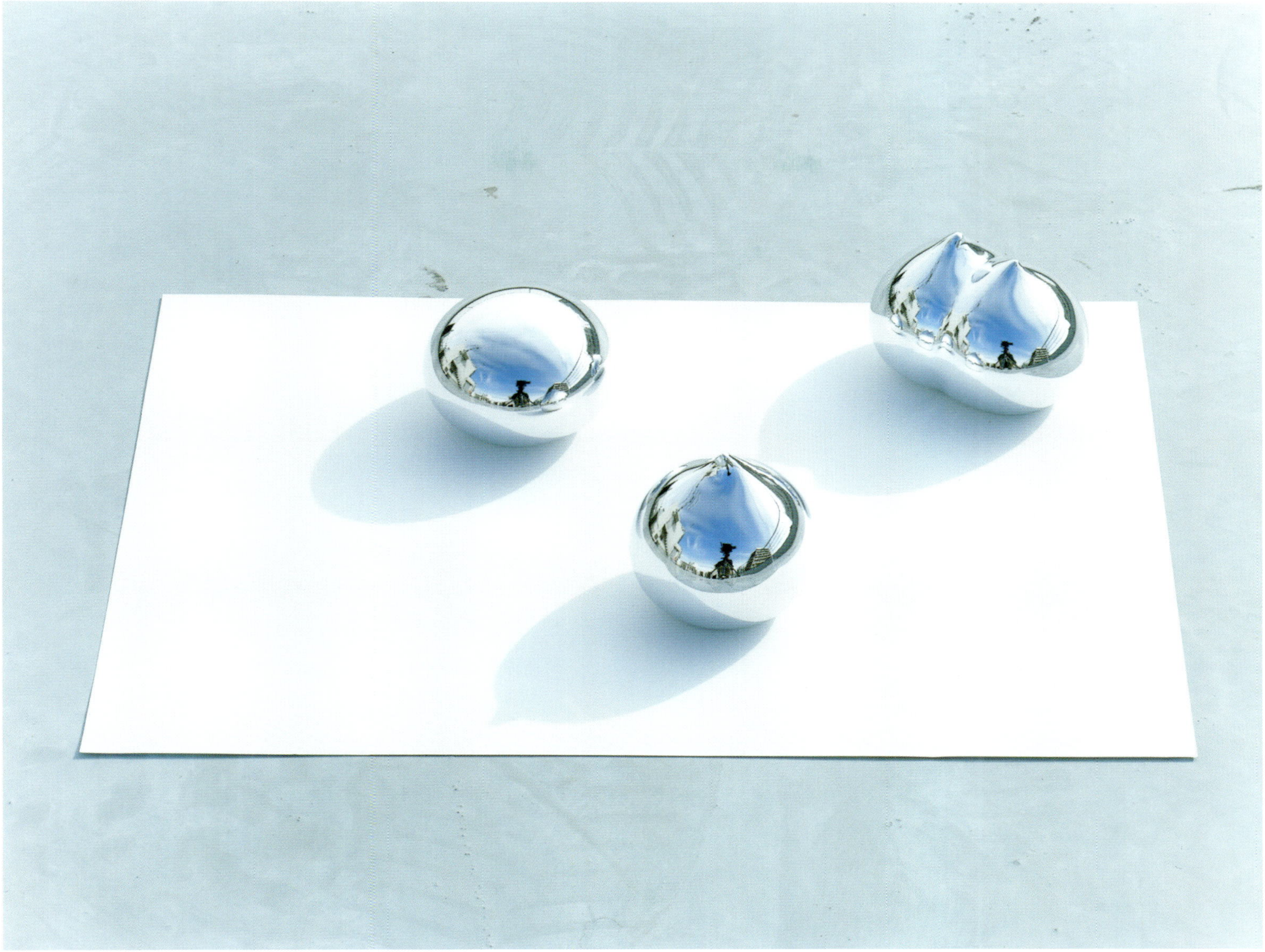

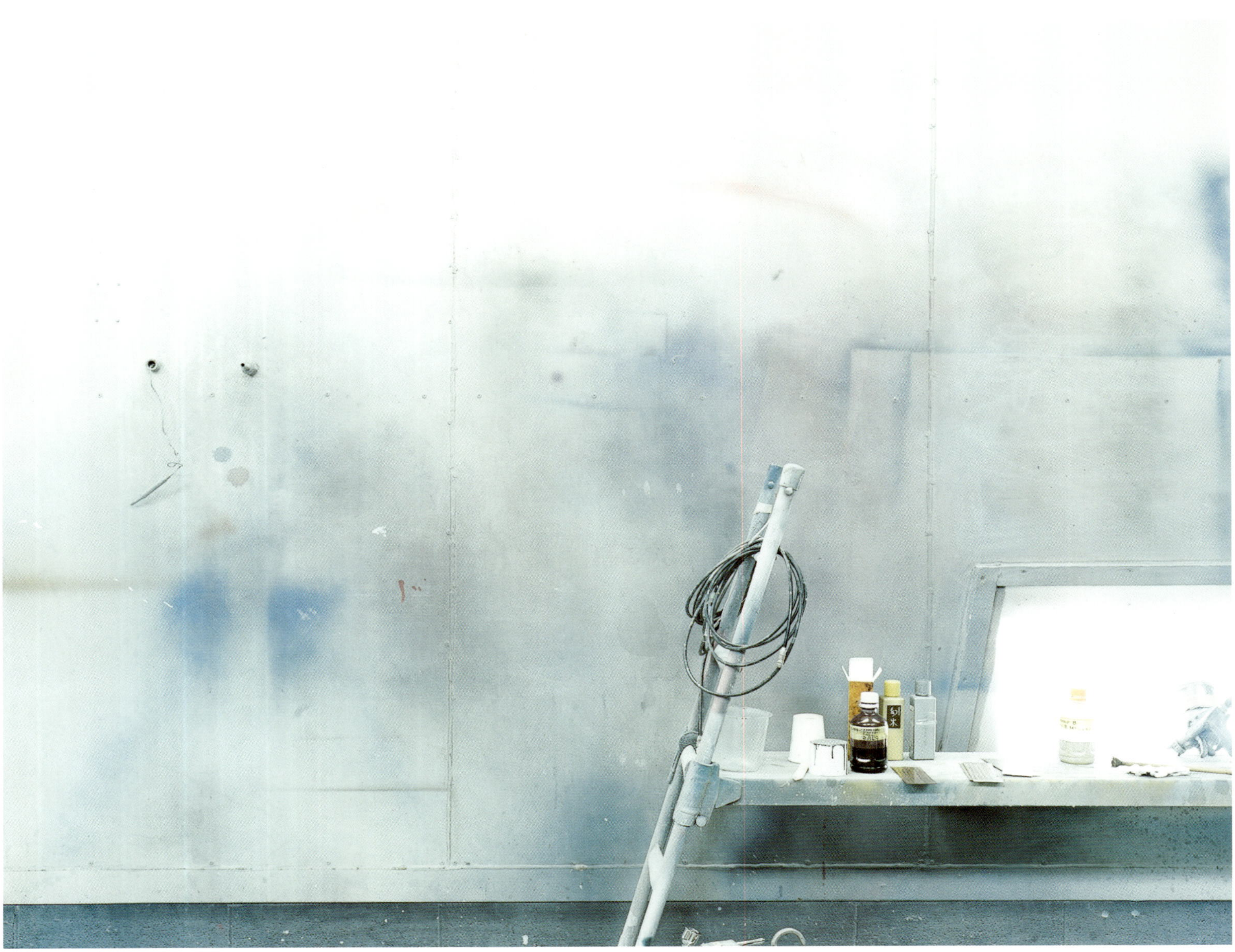

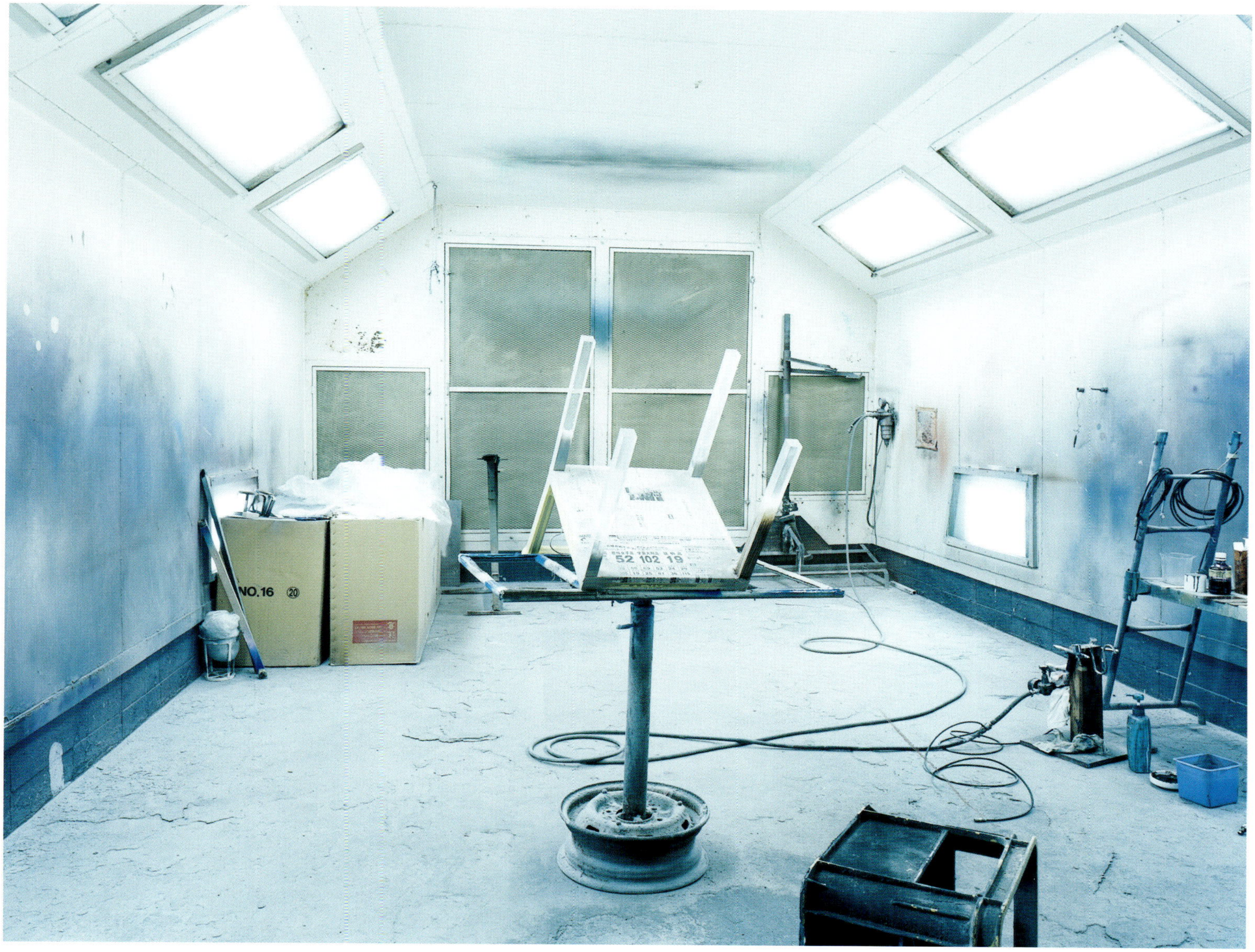
NO.16 ⑳
52 102 19

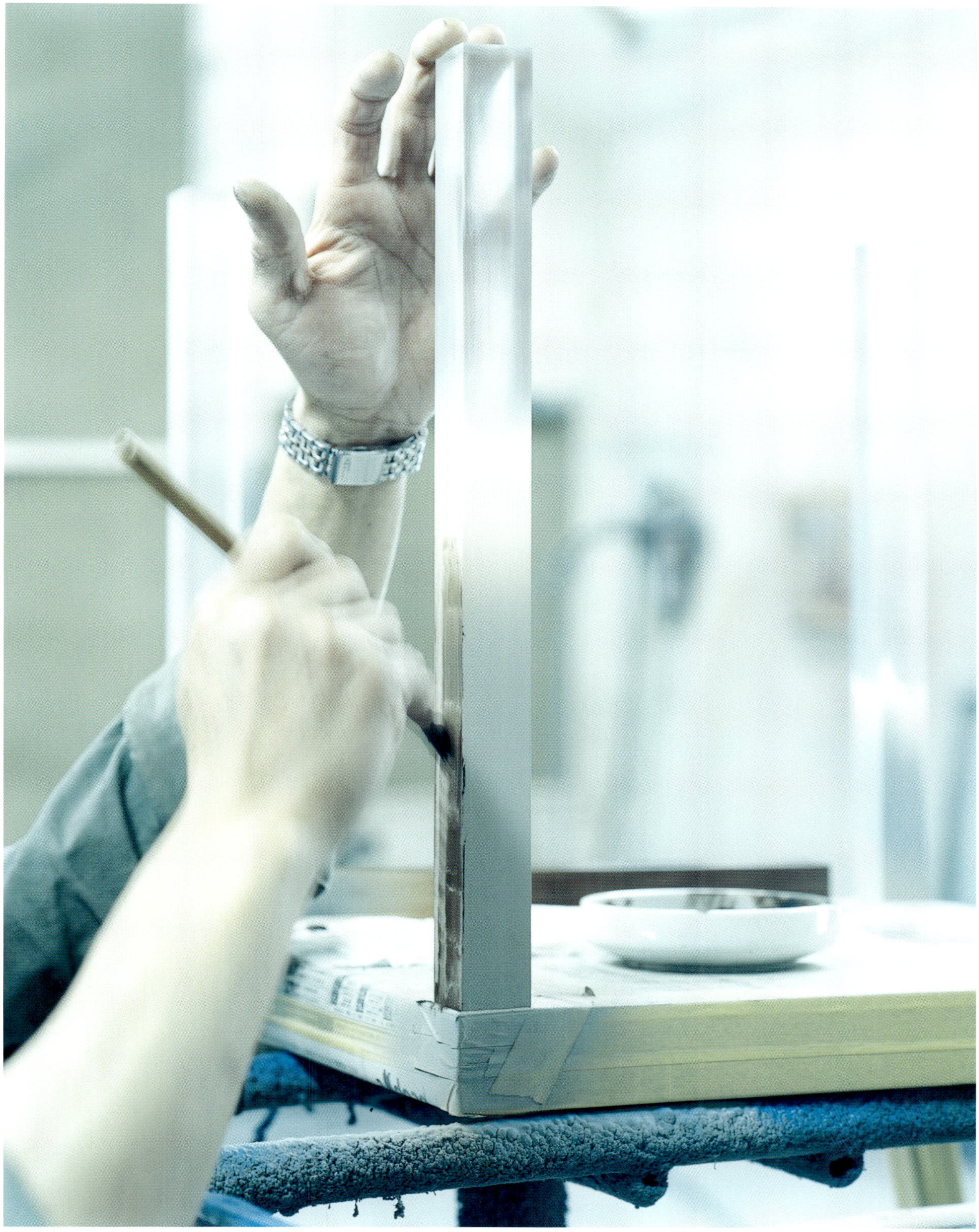

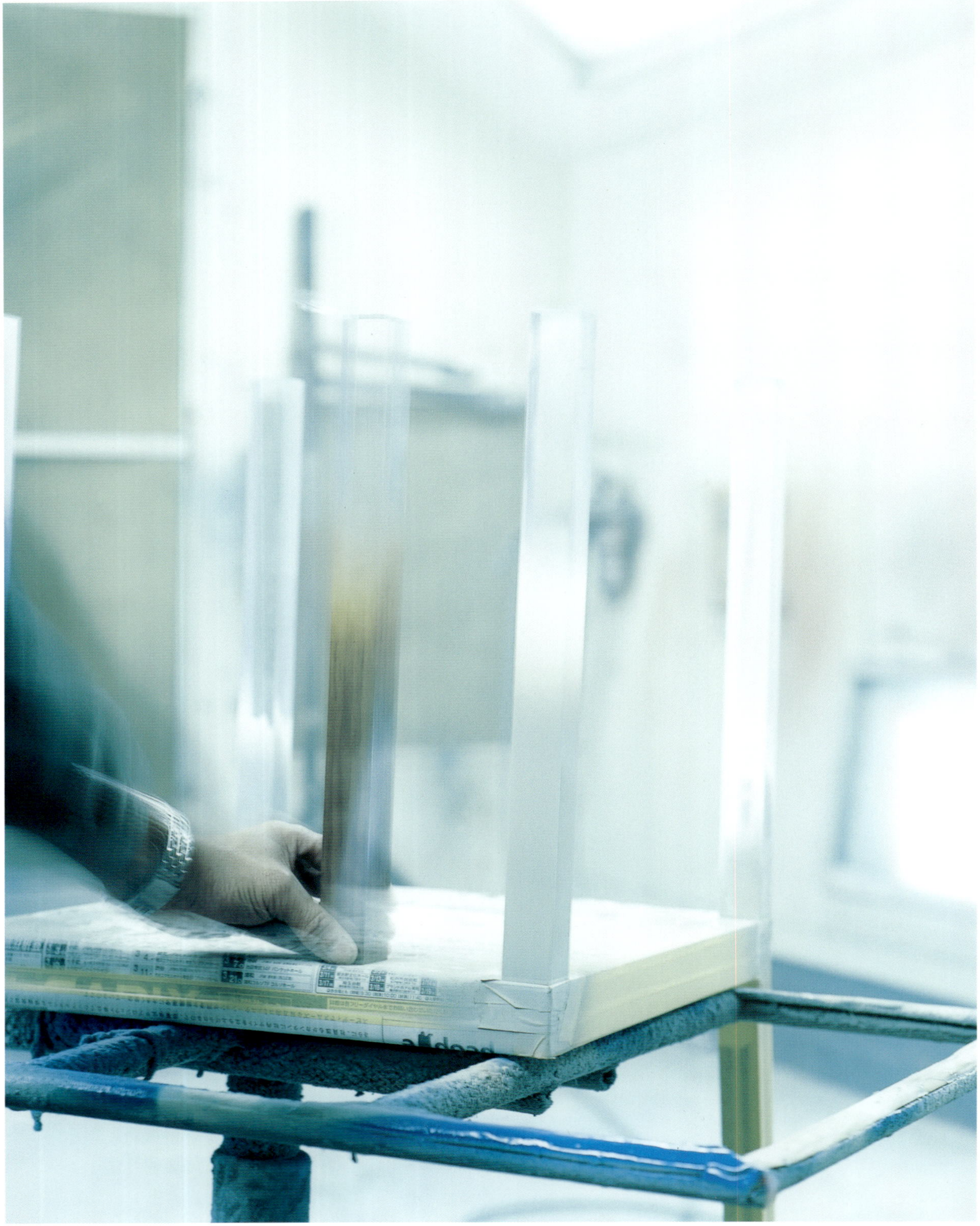

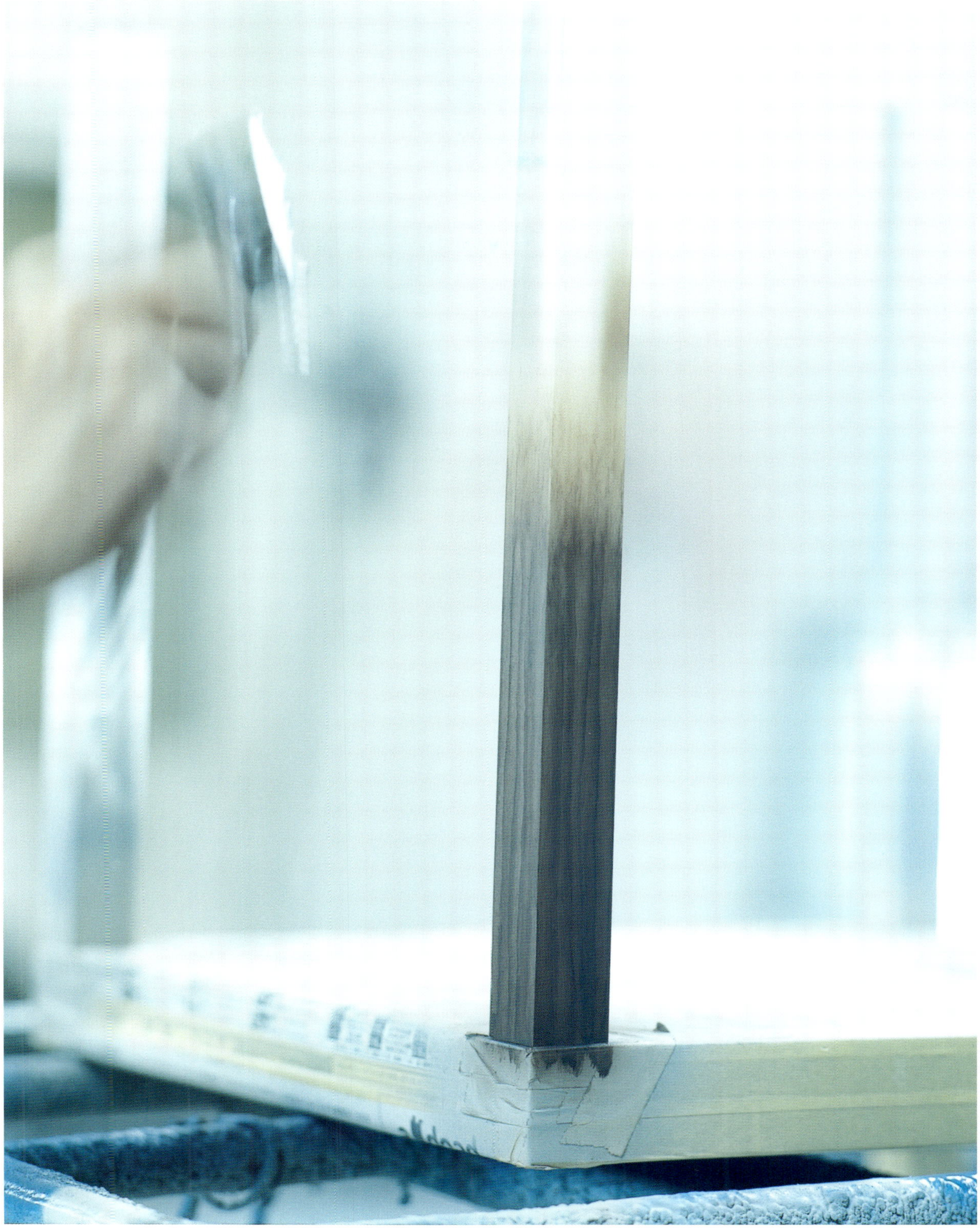

WALNUT.

001. WOOD + PAINT

002. X

003.

004. GRADATION LONGER

005. CLEAR AREA ⊕

006.-A FINAL SAMPLE

006.-B SPRAY ⊖ / BRUSH ⊕

006.-C EDGES LONGER

006.-D NARROW END.

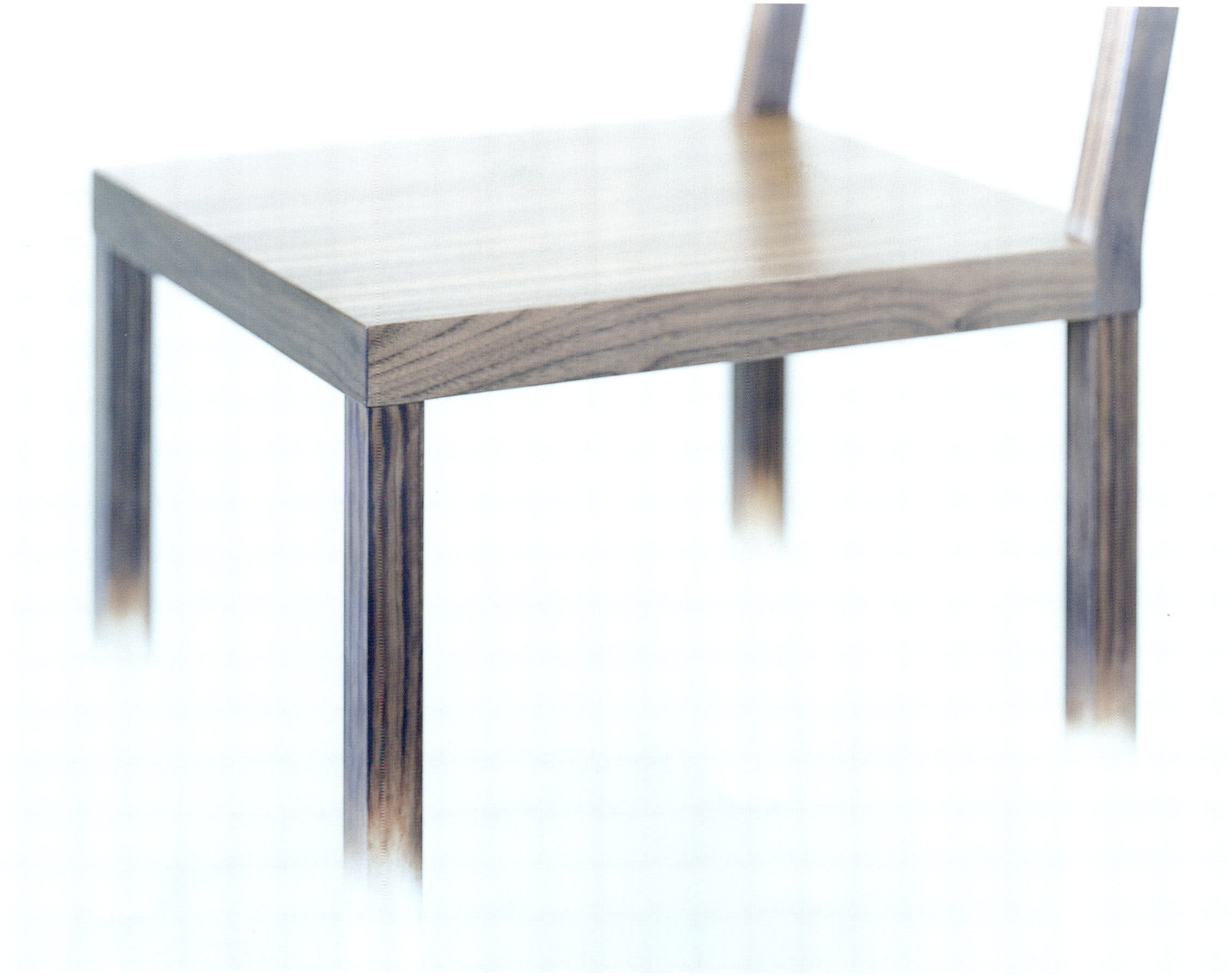

145

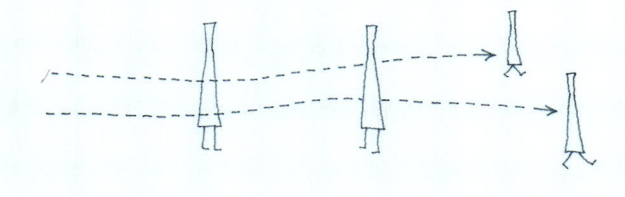

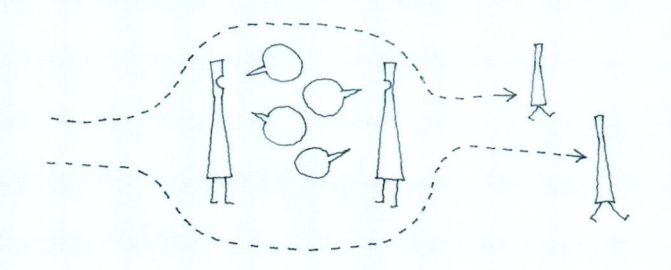

COMMUNICATION ⟶ SPACE?

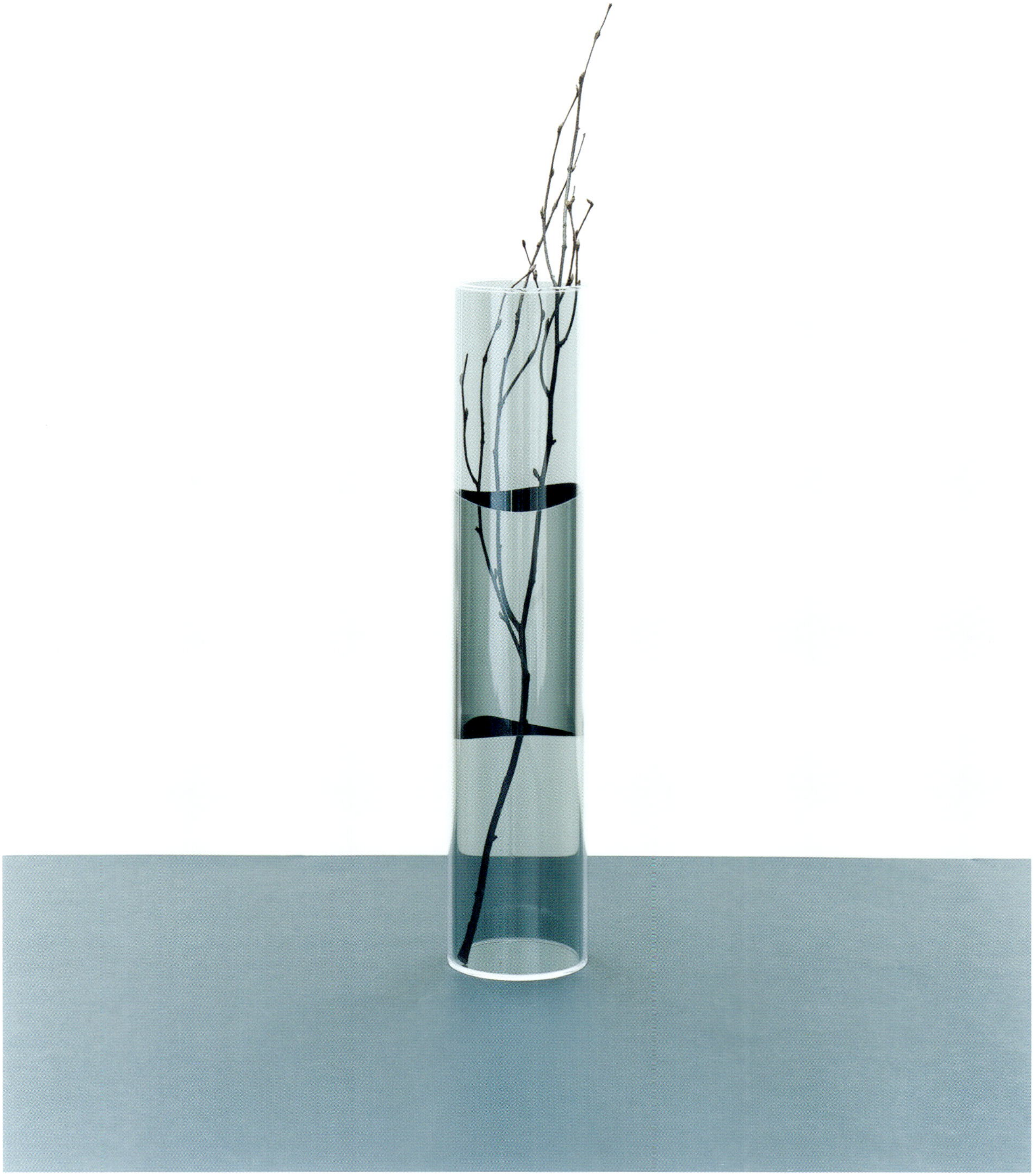

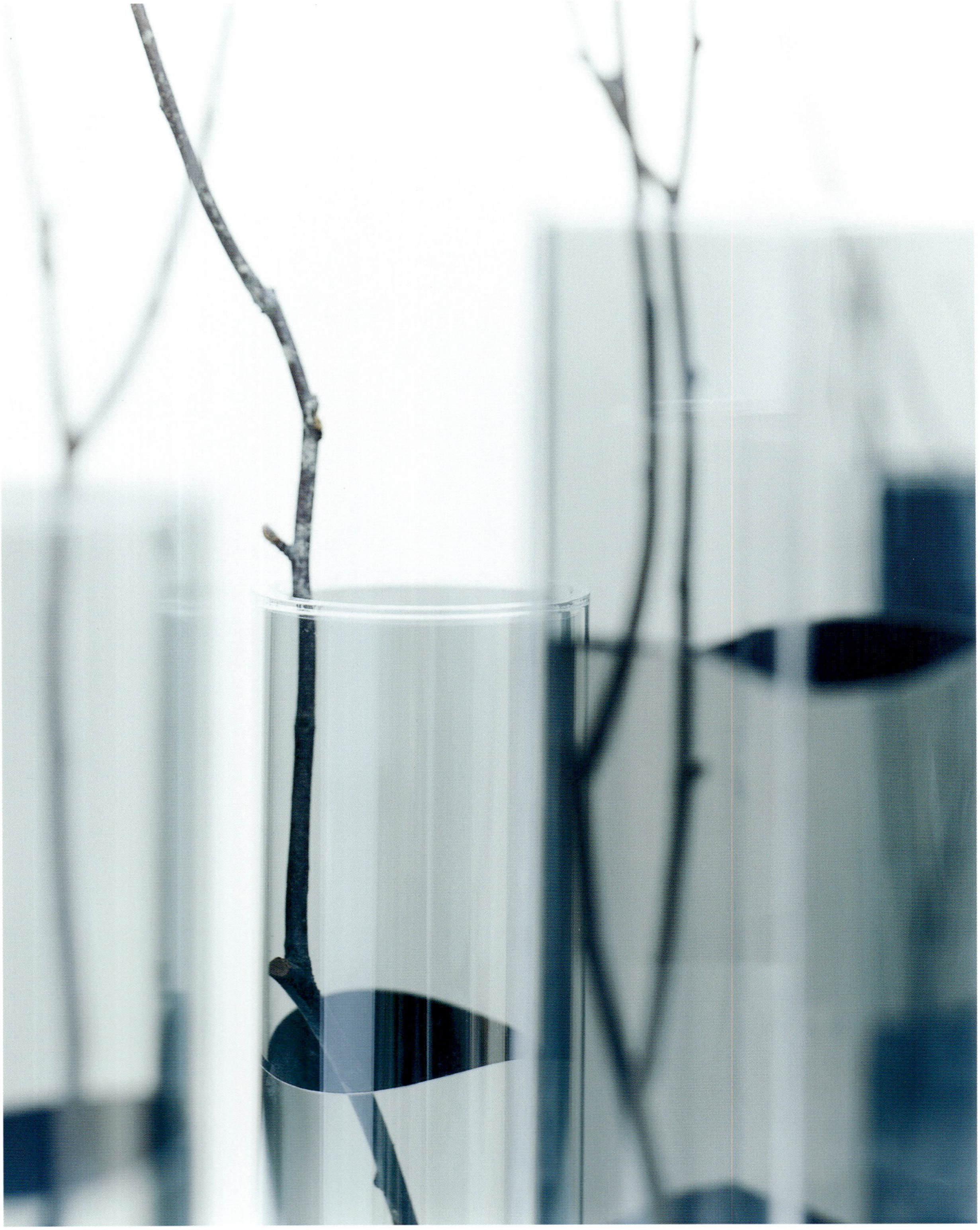

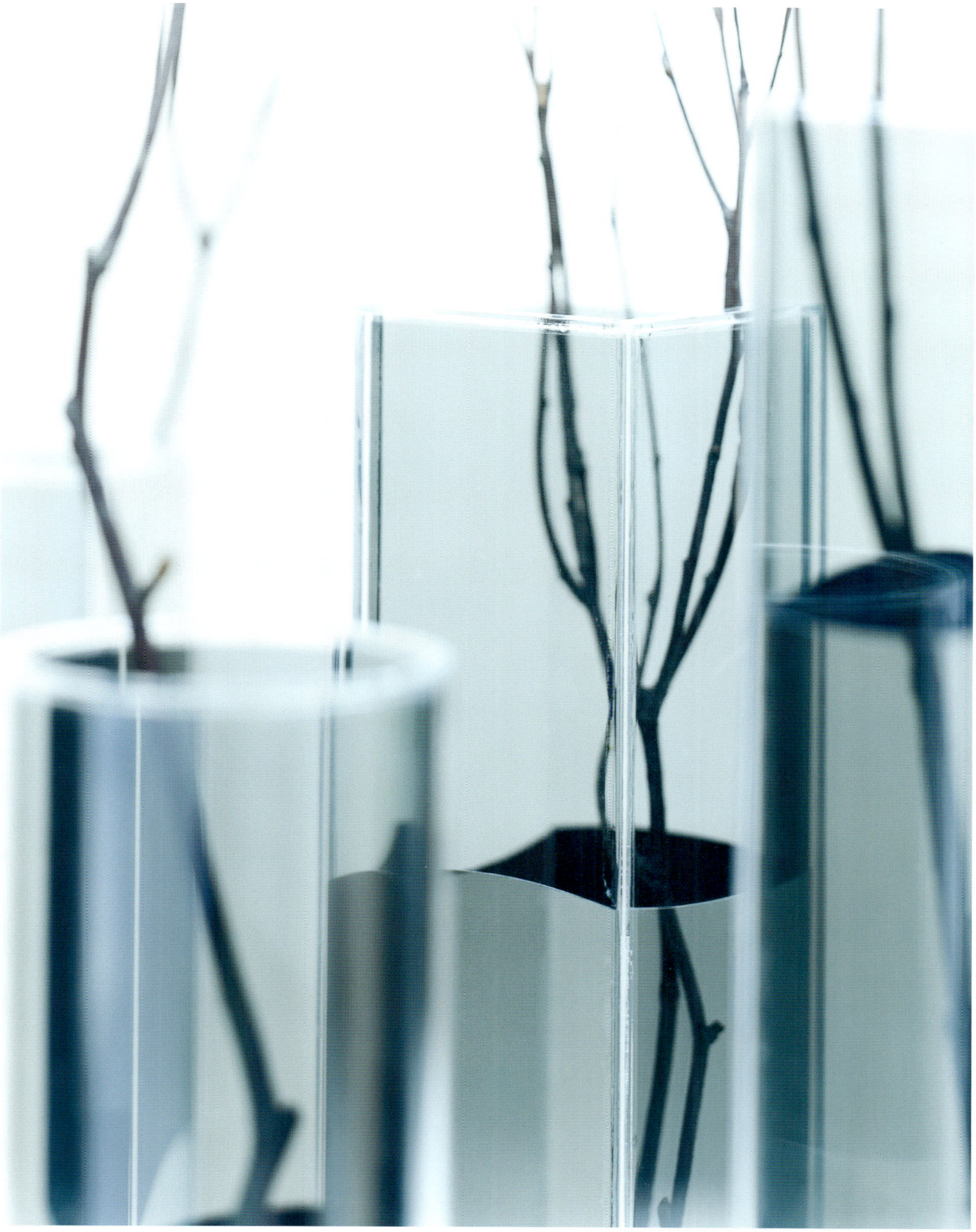

153

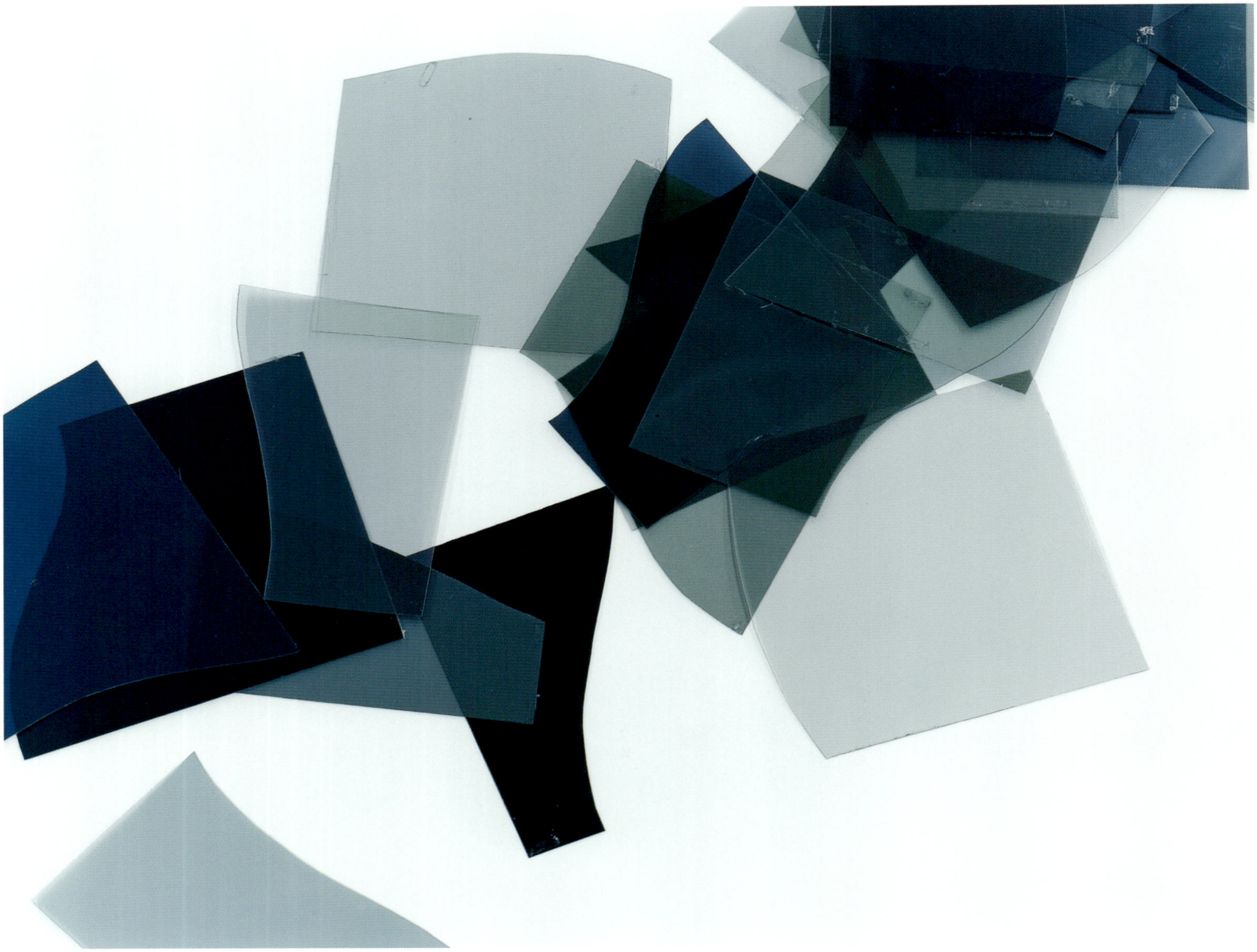

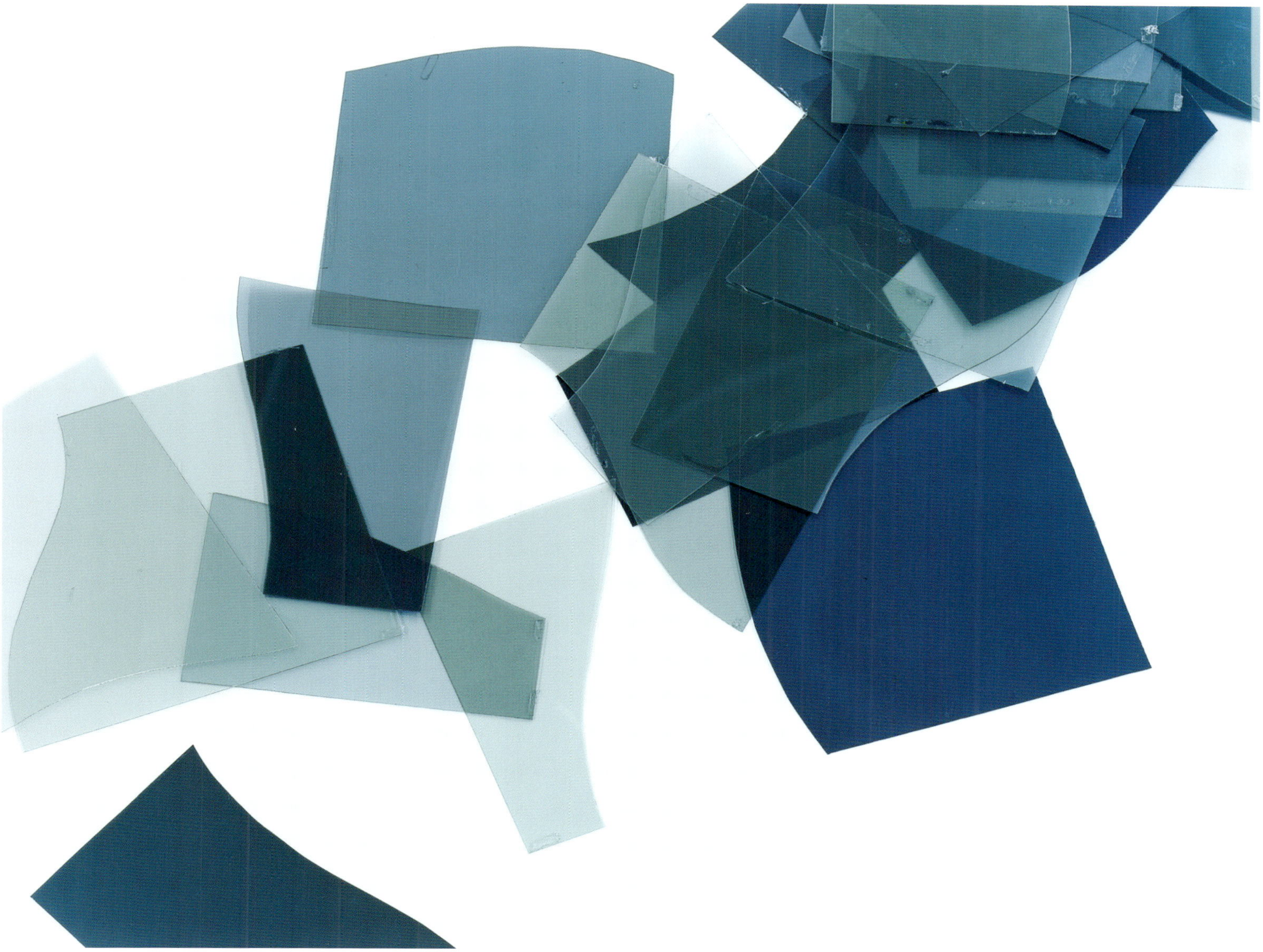

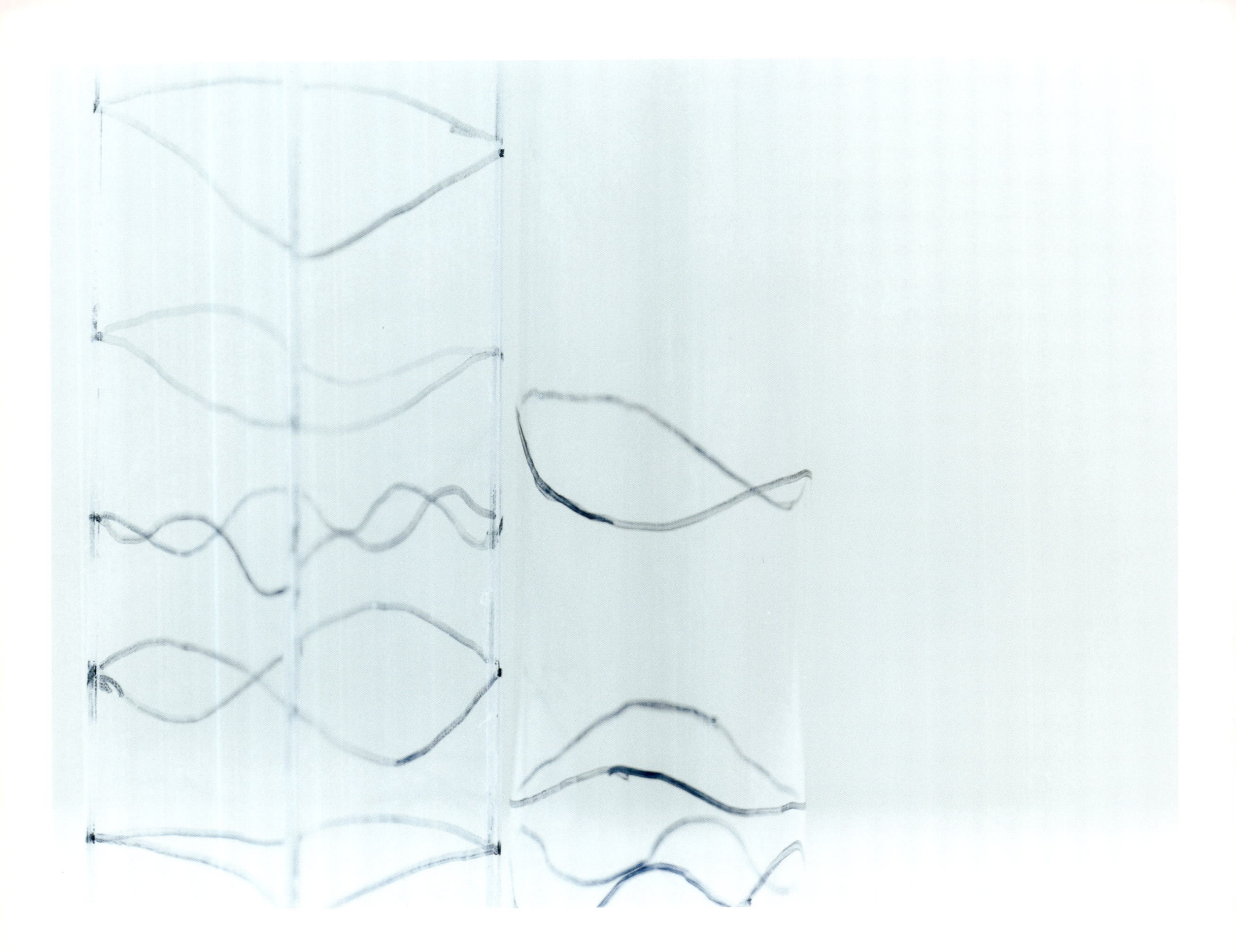

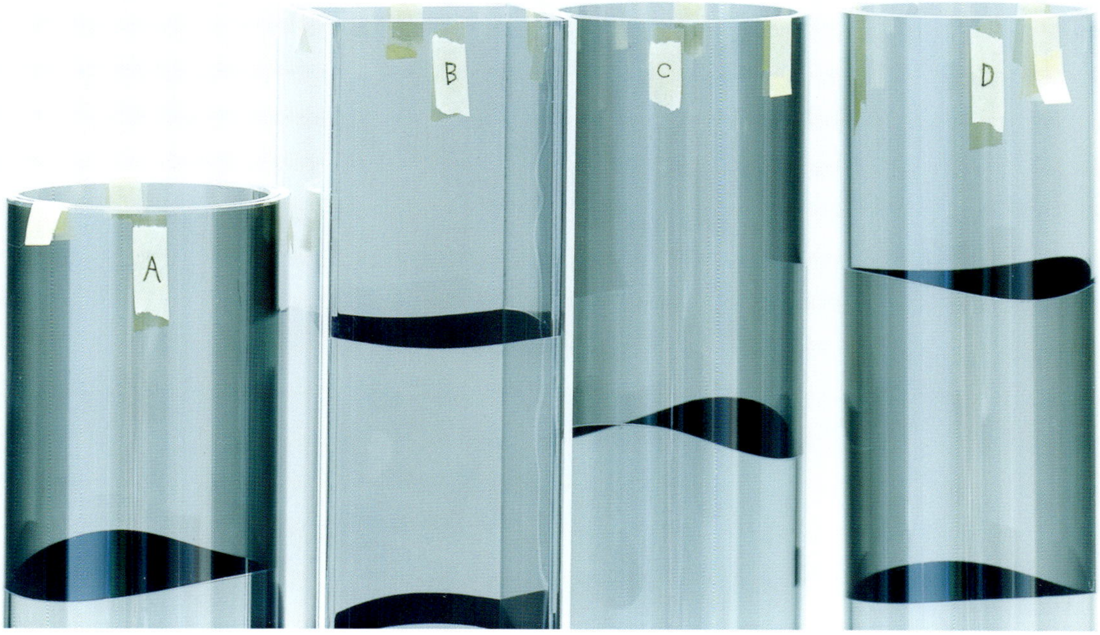
A
B
C
D

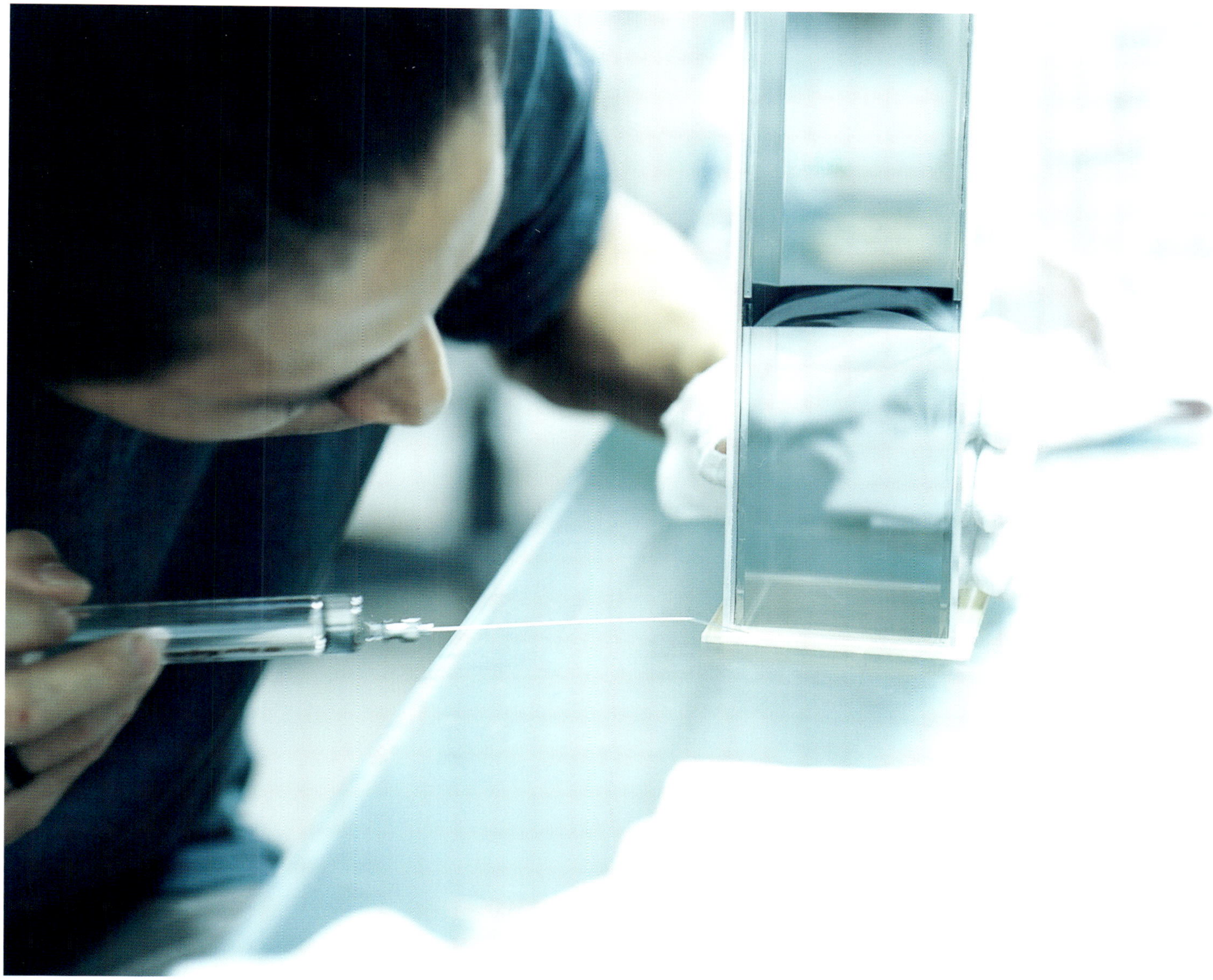

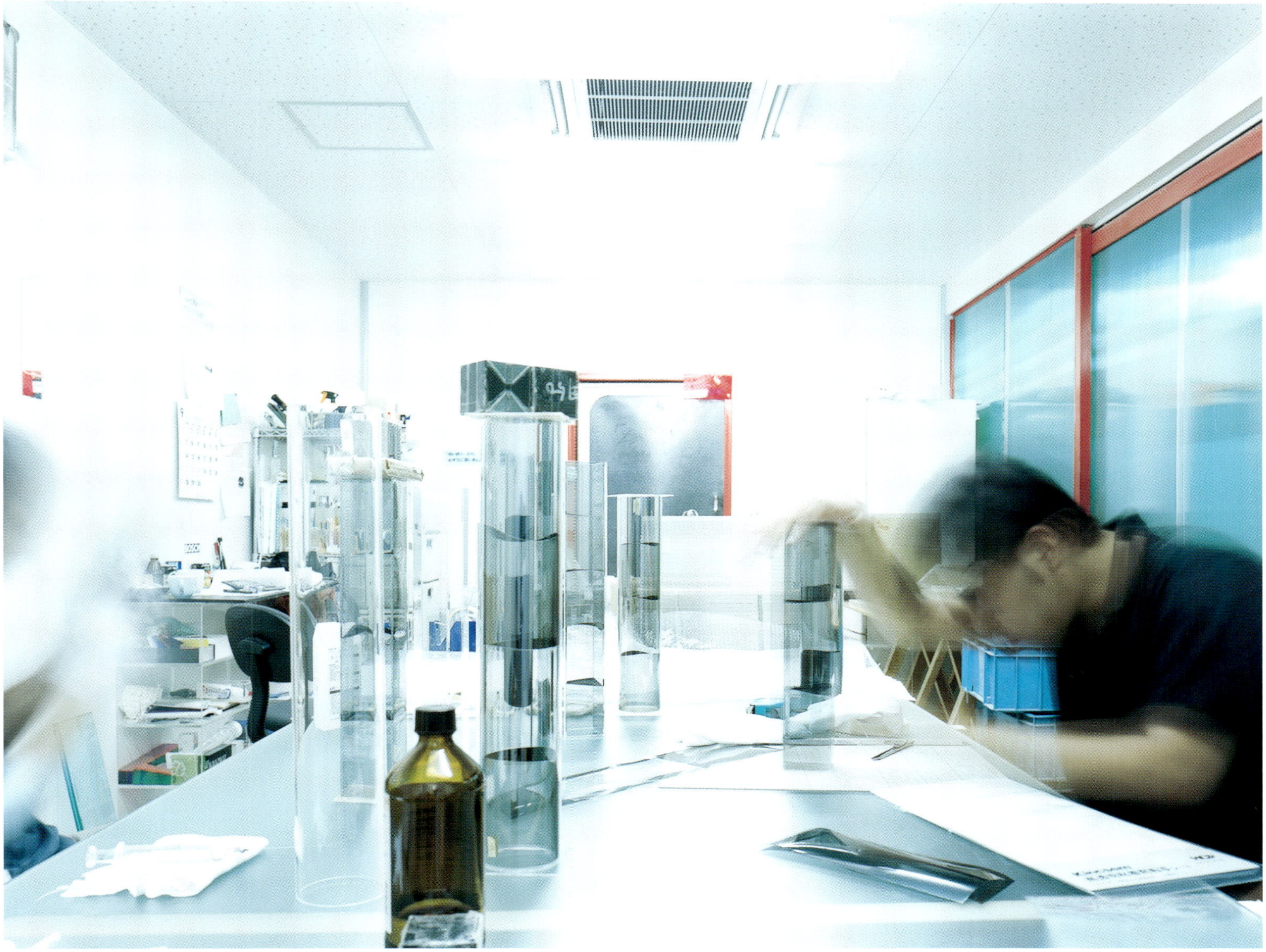

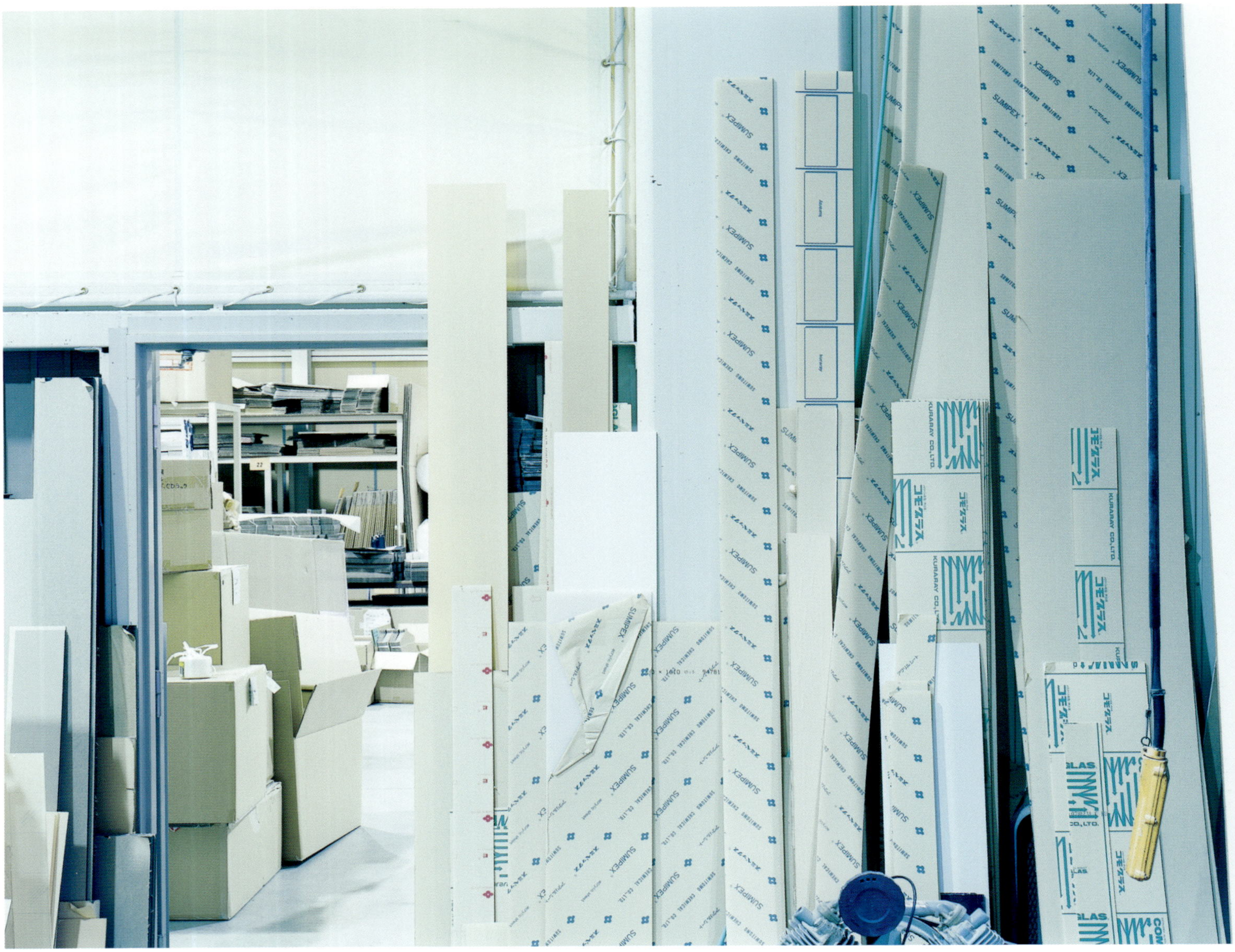
SUMPEX
KURARAY CO.,LTD.

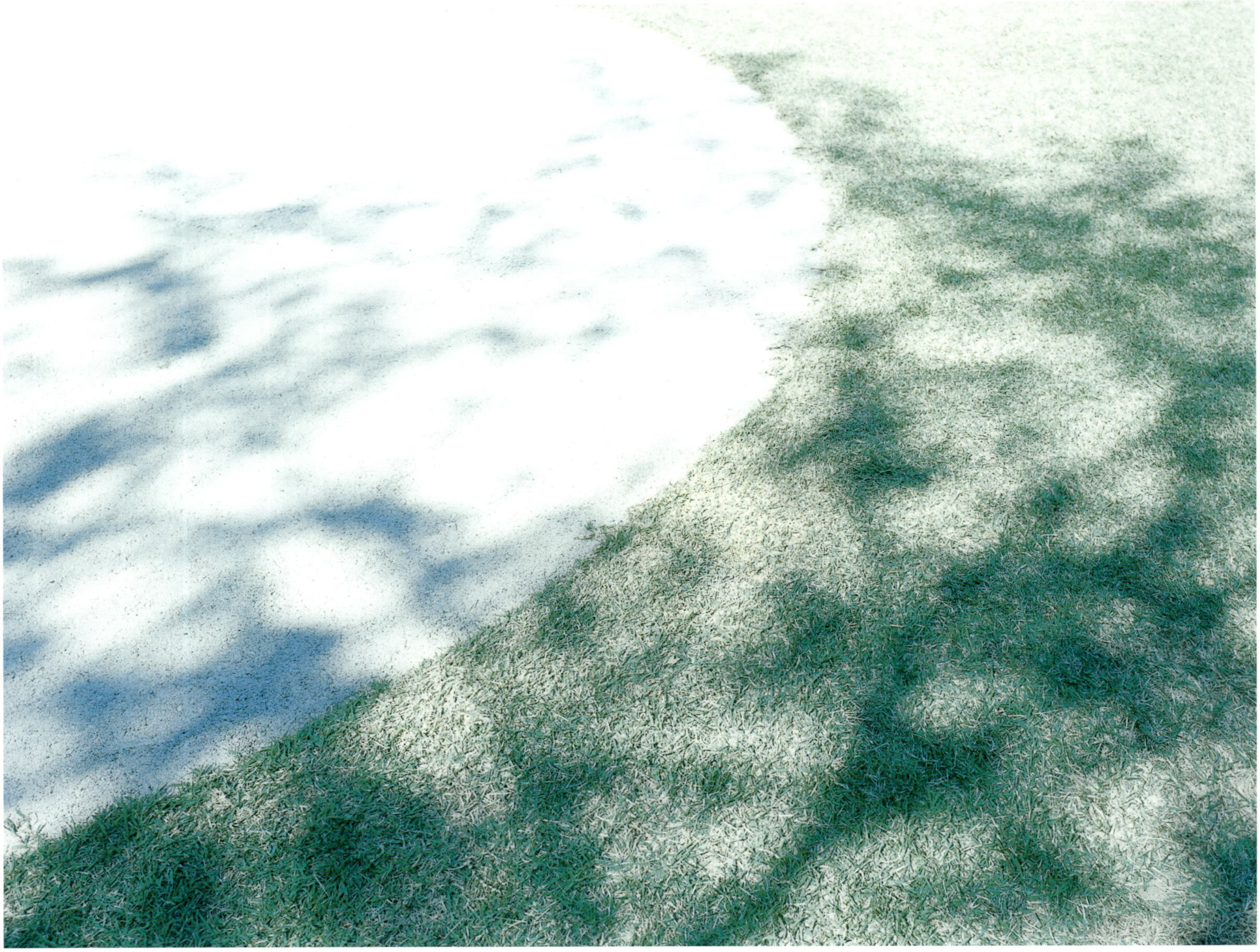

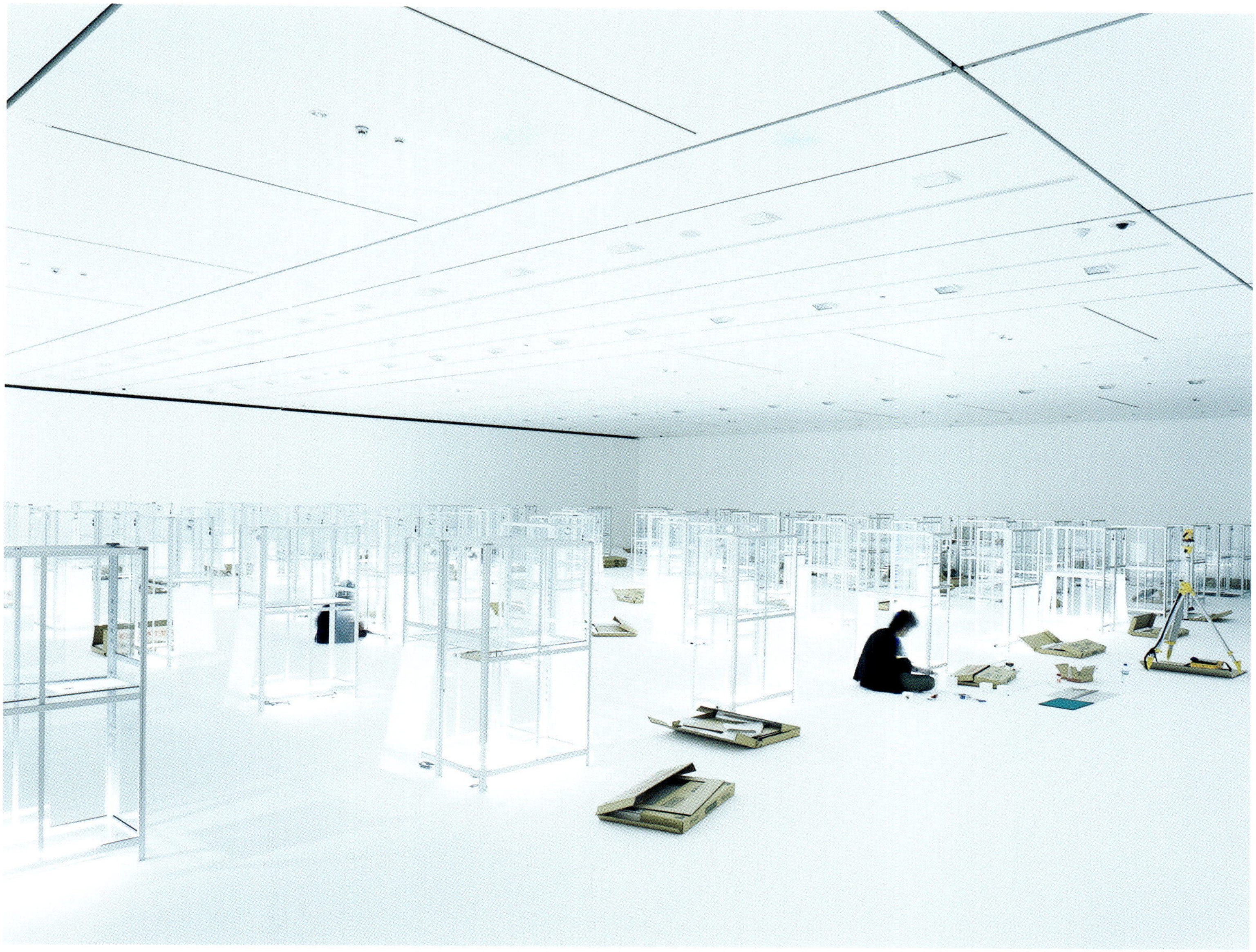

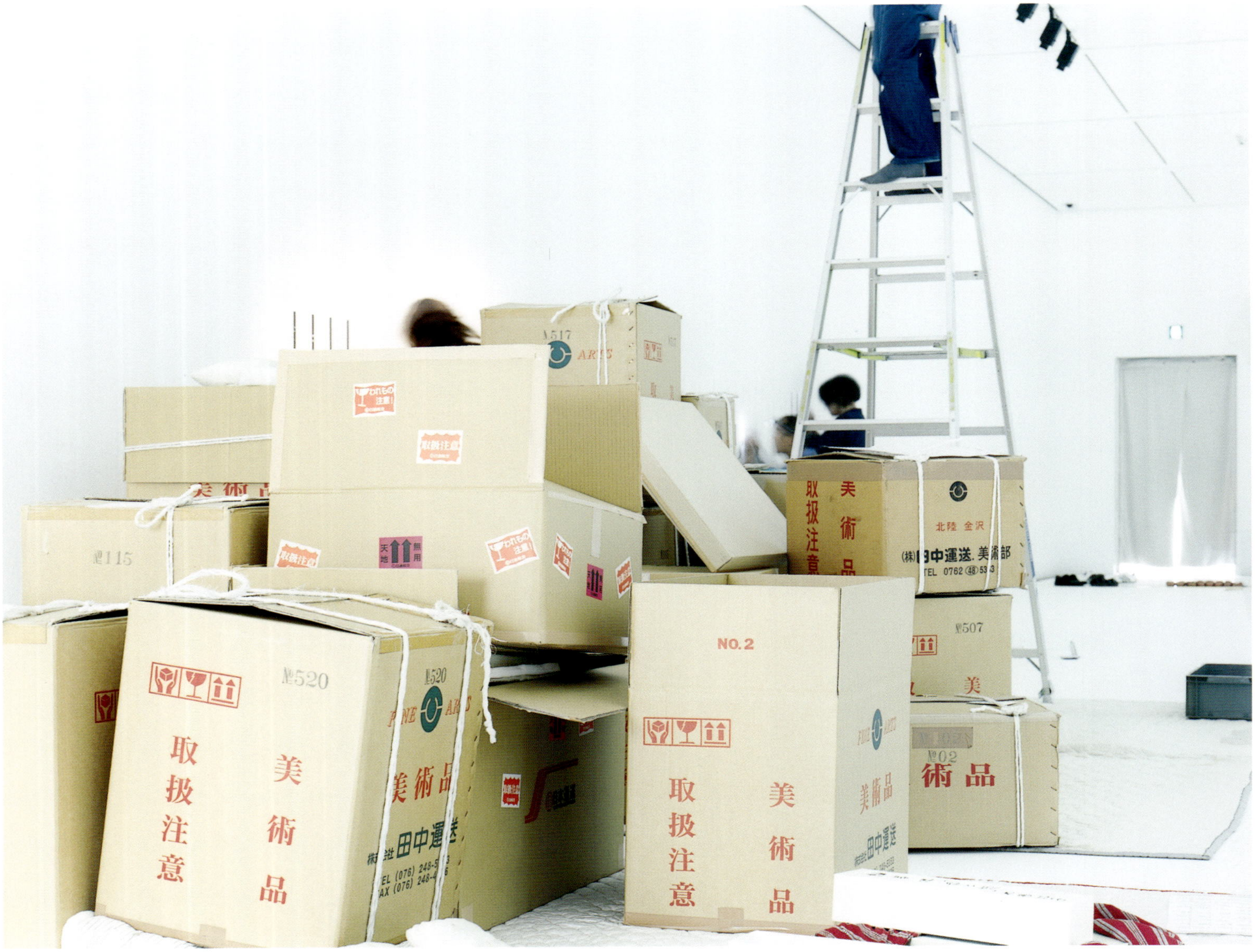
№520
取扱注意
美術品
NO.2
取扱注意
美術品
美術品
北陸 金沢
(株)田中運送. 美術部
№507
術品

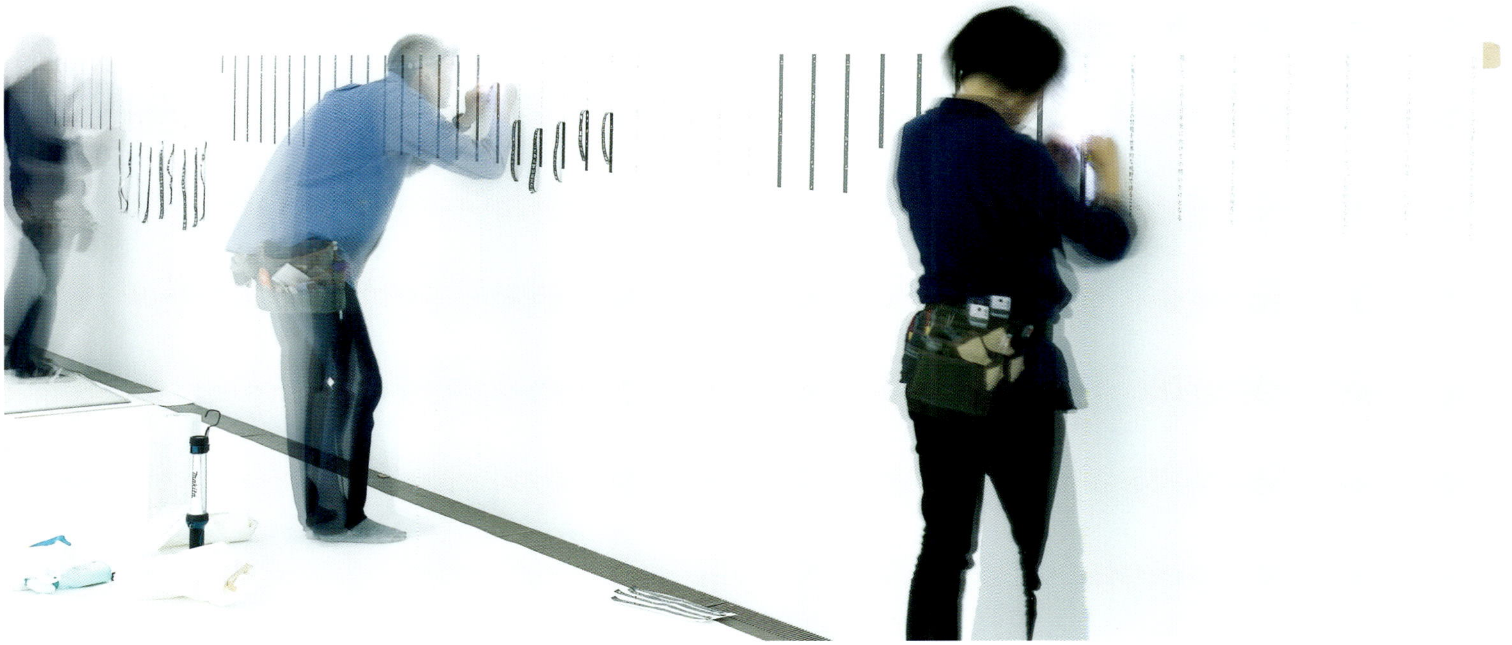

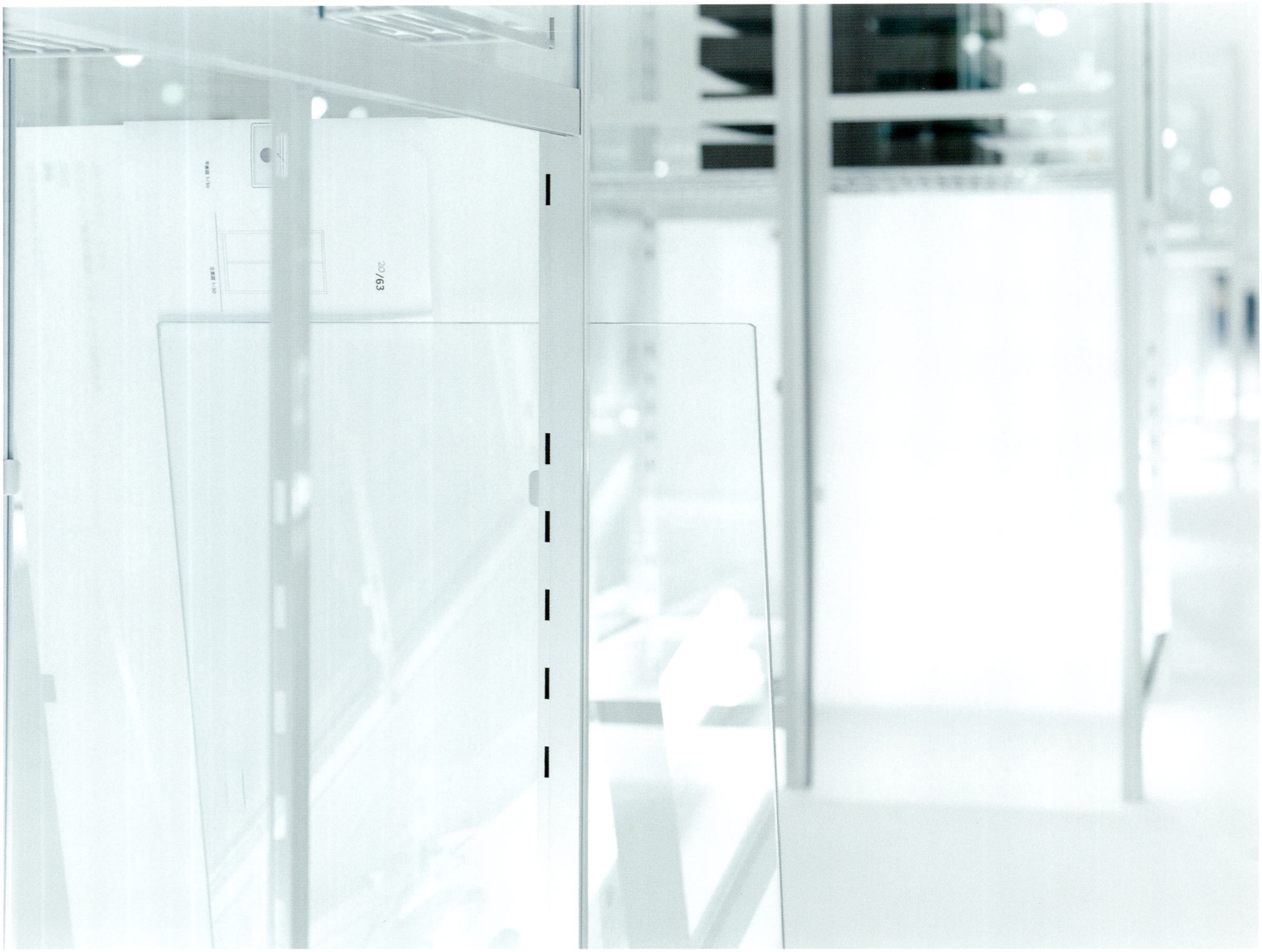

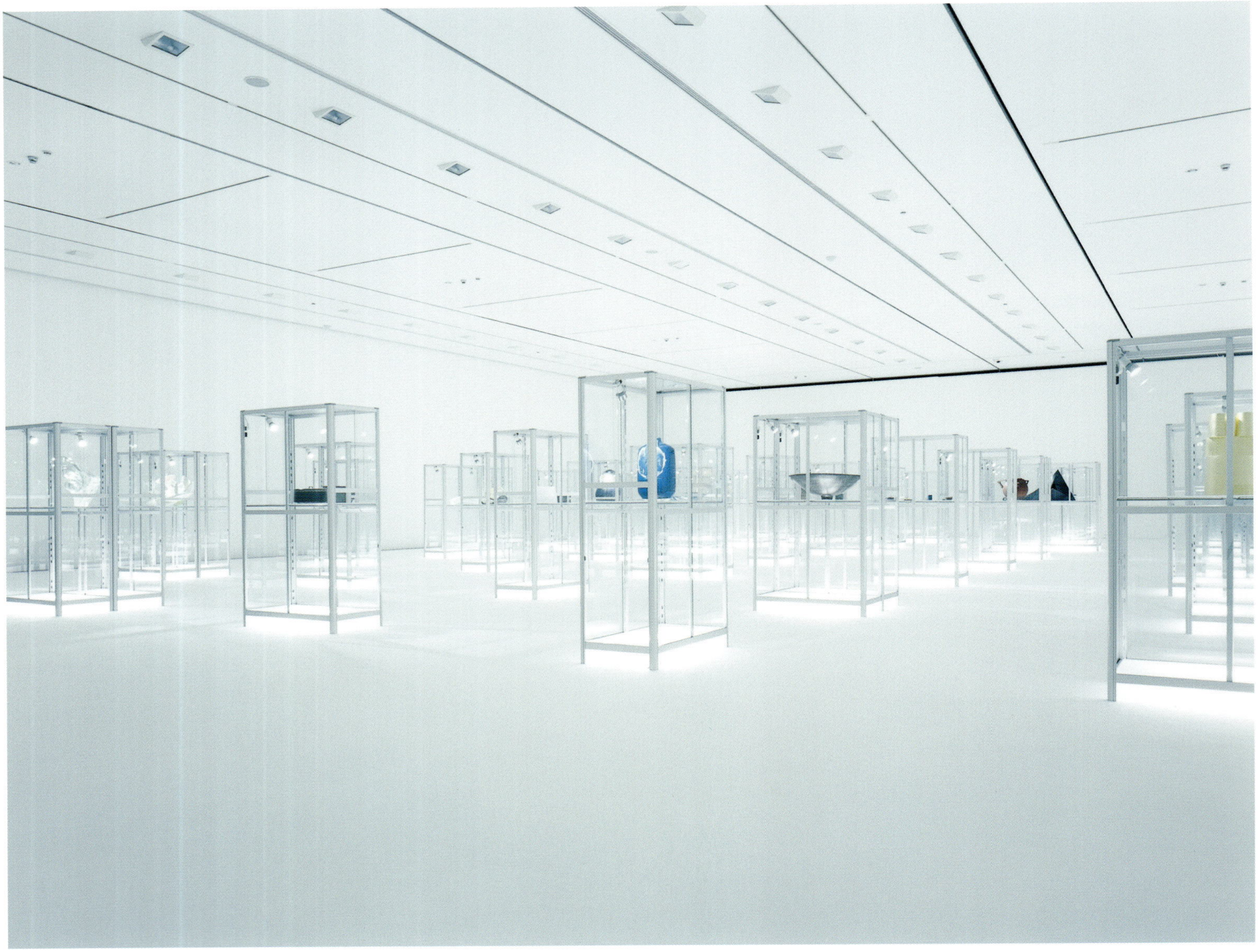

✗ TOP-DOWN

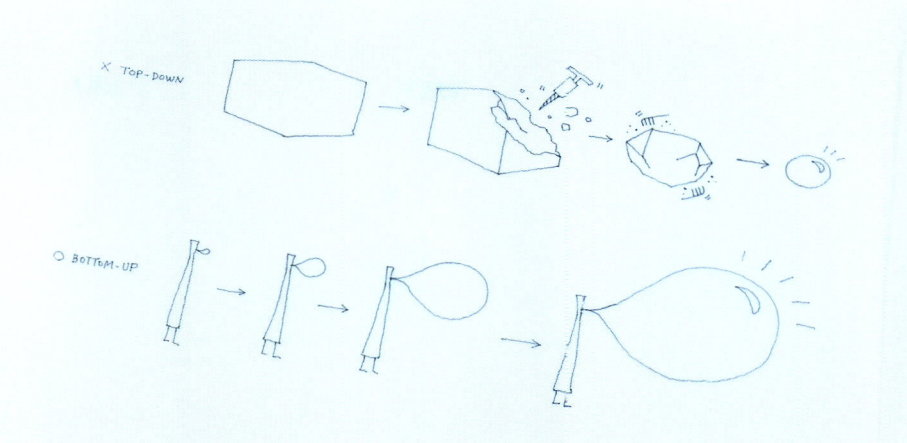

○ BOTTOM-UP

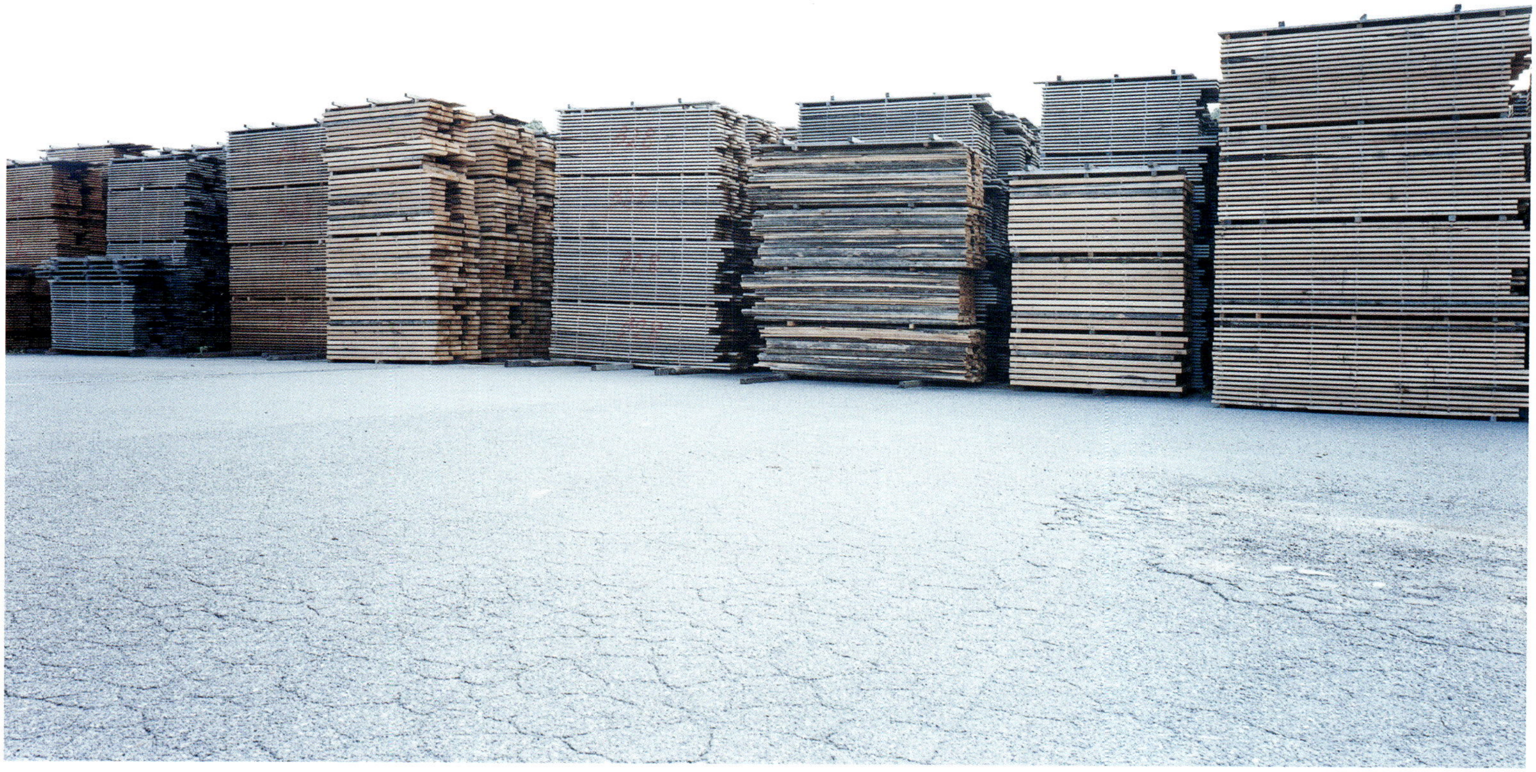

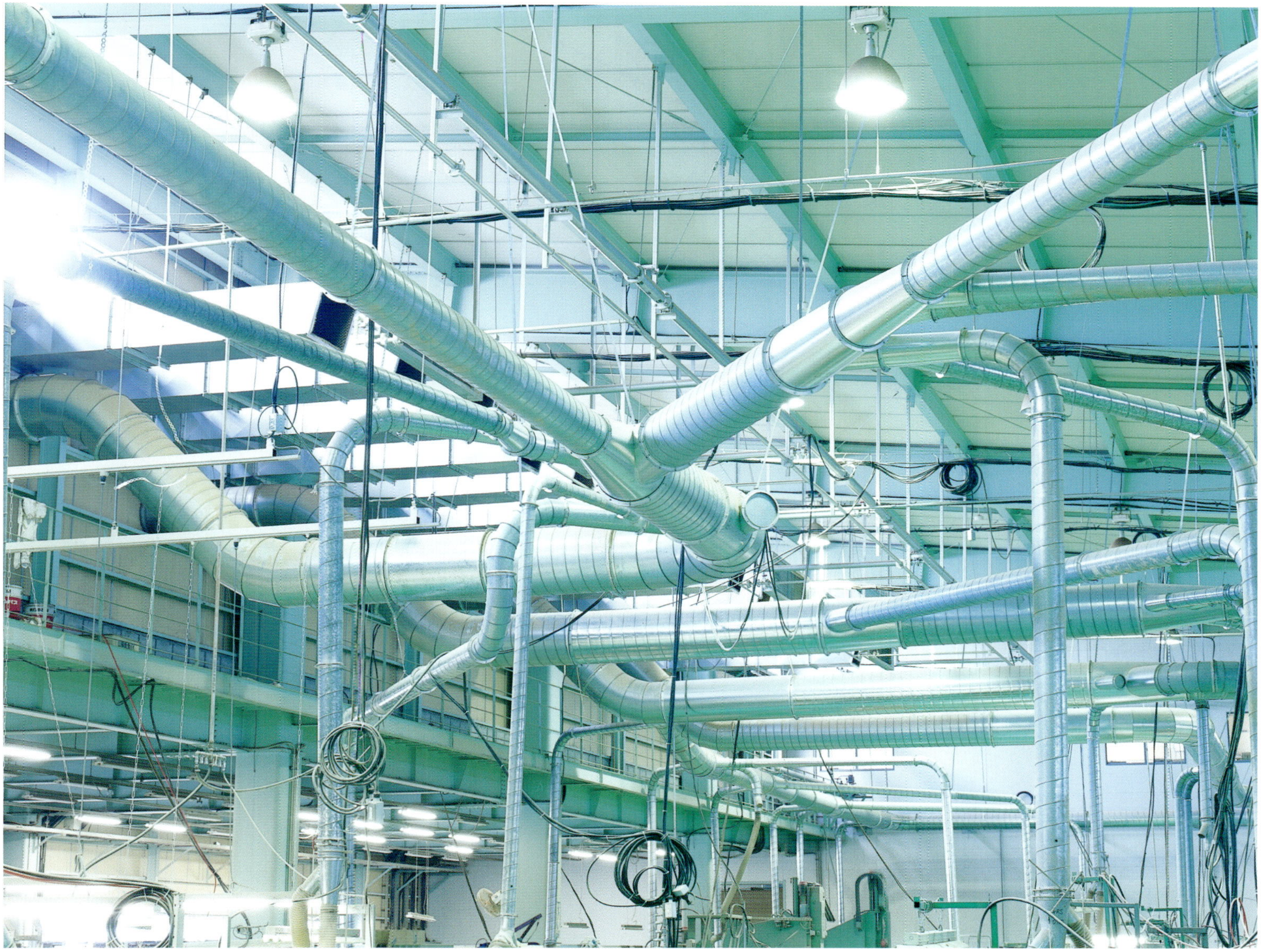

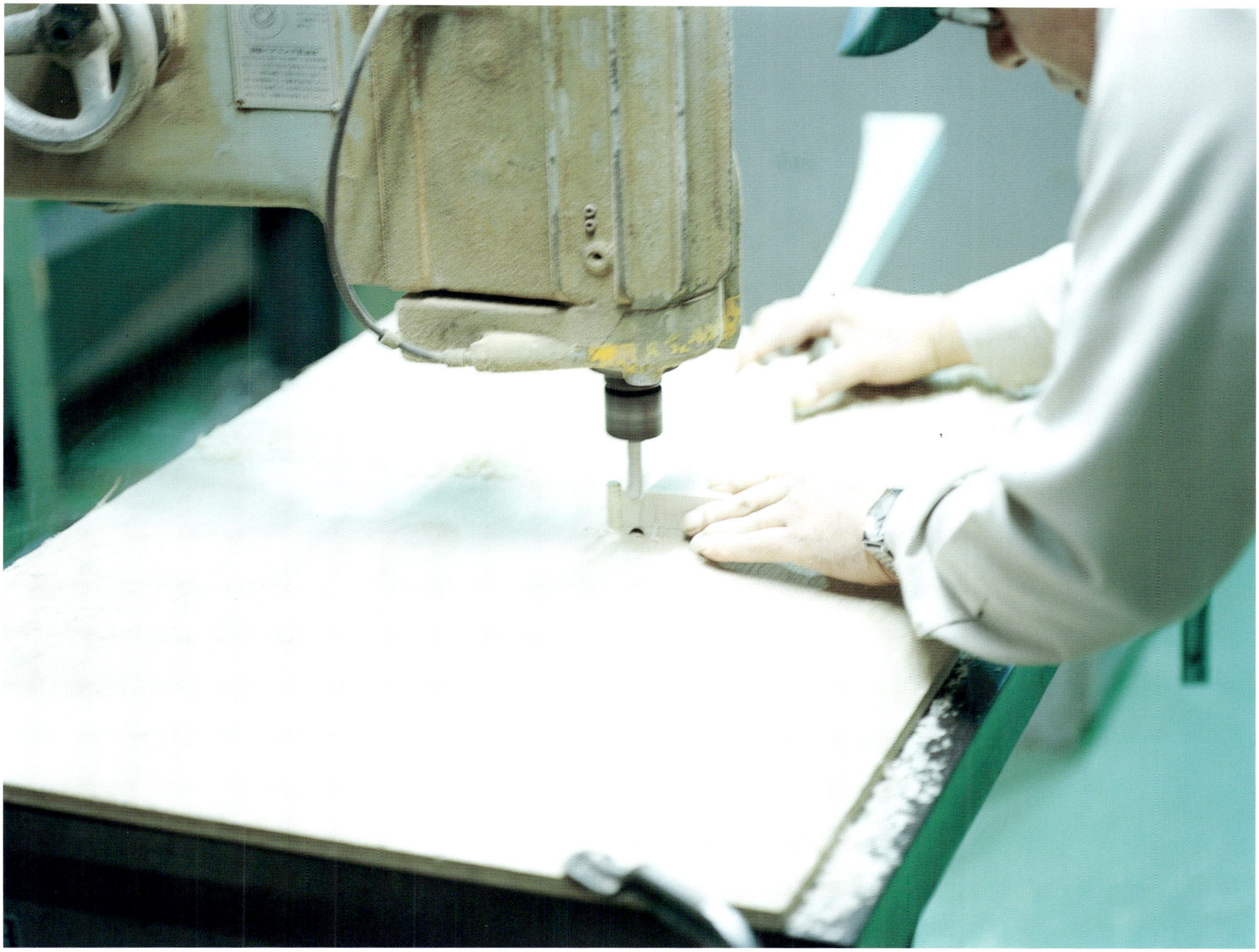

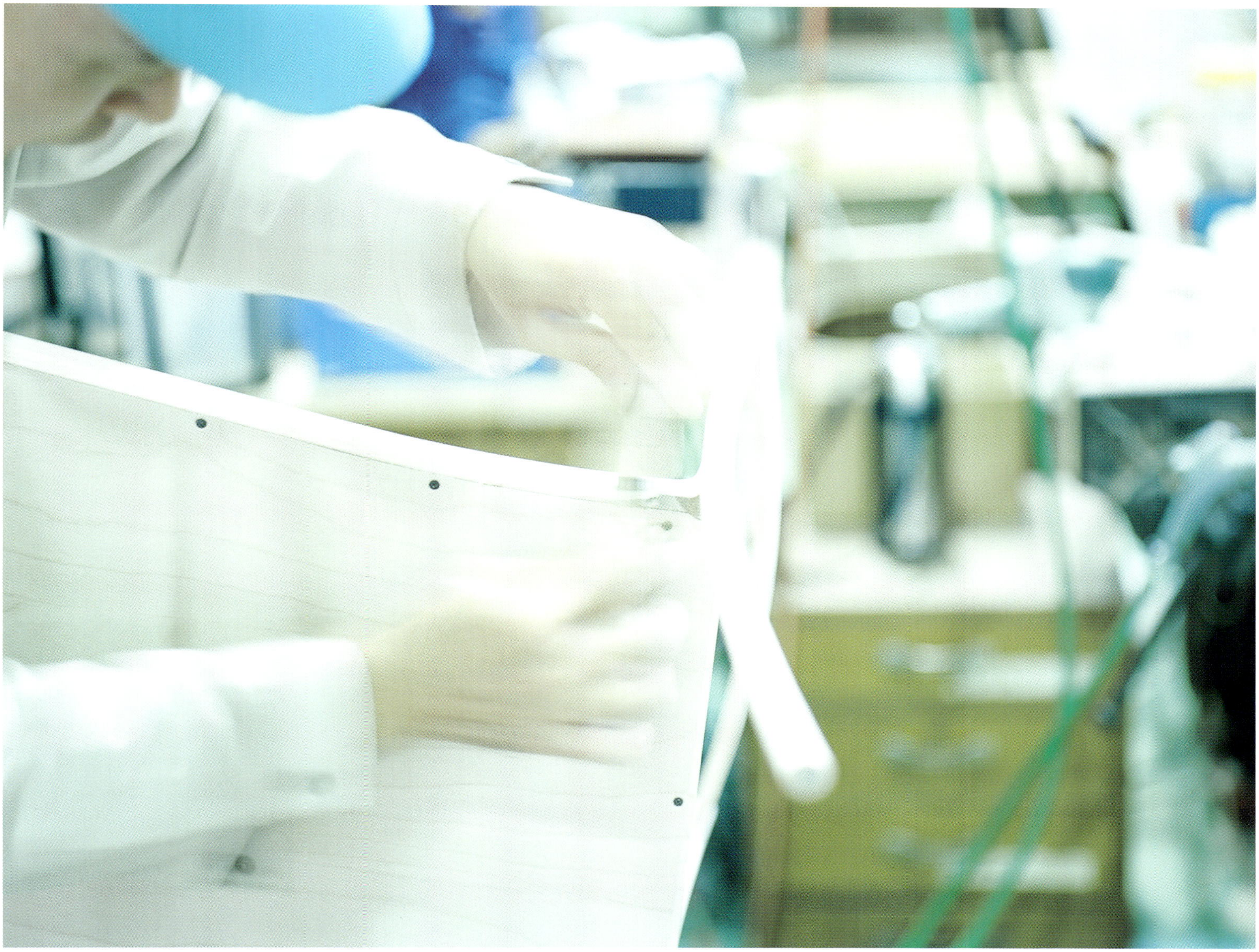

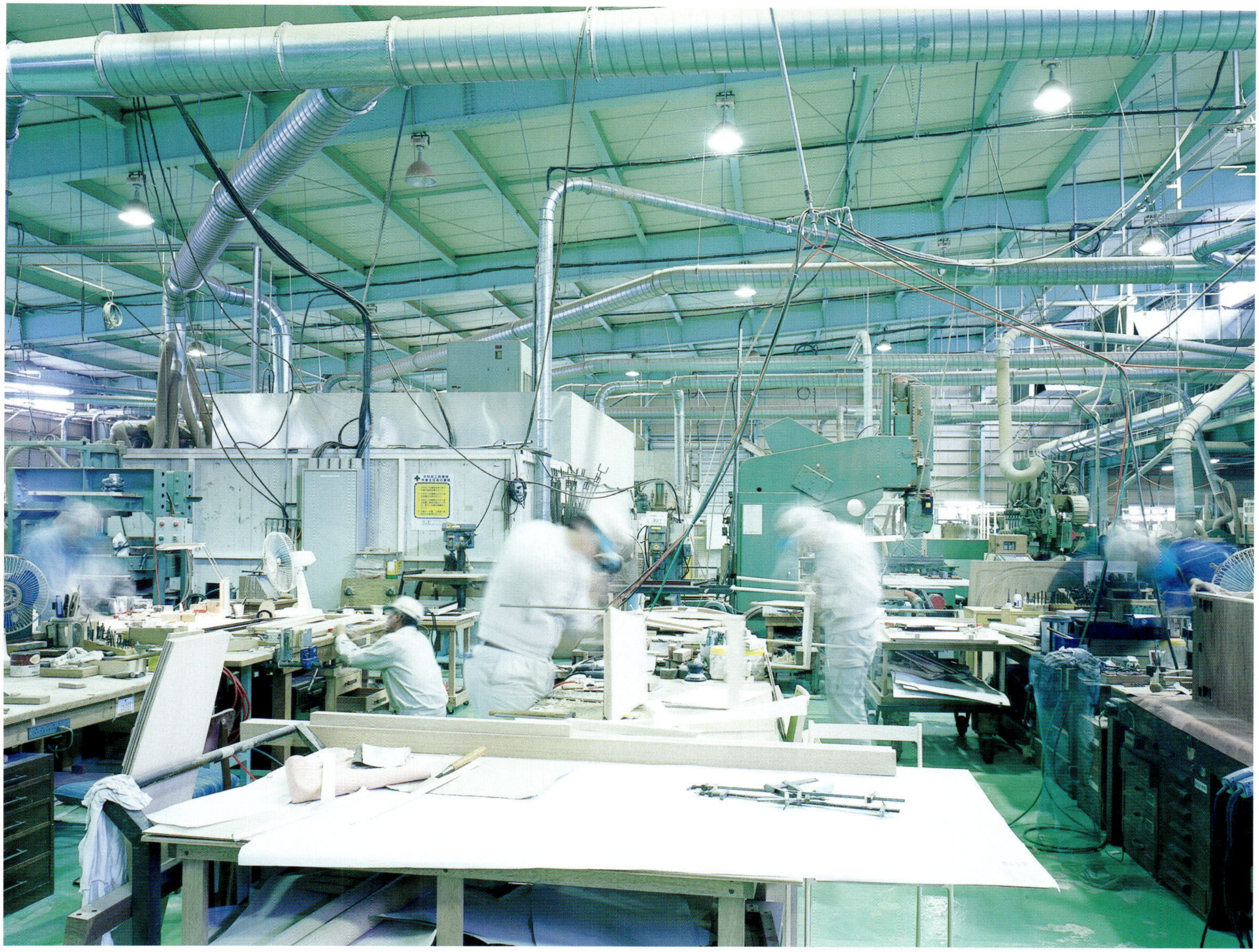

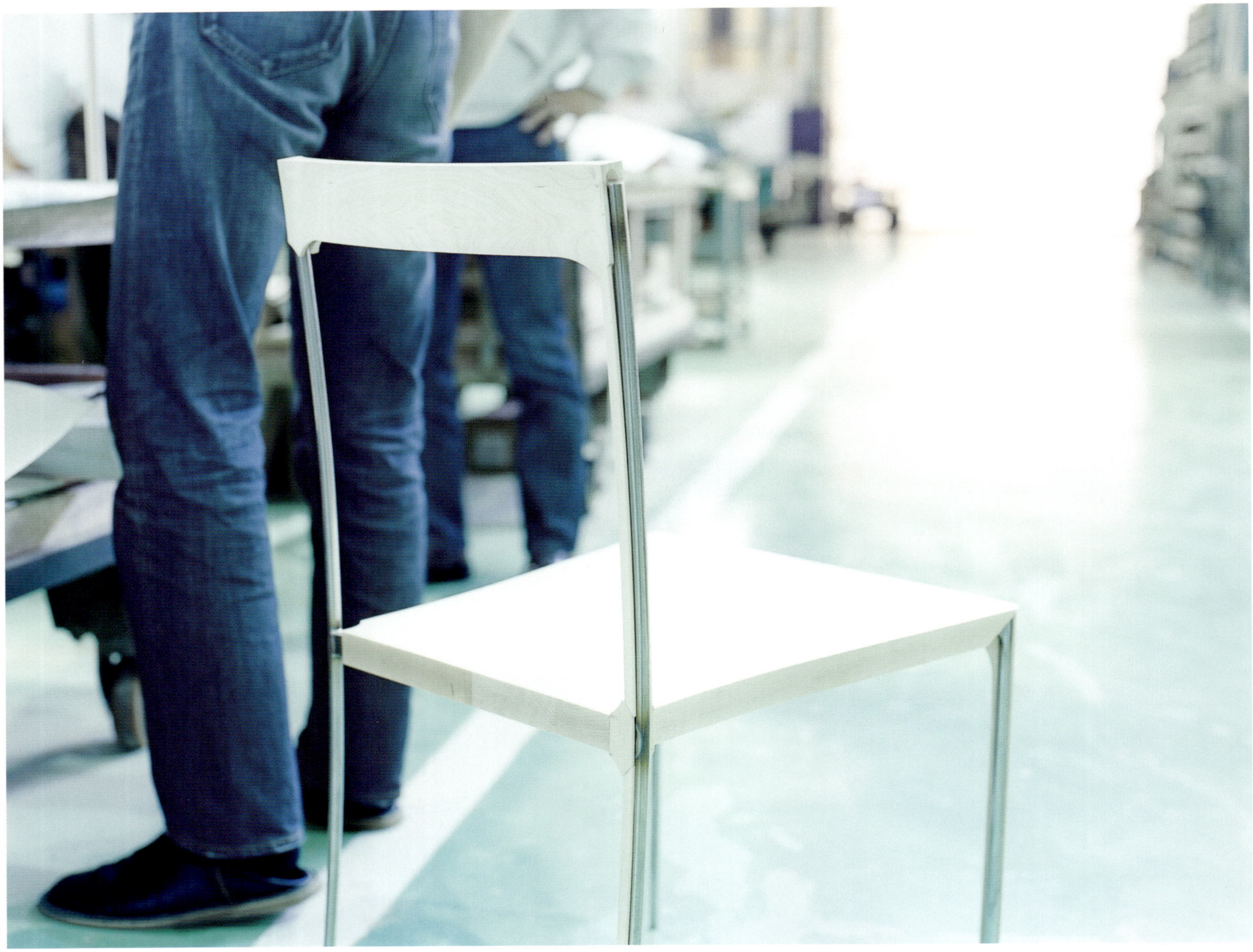

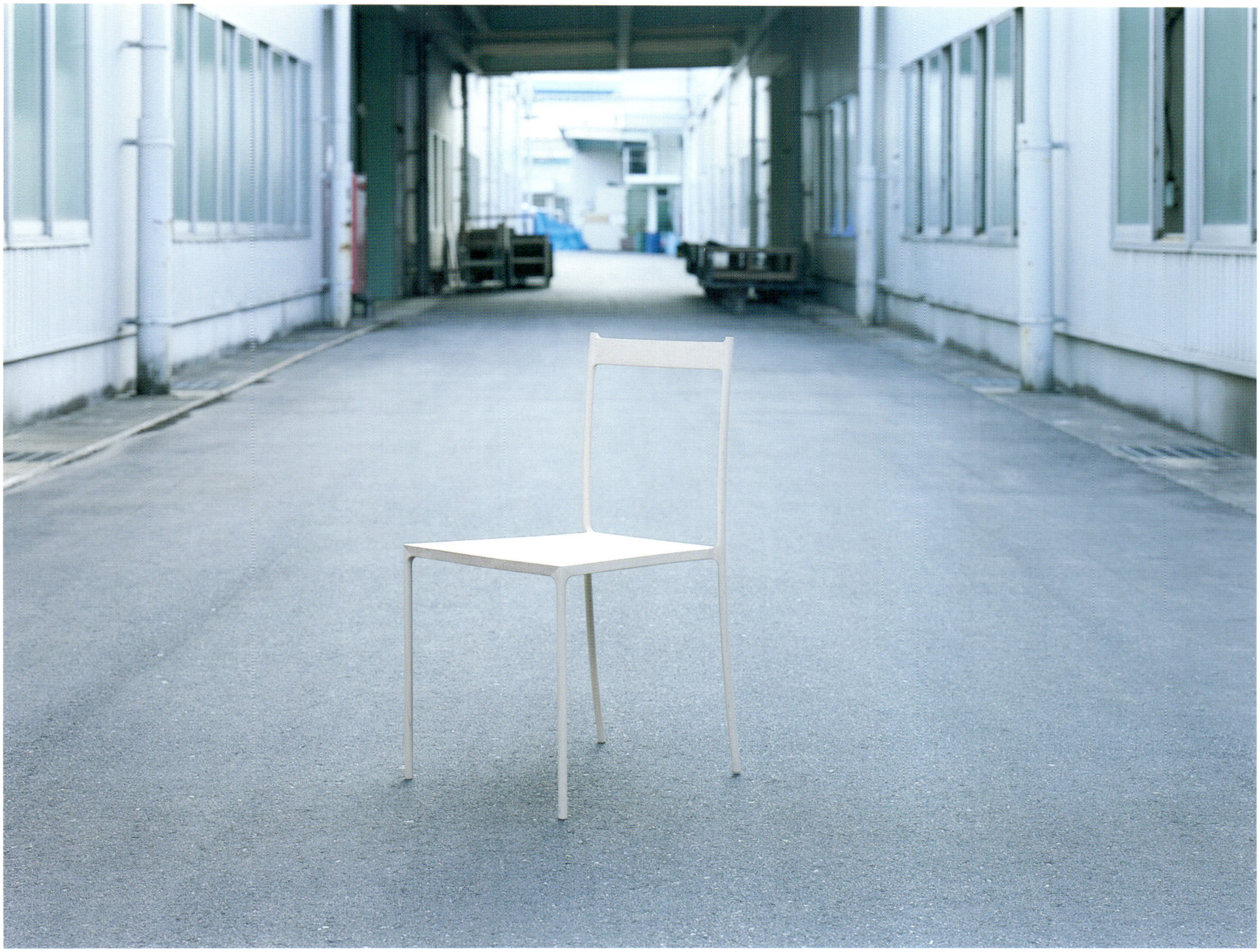

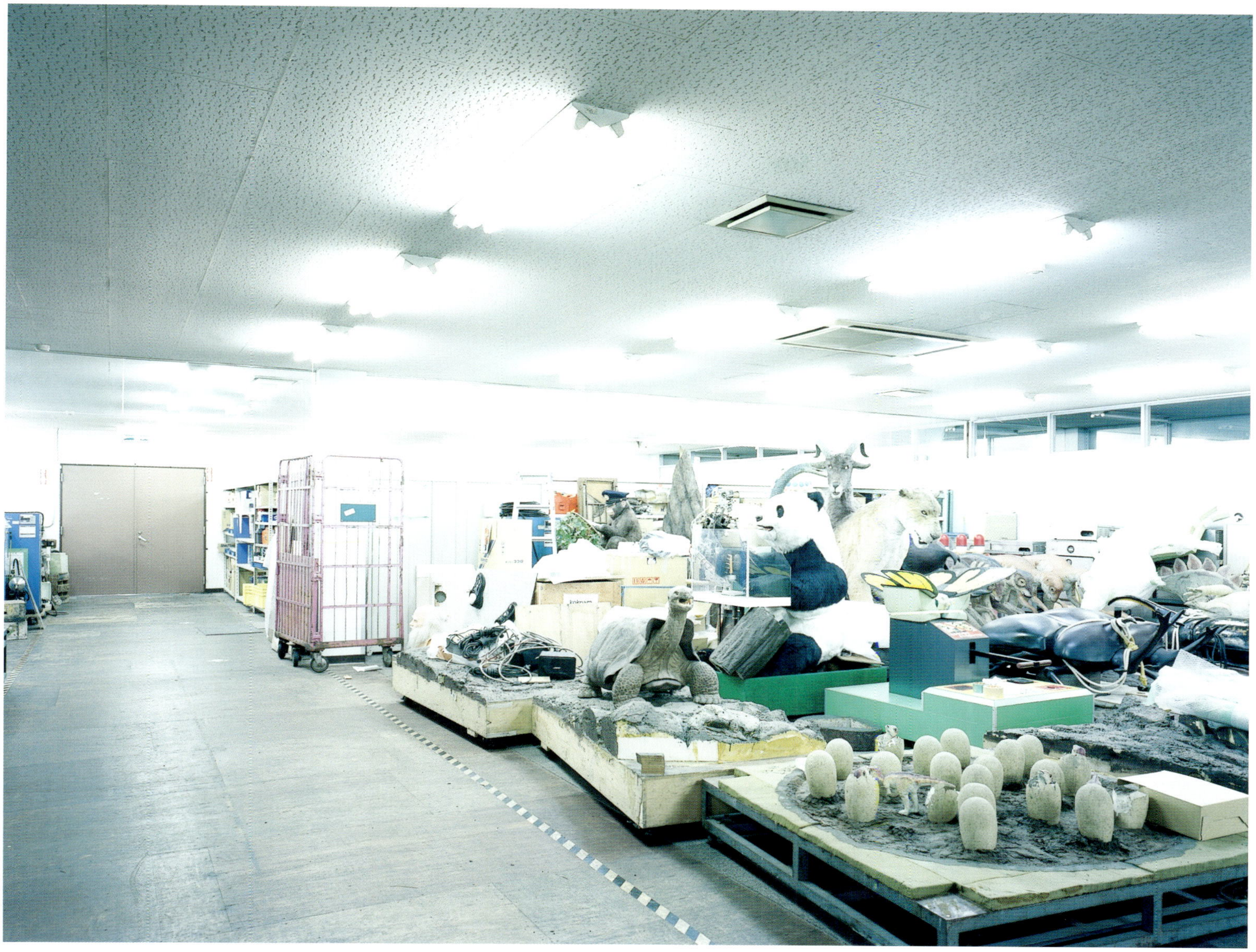

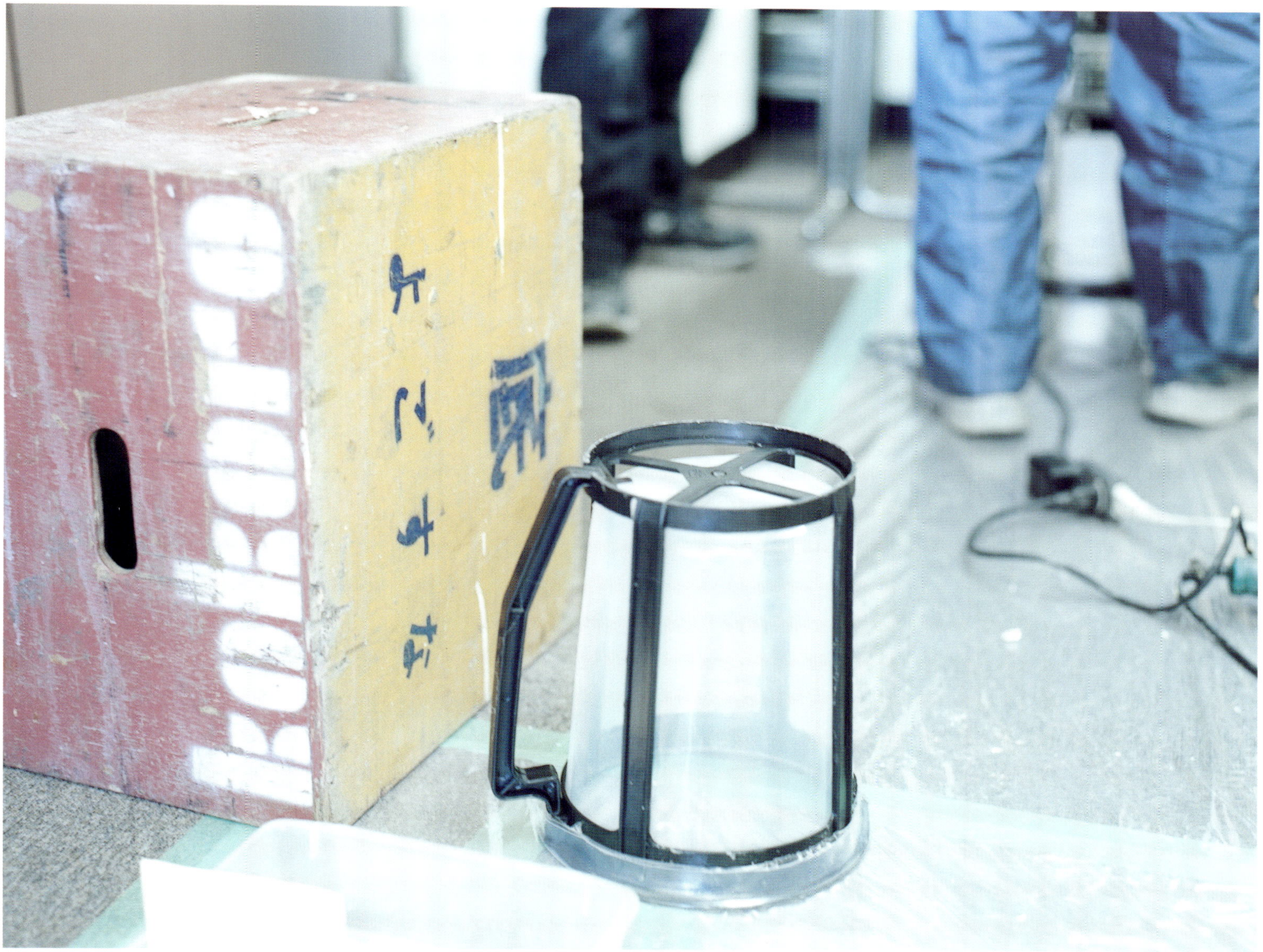

B液
2050g

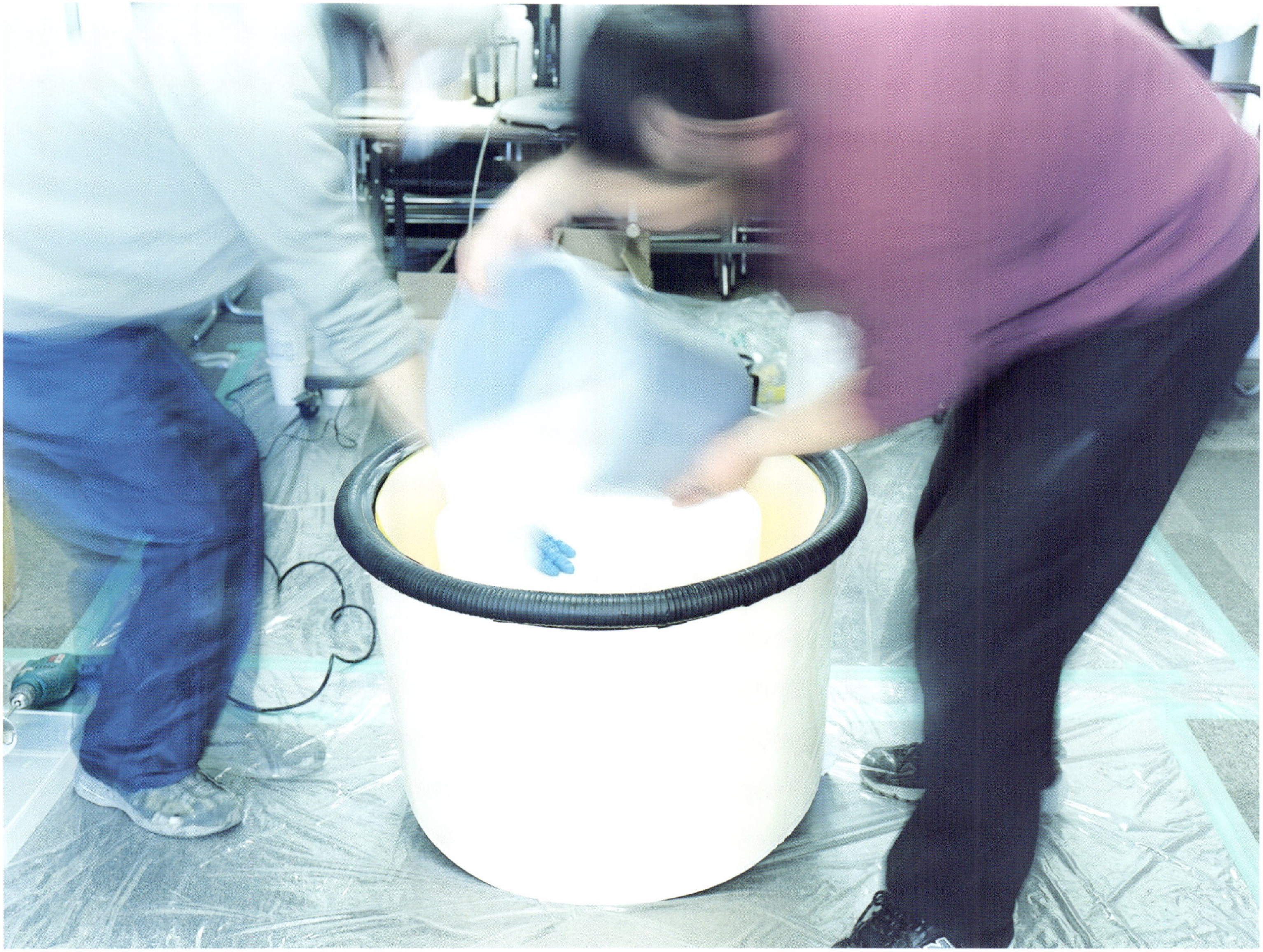

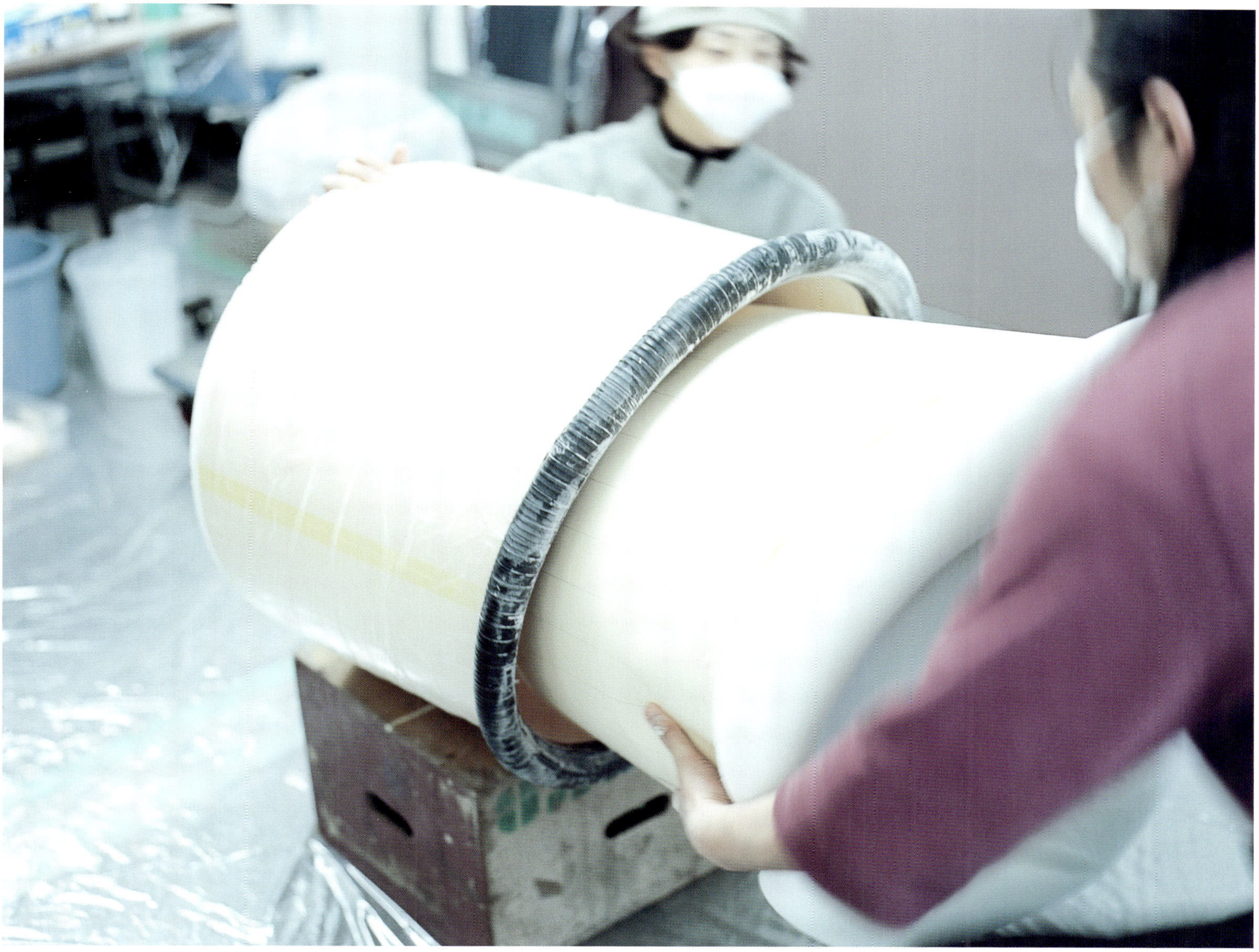

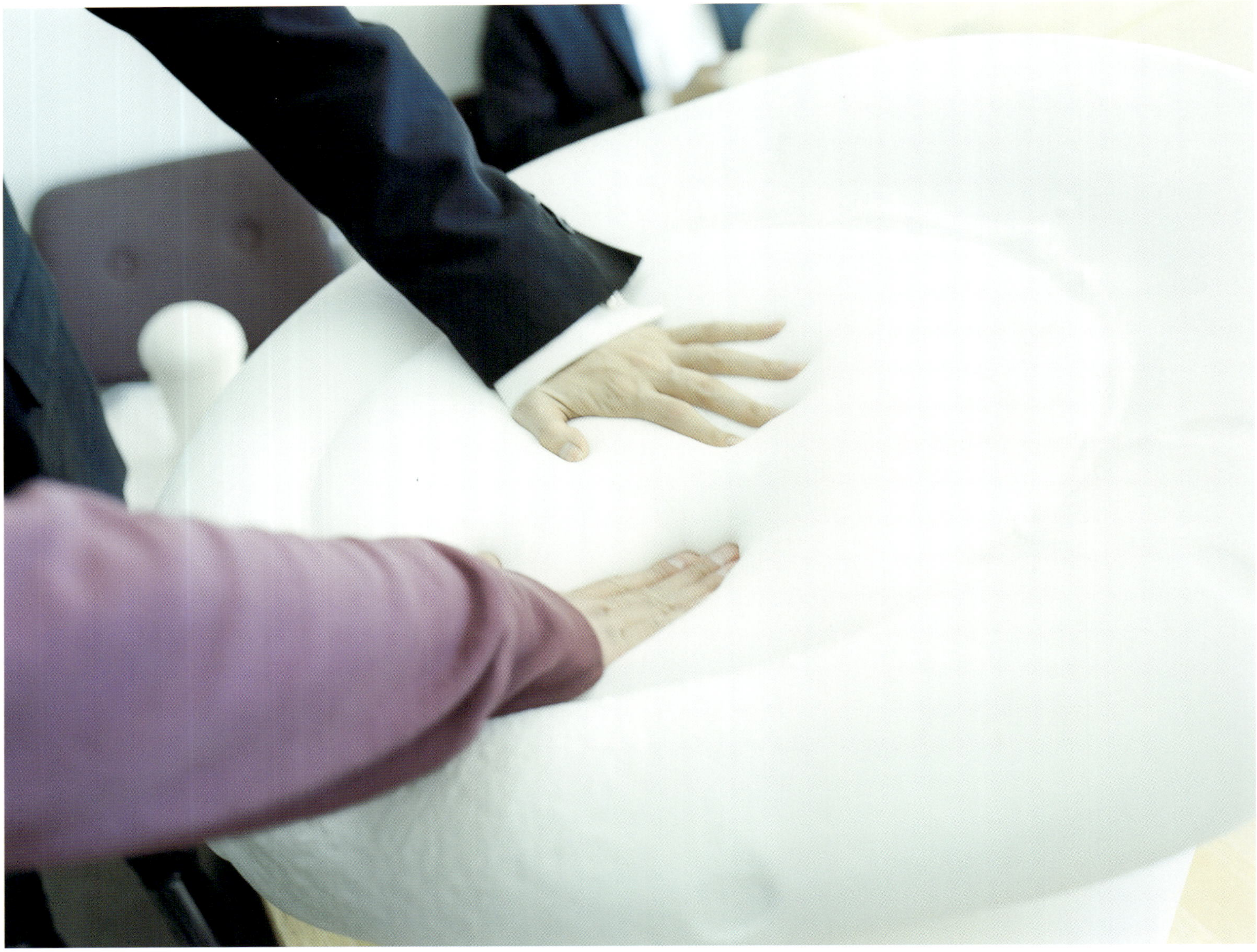

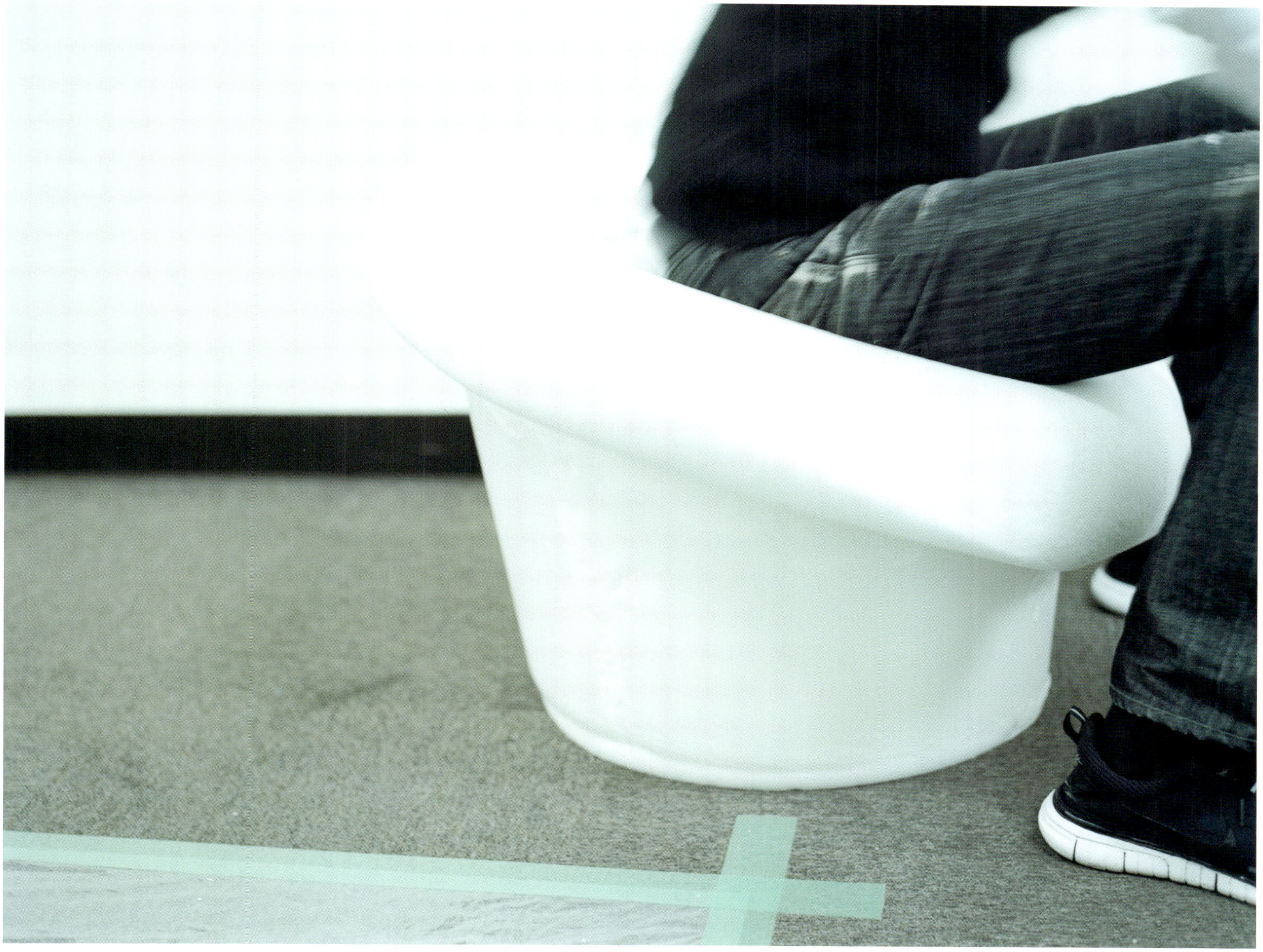

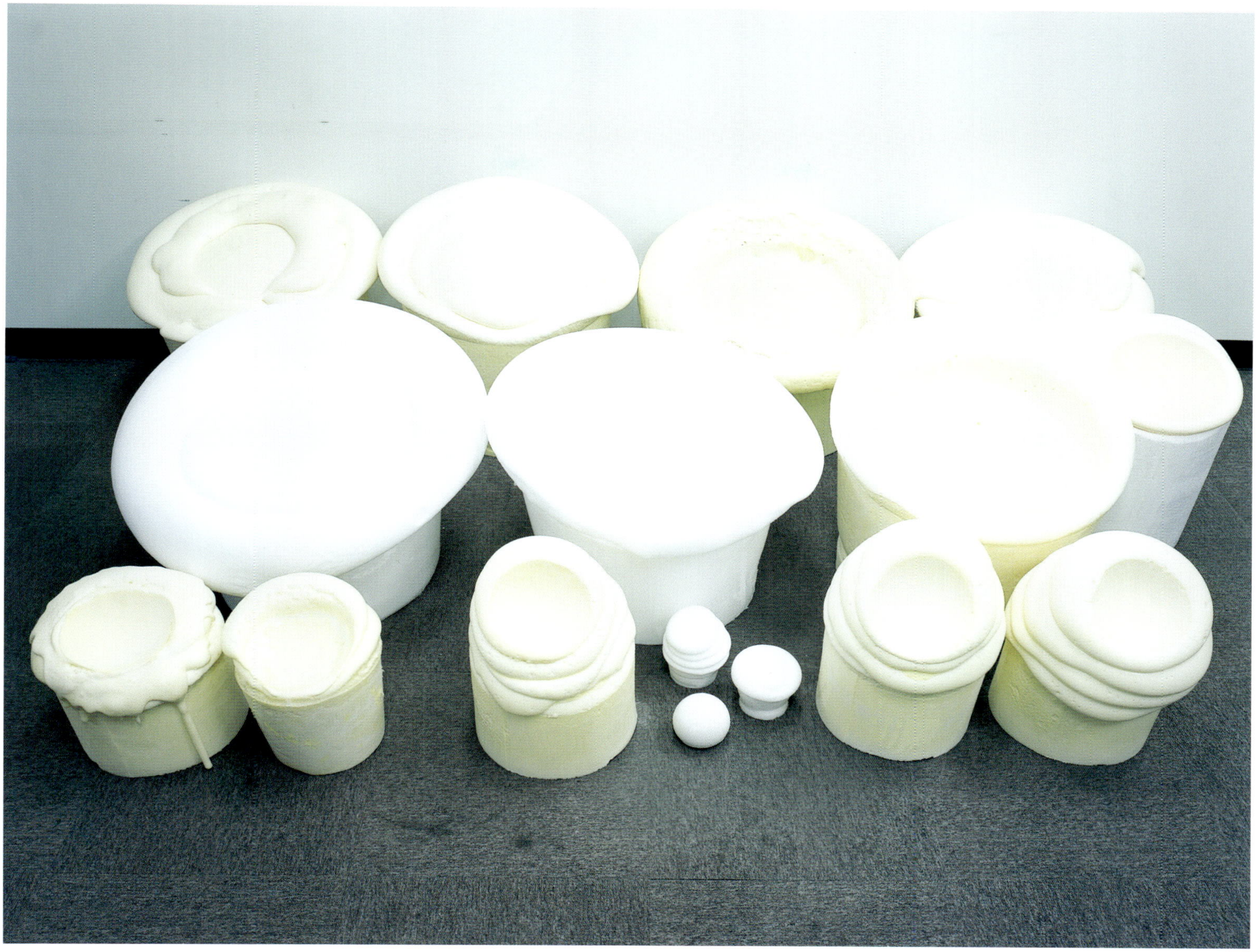

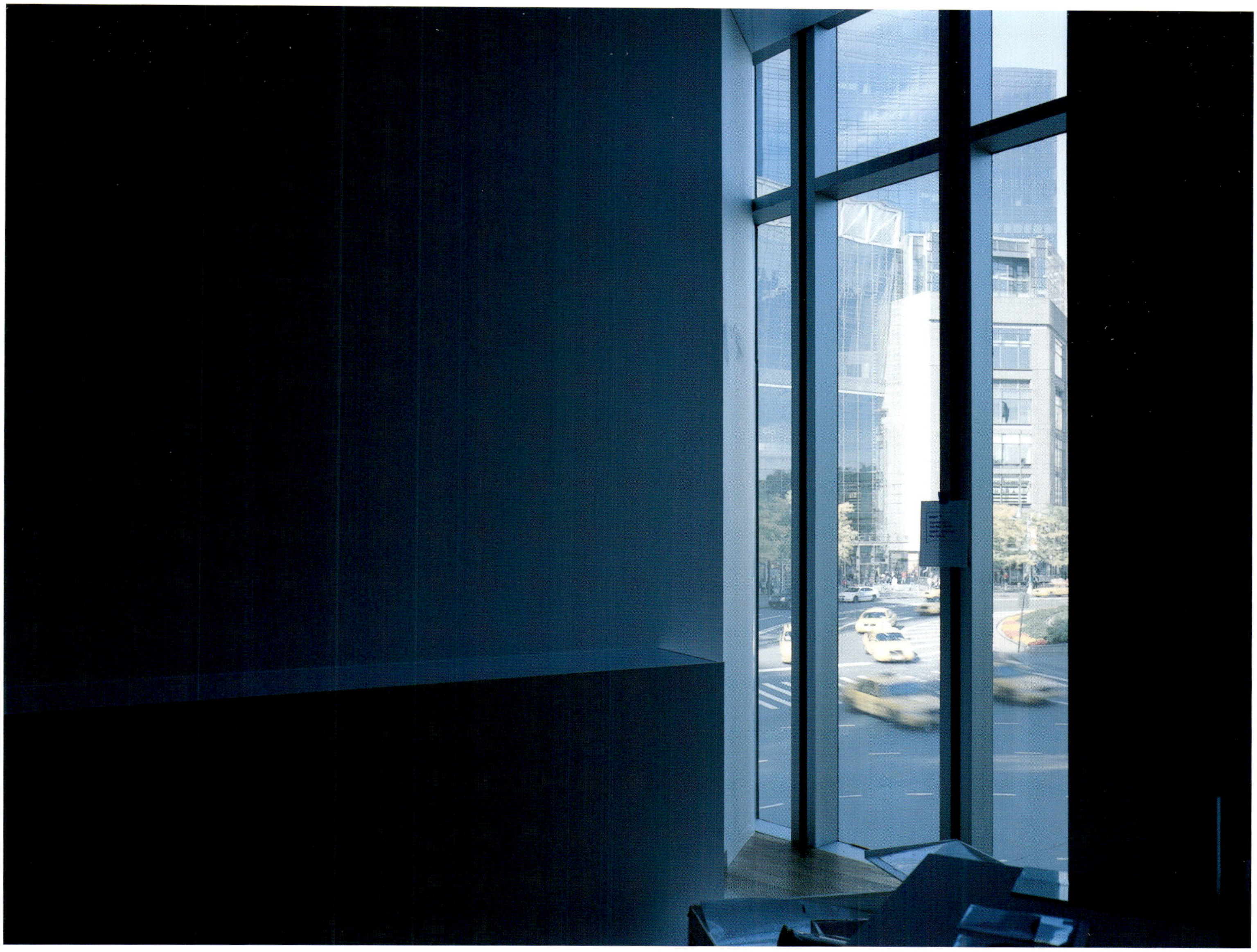

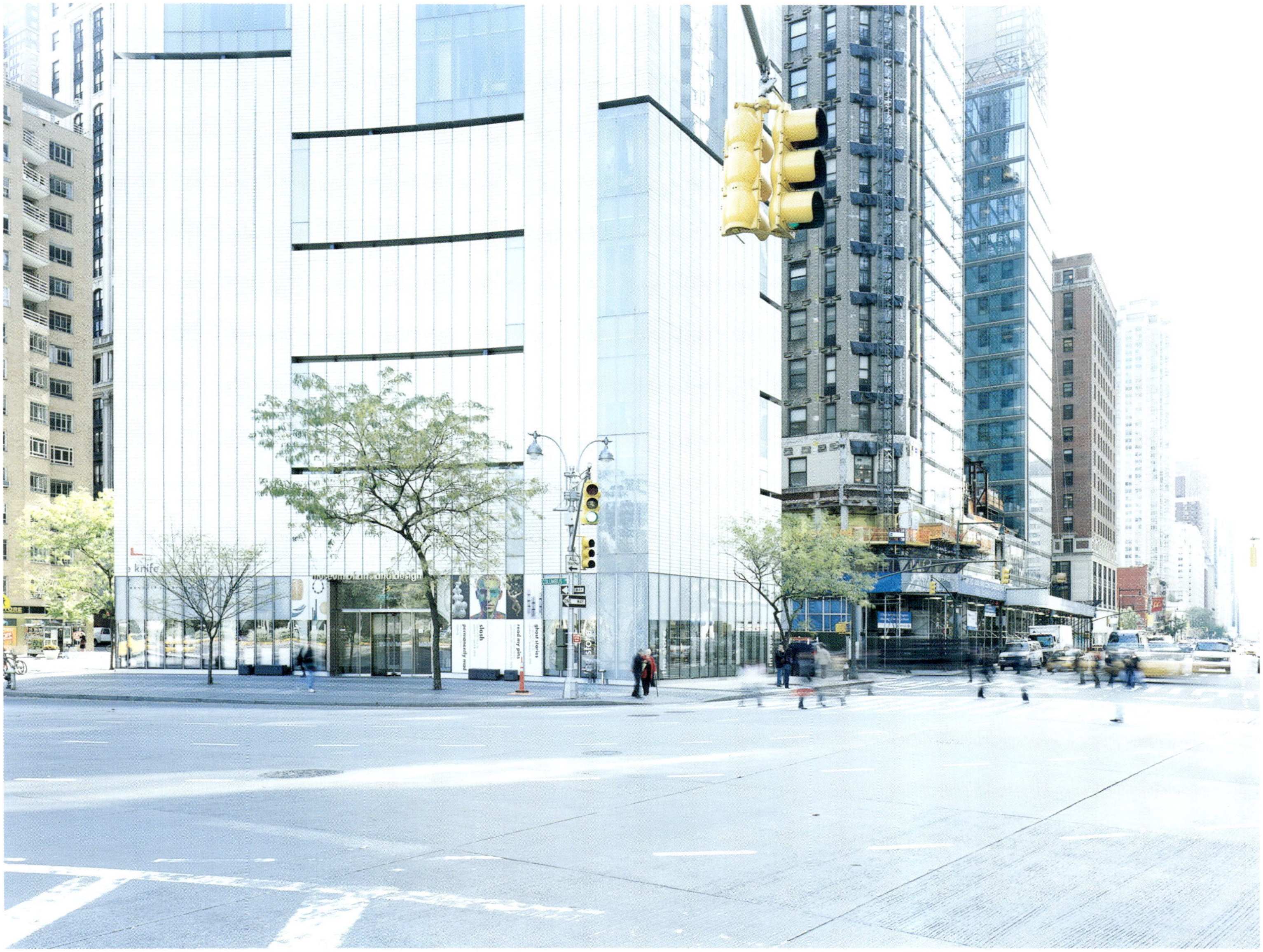

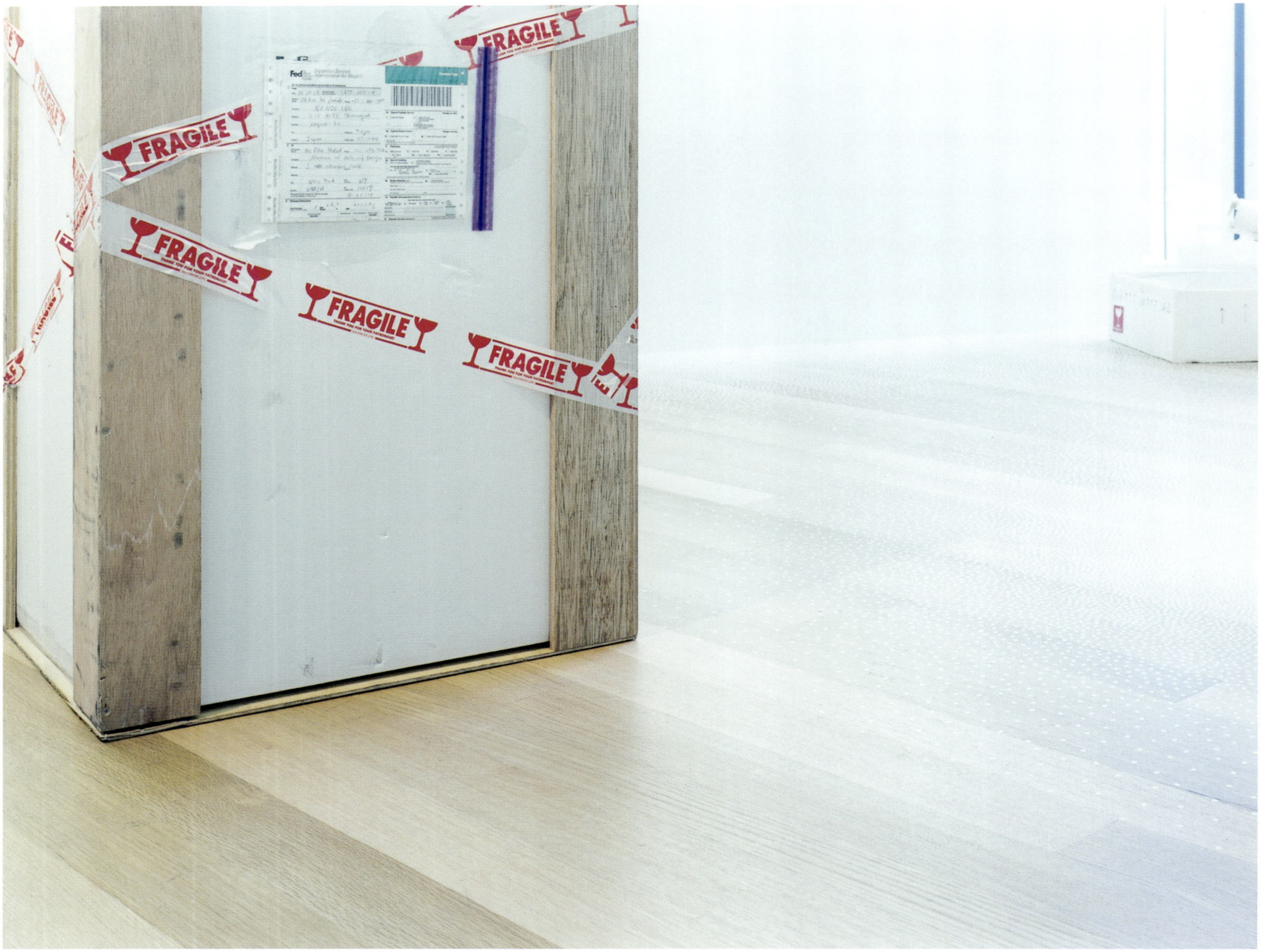
FRAGILE
FRAGILE
FRAGILE
FRAGILE
FRAGILE

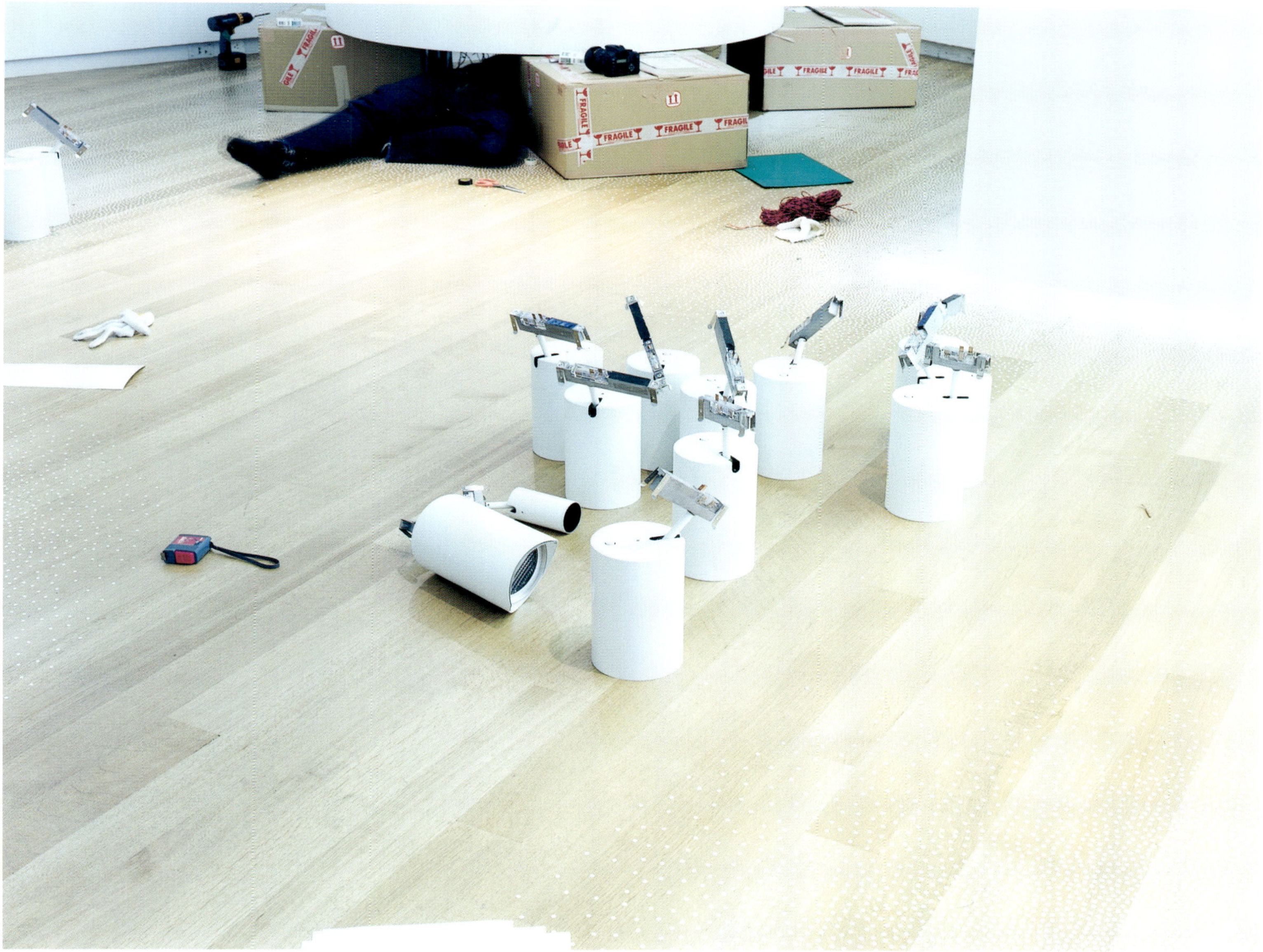
FRAGILE

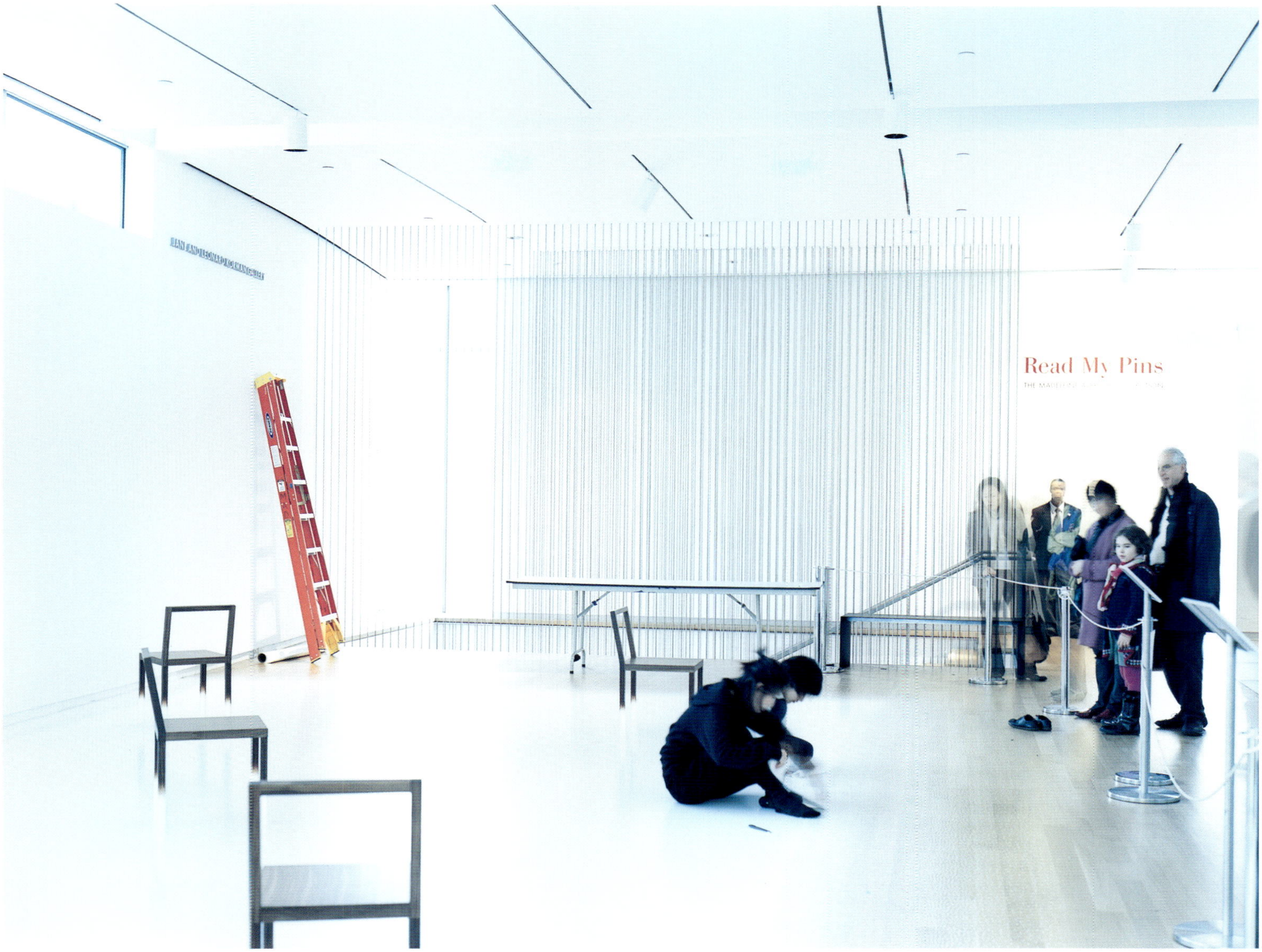
Read My Pins

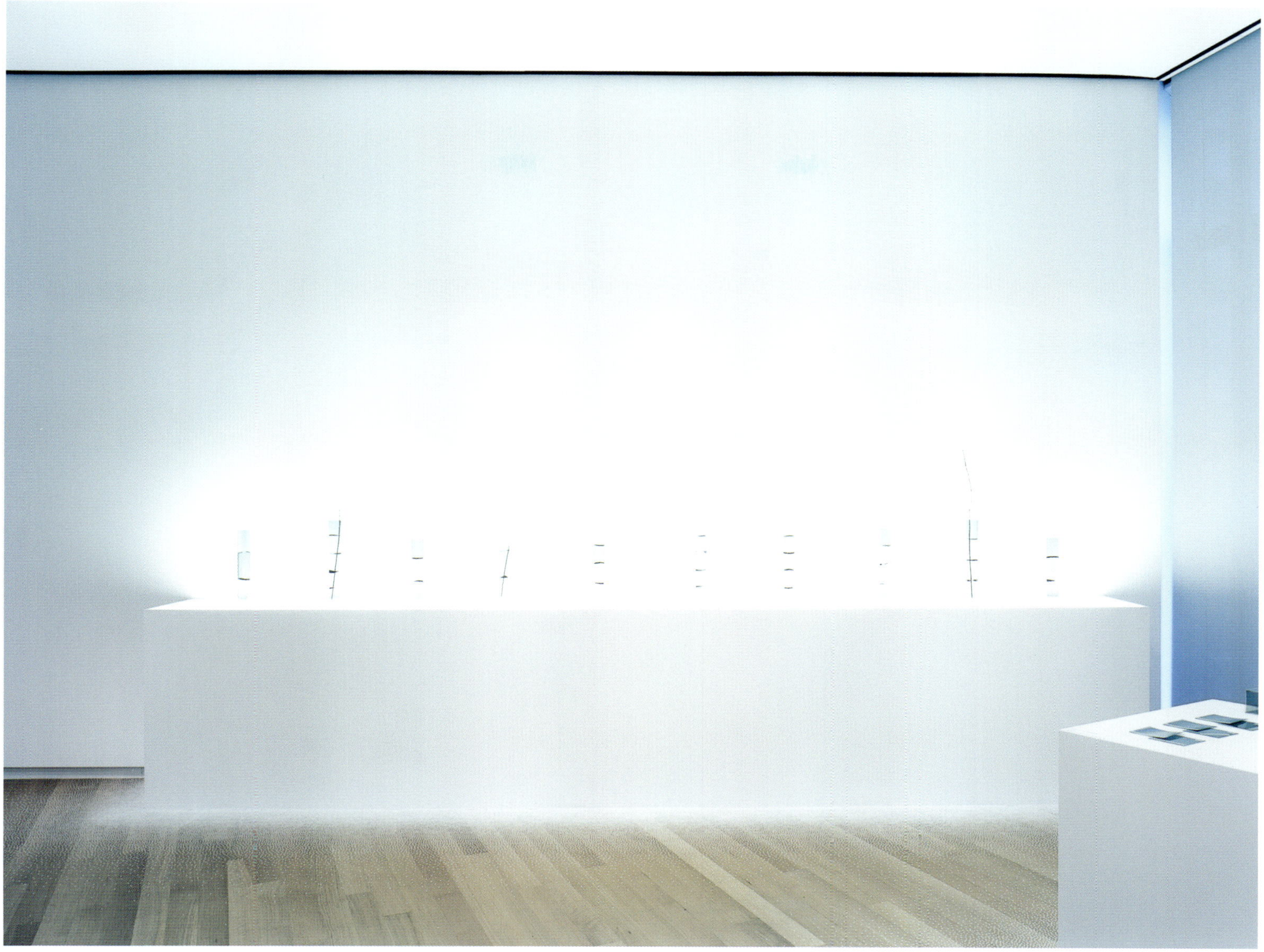

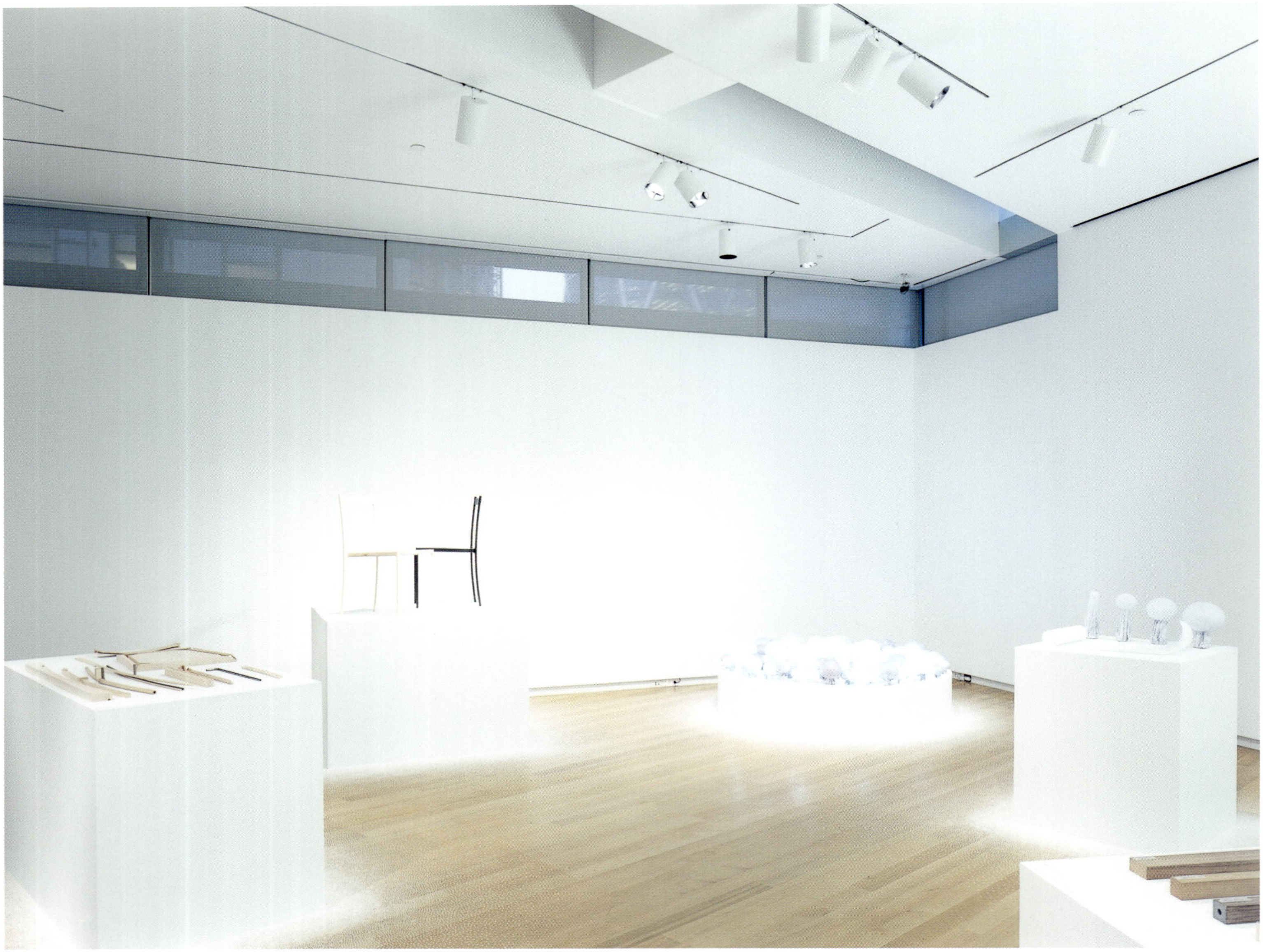

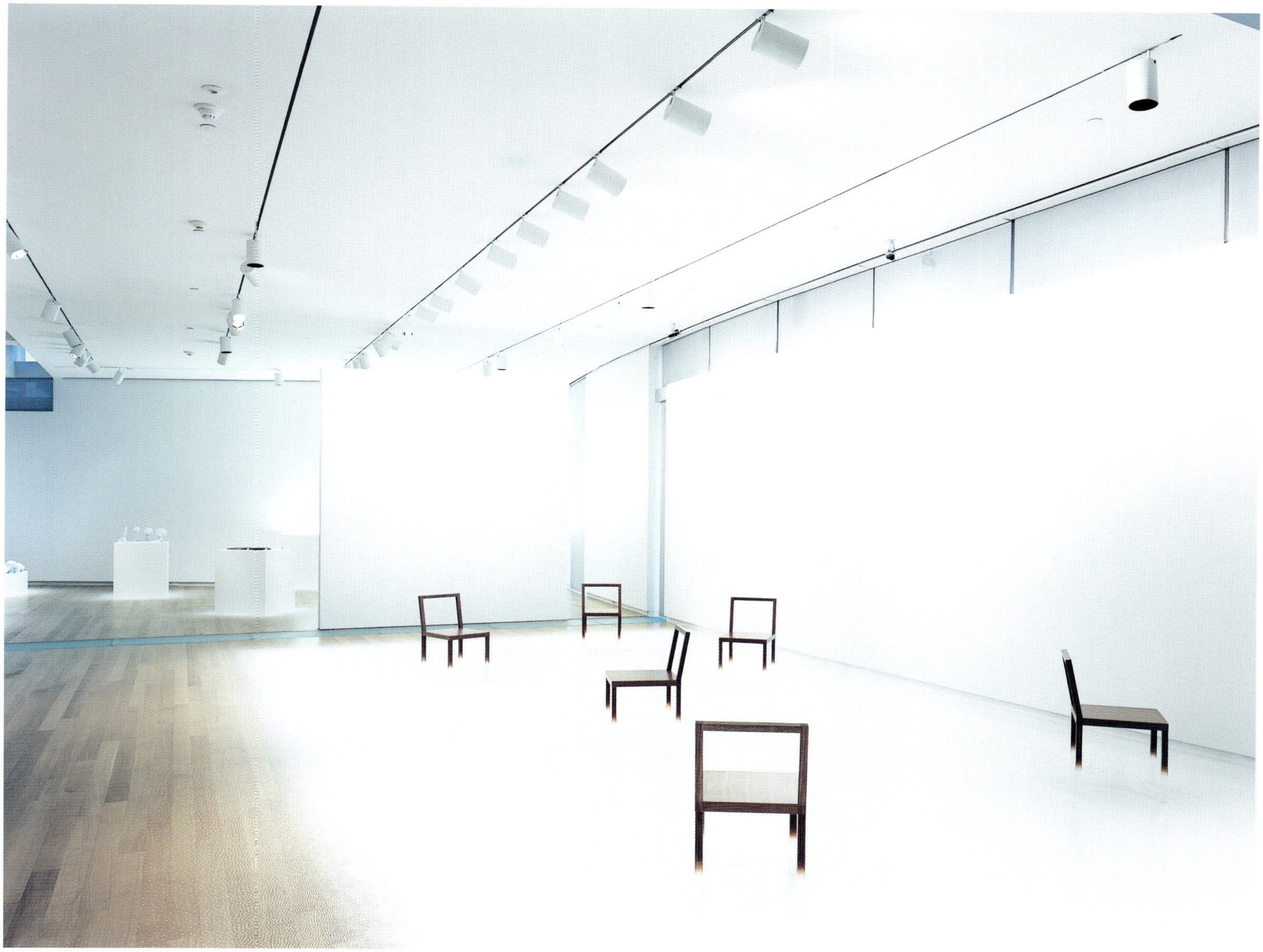

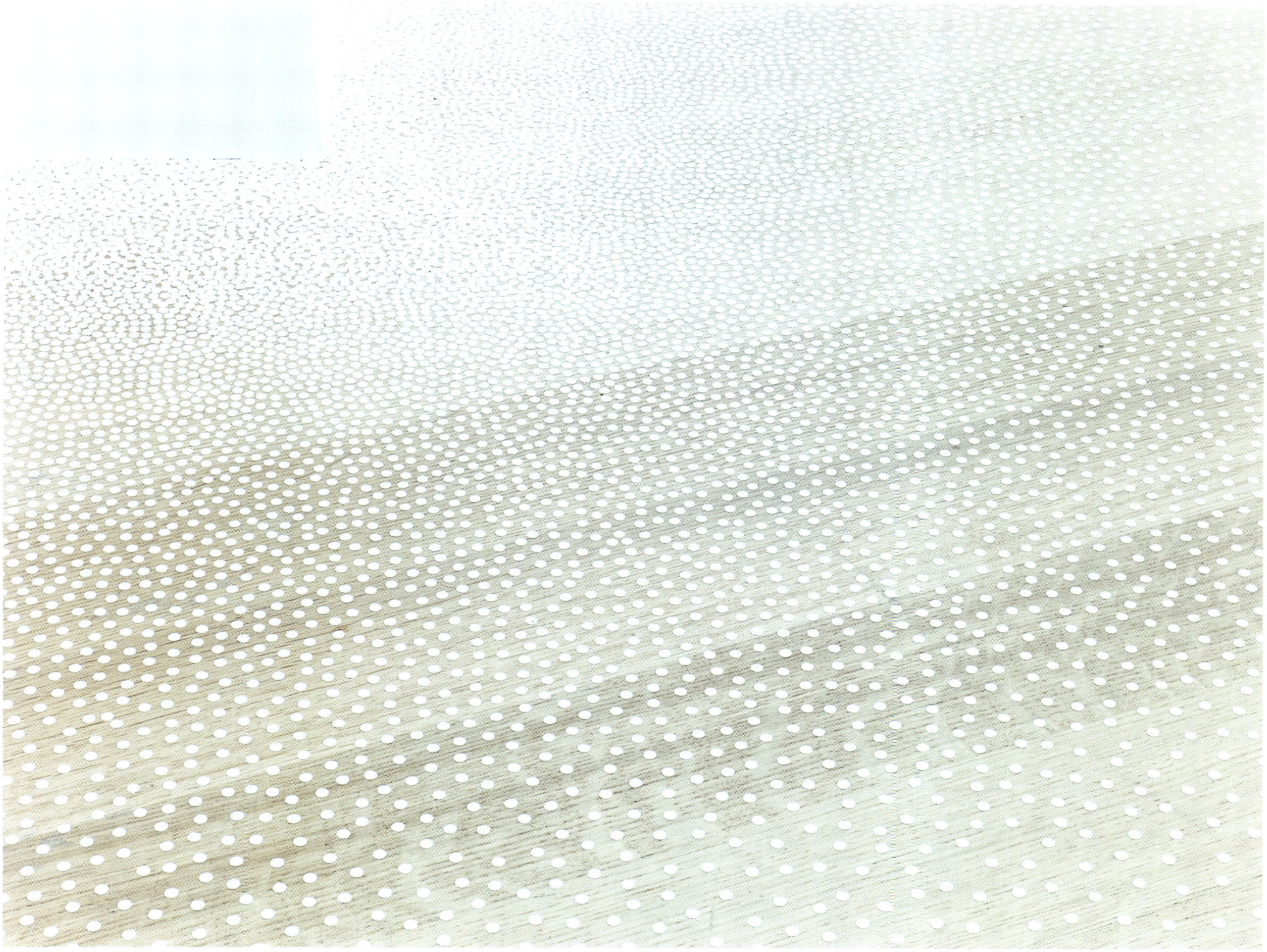

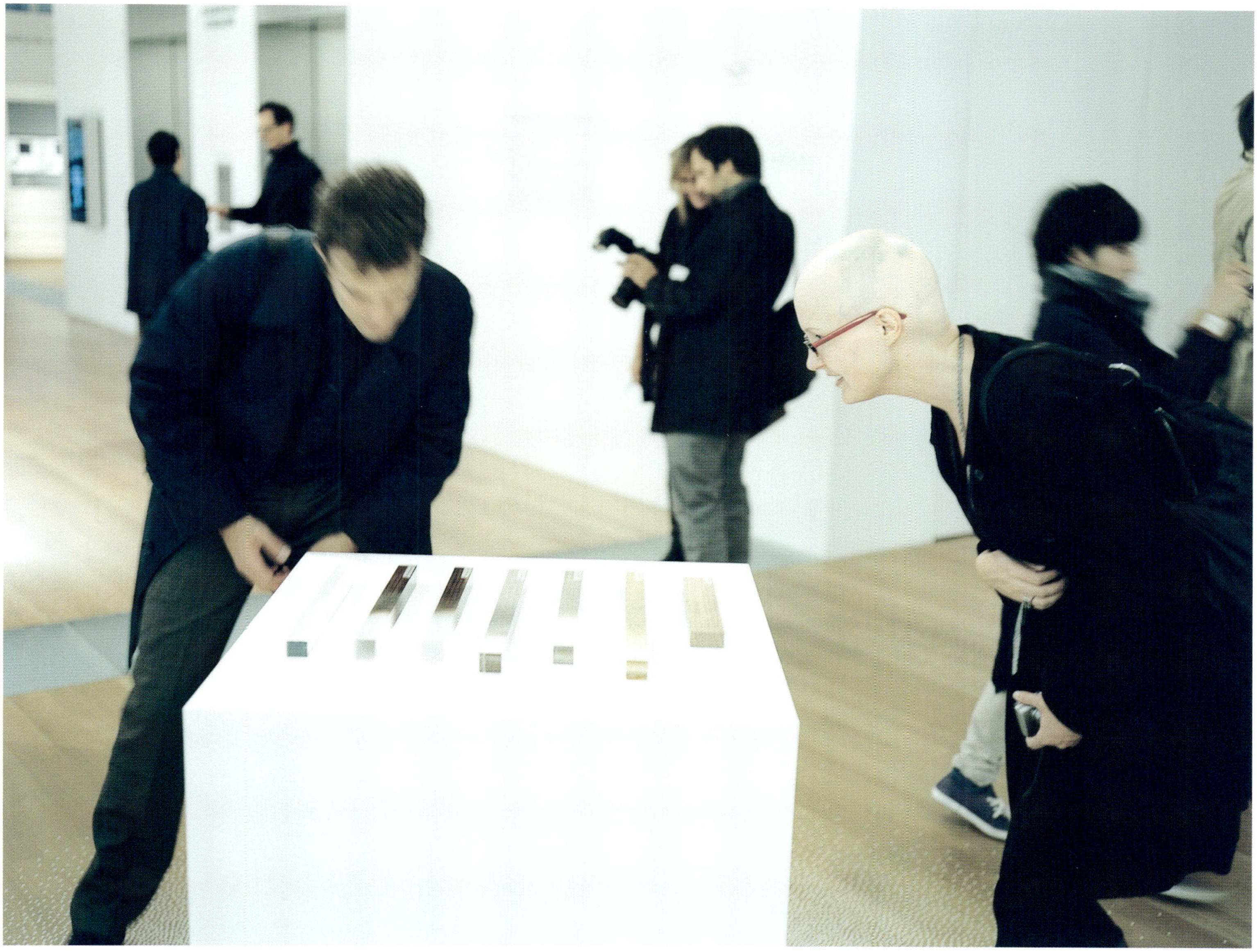

museum of arts and design
THE JEROME AND SIMONA
CHAZEN BUILDING
slash
paper under the knife
october 7 – april 4, 2010
read my pins
the madeleine albright collection
september 30 – january 31, 2010
ghost stories
new design from nendo
october 27 – january 10, 2010

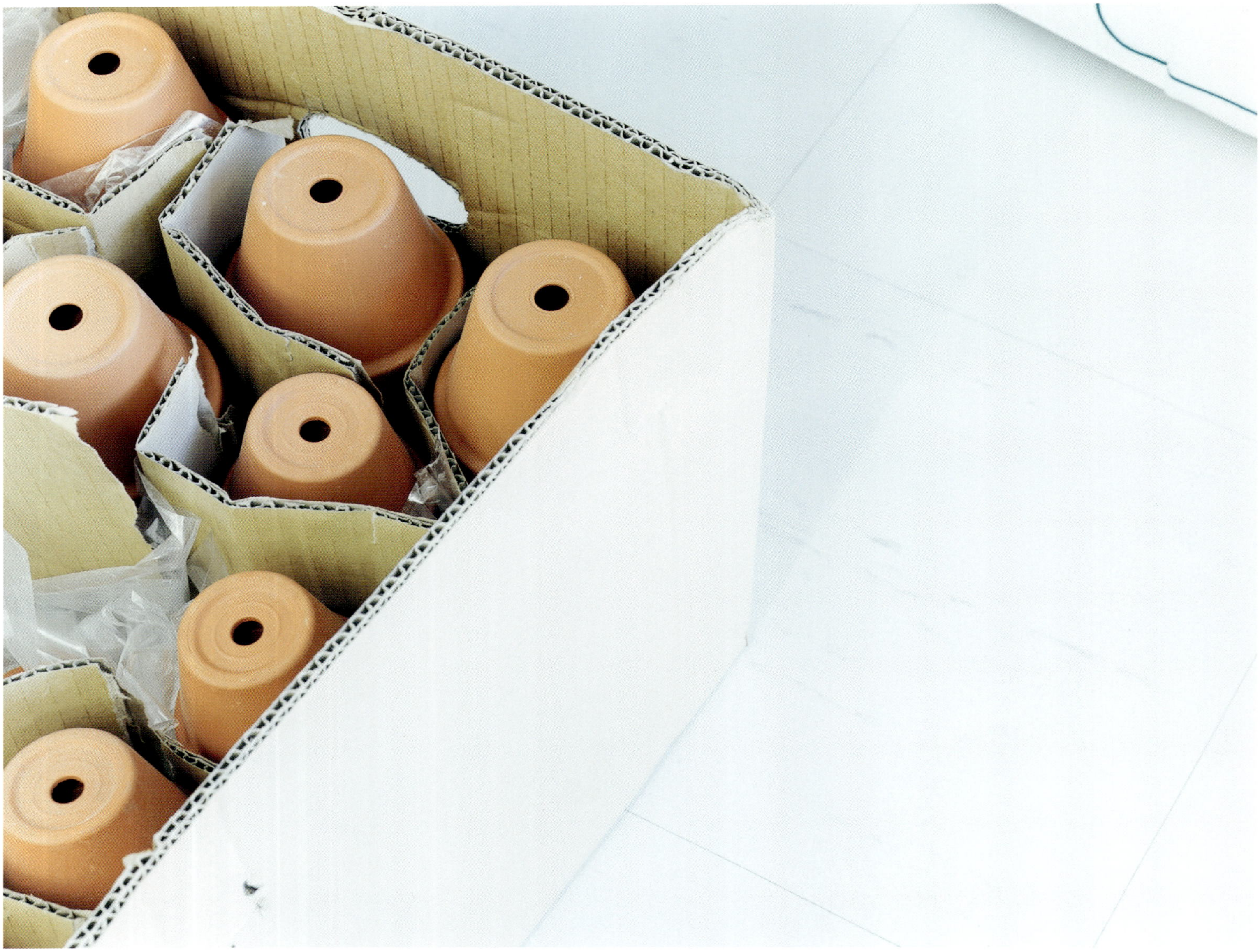

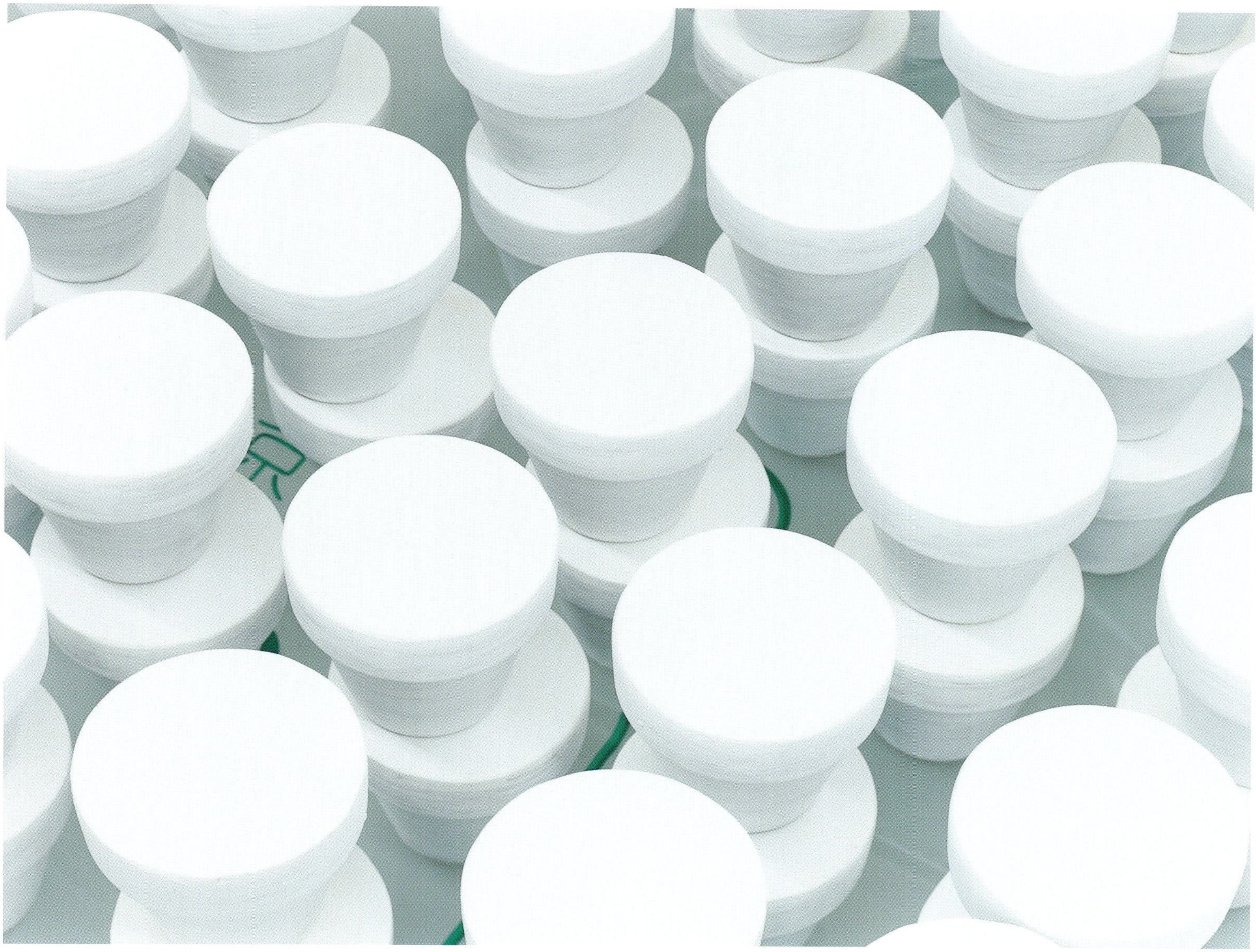

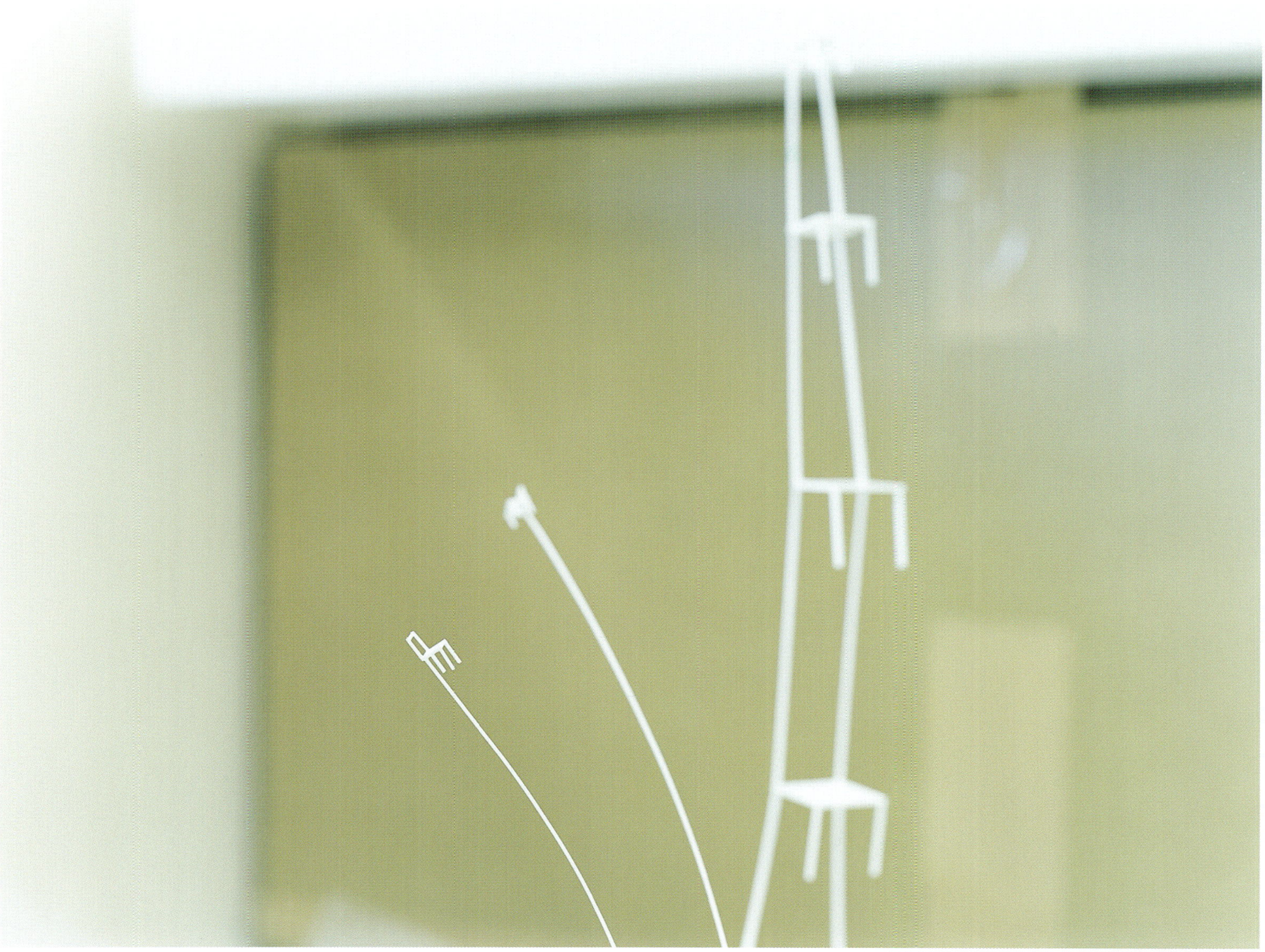

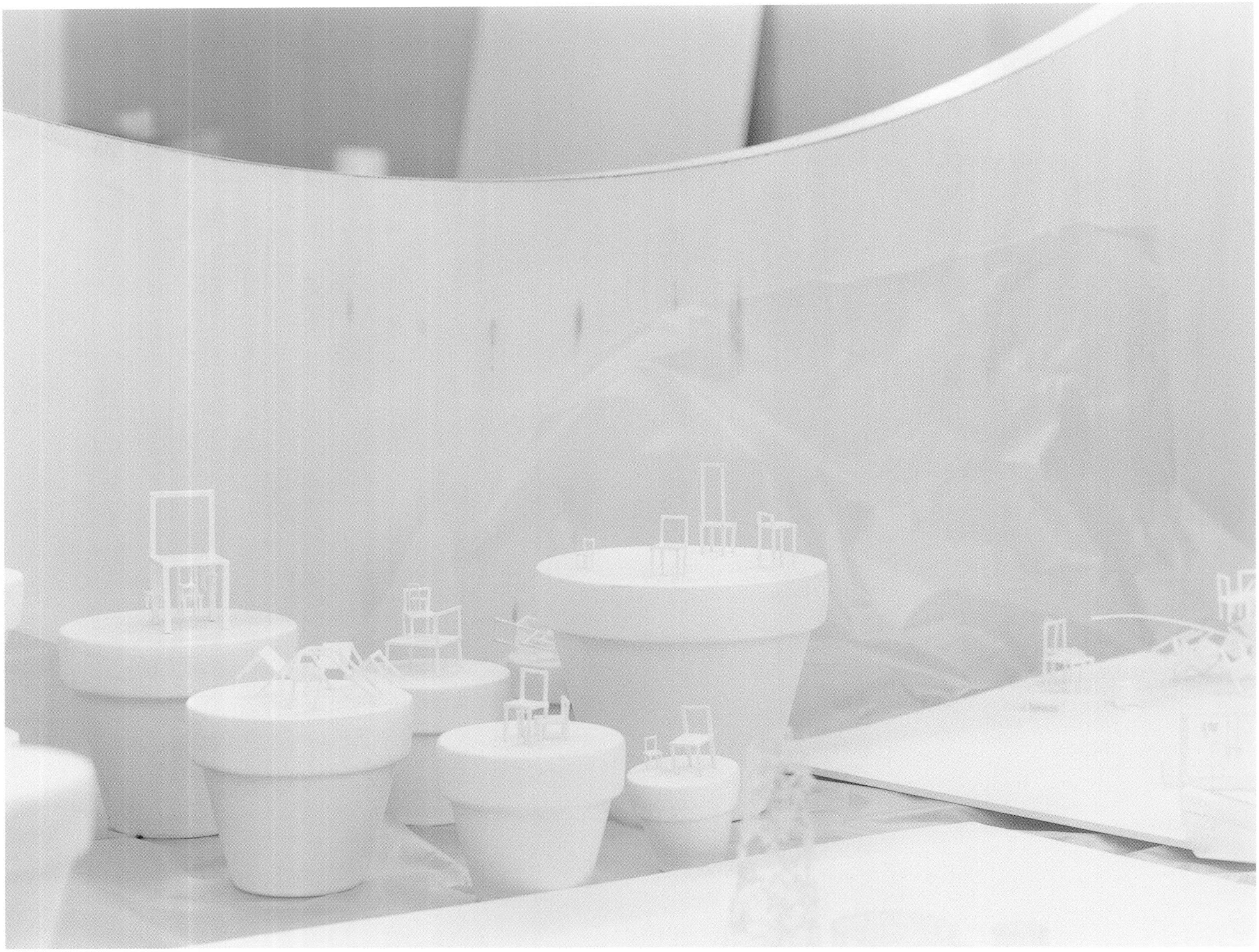

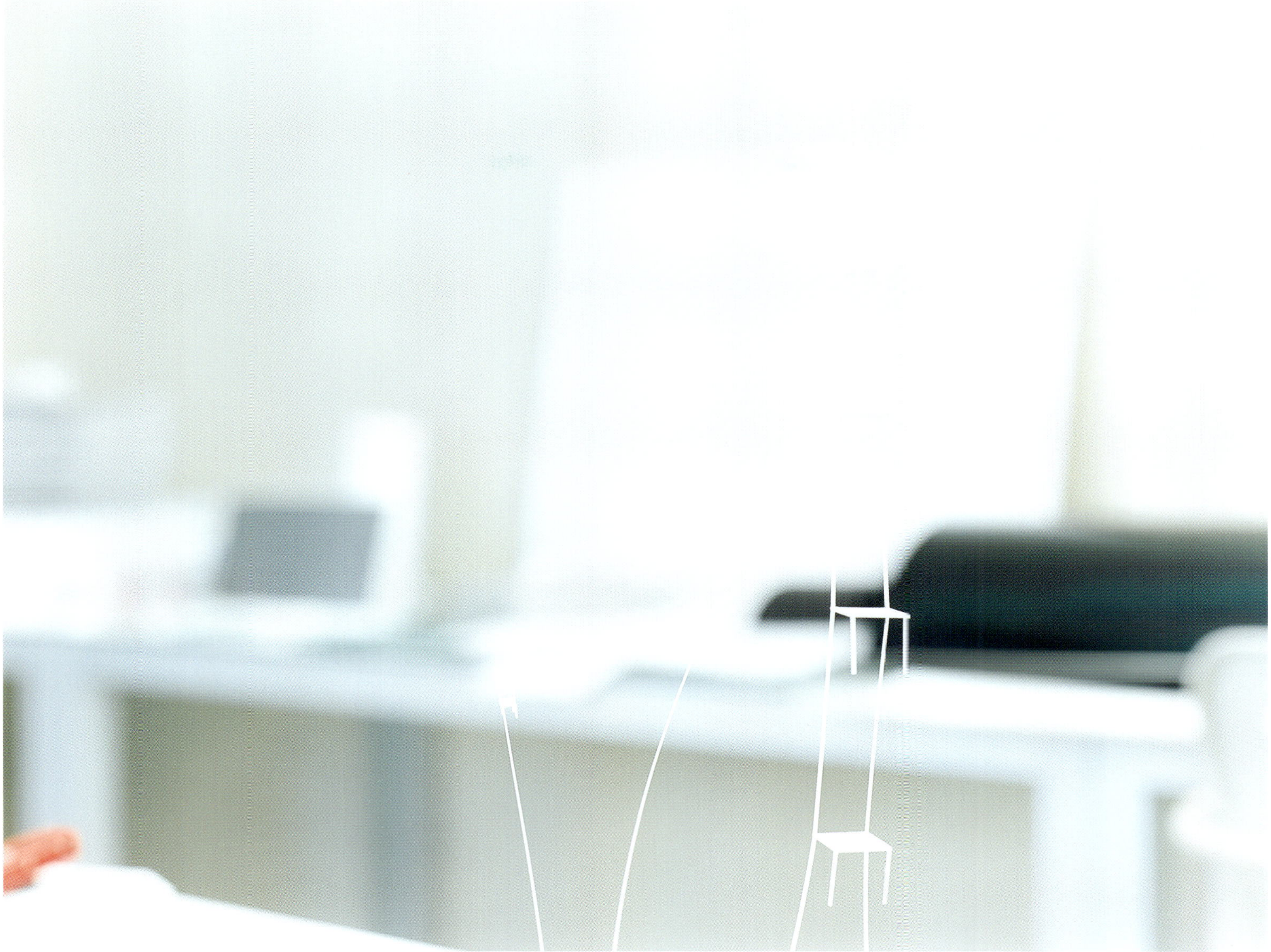

243

nendo / 佐藤 オオキ

略歴
1977年　カナダ生まれ
2002年　早稲田大学大学院理工学研究科建築学専攻修了
　　　　nendo東京オフィス設立
2005年　nendoミラノオフィス設立
2006年　昭和女子大学非常勤講師
　　　　Newsweek誌「世界が尊敬する日本人100人」選出
2007年　Newsweek誌「世界が注目する日本の中小企業100社」選出
2008年　作品集「nendo」出版（ドイツ・daab）
2009年　桑沢デザイン研究所非常勤講師

主な個展
2005年　「bloomroom」ミラノサローネ、ミラノ
2005年　「elastic diamond」ミラノサローネ、ミラノ
　　　　「kuuki」ギャラリー ルベイン、東京
2009年　「ghost stories」フリードマンベンダ ギャラリー、ニューヨーク
　　　　「ghost stories」ニューヨークデザイン美術館、ニューヨーク
2010年　「chair garden」アントニアジャンノーネ ギャラリー、ミラノ

作品収蔵美術館
ニューヨーク近代美術館
パリ装飾美術館
ニューヨークデザイン美術館
クーパーヒューイット美術館、ニューヨーク
モントリオール美術館
ホロンデザイン美術館、ホロン、イスラエル

Oki Sato / nendo

Profile
1977　Born in Toronto, Canada
2002　M.A.in Architecture, Waseda University, Tokyo
　　　Established "nendo" Tokyo office
2005　Established "nendo" Milan office
2006　Lecturer for Showa Women's University, Tokyo
　　　"The 100 Most Respected Japanese" (Newsweek magazine)
2007　"The Top 100 Small Japanese Companies" (Newsweek magazine)
2008　Collection of works "nendo" (daab)
2009　Lecturer for Kuwasawa Design School, Tokyo

Selected Solo Exhibitions
2005　"bloomroom" Milan Design Week, Milan
2008　"elastic diamond" Milan Design Week, Milan
　　　"kuuki" Le Bain gallery, Tokyo
2009　"ghost stories" Friedman Benda gallery, New York
　　　"ghost stories" Museum of Arts and Design, New York
2010　"chair garden" Antonia Jannone gallery, Milan

Public Collections
The Museum of Modern Art, New York
Musée des Arts décoratifs, Paris
Museum of Arts and Design, New York
Cooper-Hewitt, National Design Museum, New York
The Montreal Museum of Fine Arts, Montreal
Design Museum Holon, Holon, Israel

樋口 兼一（写真家）

略歴
1975年　東京生まれ
1999年　瀧本幹也氏に師事
2004年　独立

Kenichi Higuchi (Photographer)

Profile
1975　Born in Tokyo
1999　Studied photograph under Mikiya Takimoto
2004　Became independent

ゴースト・ストーリーズ
ghost stories

発行日　2010年4月12日

著者　nendo（ネンド）

撮影　樋口兼一

ブックデザイン　山田信男（CENTRAL PARK）

プリンティングディレクション　田中一也（凸版印刷株式会社）

発行者　久保田啓子

発行所　株式会社ADP｜Art Design Publishing
169-0075 東京都新宿区高田馬場4-38-17-1003
tel：03-5332-2099　fax：03-5332-6940
http://www.ad-publish.com
郵便振替　0160-2-355359

印刷・製本　凸版印刷株式会社

©nendo 2010
Printed in Japan
ISBN978-4-903348-15-5　C0072　¥5000E

本書の無断複写（コピー）は著作権上での例外を除き、禁じられています。

ghost stories

Date of Publication　April 12, 2010

Author　nendo

Photo　Kenichi Higuchi

Book Design　Nobuo Yamada (CENTRAL PARK)

Printing Direction　Kazuya Tanaka (Toppan Printing Company Limited)

Publisher　Keiko Kubota

Publishing House　ADP Company | Art Design Publishing
4-38-17-1003, Takadanobaba, Shinjuku-ku, Tokyo 169-0075, Japan
tel: +81-3-5332-2099　fax: +81-3-5332-6940
http://www.ad-publish.com

Printing & Binding　Toppan Printing Company Limited

©nendo 2010
Printed in Japan
ISBN978-4-903348-15-5 C0072

All right reserved.
No part of this publication may be reproduced or transmitted in any form or by any means,
electric or mechanical, including photocopy, or any other information storage and retrieval system,
without prior permission in writing from the ADP Company.